Y0-GFP-874

Abandoning American Neutrality

Abandoning American Neutrality

Woodrow Wilson and the Beginning of the Great War, August 1914–December 1915

M. Ryan Floyd

WITHDRAWN

palgrave
macmillan

OHIO UNIVERSITY LIBRARY ATHENS OHIO

ABANDONING AMERICAN NEUTRALITY

Copyright © M. Ryan Floyd, 2013

All rights reserved.

First published in 2013 by PALGRAVE MACMILLAN® in the United States—a division of St. Martin's Press LLC, 175 Fifth Avenue, New York, NY 10010.

Where this book is distributed in the UK, Europe, and the rest of the world, this is by Palgrave Macmillan, a division of Macmillan Publishers Limited, registered in England, company number 785998, of Houndmills, Basingstoke, Hampshire RG21 6XS.

Palgrave Macmillan is the global academic imprint of the above companies and has companies and representatives throughout the world.

Palgrave® and Macmillan® are registered trademarks in the United States, the United Kingdom, Europe and other countries.

ISBN: 978-1-137-33411-4

Library of Congress Cataloging-in-Publication Data

Floyd, M. Ryan, 1974–
Abandoning American neutrality : Woodrow Wilson and the beginning of the Great War, August 1914-December 1915 / by M. Ryan Floyd.
pages cm
ISBN 978-1-137-33411-4 (alk. paper)
1. World War, 1914-1918—United States. 2. World War, 1914-1918—Diplomatic history. 3. Neutrality—United States—History—20th century. 4. United States—Foreign relations—1913-1921. 5. Wilson, Woodrow, 1856–1924. I. Title.

D619.F57 2013
940.3'2273—dc23 2013011369

A catalogue record of the book is available from the British Library.

Design by Scribe Inc.

First edition: September 2013

10 9 8 7 6 5 4 3 2 1

For my children Delaney, Michael, and Riley

Contents

Acknowledgments

I could not have completed this project without the support and encouragement of many people. My wife Elizabeth's love and patience have played an integral role in helping me to spend the time necessary to research and write day in and day out. I cannot imagine doing this without her by my side. I owe my parents, Dr. Hugh and Paula Floyd, an enormous debt of gratitude as well. They have always encouraged me to find something that makes me happy and do it to the best of my ability. My brother Stephen was also a great help. I appreciated his willingness to act as a sounding board as I worked out many of the arguments in this book. I will always admire his passion for working in the trenches of secondary education.

I would like to thank Dr. Howard Jones for his guidance on this project and during my graduate career as a whole. I have sincerely appreciated his support and friendship. It was a privilege to work with him at the University of Alabama and I hope that in the years to come that I can provide my students with the same quality of teaching and attention that he gave me.

There are also numerous others who have supported me along the way. Waist-deep in their own projects, my friends and colleagues were a great support group when I could not see the end of the tunnel. Standing out among many are Joe Danielson and Matthew Downs. As fellow graduate students and again as professional scholars, Joe and Matthew took the time to read my work from beginning to end and provide honest and valuable feedback. Their close friendship and editorial eye have been indispensable. I only hope that I was able to help them half as much as they helped me. At the University of Alabama, John Beeler, Andrew Huebner, Harold Selesky, and Donald Snow also provided a considerable amount of advice and I would like to thank them for everything they did to help me along. I also want to recognize my colleagues at Lander University, Kevin Witherspoon, William Ramsey, Robert Figuera, Frank Rausch, John Moore, and Mathew Faust, who either read parts of the manuscript or gave me encouragement in this endeavor. Additionally I want to thank Chris Chappell, Sarah Whalen, and the rest of the editorial staff at Palgrave Macmillan for working with me to bring this book together.

Last but certainly not least I would like to thank a number of archivists and librarians in the United States and Great Britain. Special thanks go out to Brett Spencer at the University of Alabama, Gail Barton at Samford University, and Michael Berry and Adam Haig at Lander University who always seemed to locate those elusive files.

Introduction

In the summer of 1914, decades of growing tension over the balance of power in world politics provoked the major European states to mobilize massive armies and march them into battle across the globe. Caught up in the moment, numerous men and women expressed enthusiasm about the outbreak of the conflict. Newspaper editors, generals, and statesmen wrote patriotic articles and gave speeches about the justness of their nations' decisions to go to war. Hearing the call to arms, young men, fresh from civilian life, signed up to partake in what they perceived as an opportunity to obtain honor for themselves and their countries. Some of the newly minted soldiers walked or rode into battle wearing breastplates and horsehair plumes in their helmets—uniforms of a bygone era. Many of them expected to fight in a war similar to engagements of the past and assumed that the conflict would end in a matter of weeks or, at the most, several months. "It was the glamour of it all," Len Whitehead recalled years later about his older brother's decision to join the British Army. "[N]obody sort of gave a second thought that they might never come back."[1]

The Great War, however, was unlike anything the world had experienced before. During the hostilities that engulfed Europe, Asia, and Africa from 1914 through 1918, the use of new weapons like the machine gun and powerful artillery caused massive military and civilian casualties. Additionally the enormity of the conflict forced states to organize more than armies and navies. To support their soldiers at the front, governments focused almost all aspects of domestic life on the war effort. Women and men who were either too old or unfit for duty entered factories to produce the weapons and supplies that were desperately needed by the soldiers. If states could not produce enough war material at home they looked to neutral countries for help.

The growing reliance on neutrals brought about its own problems for the belligerents. The Allies and Central Powers wanted to ensure their own access to foreign-made goods while simultaneously preventing the other from doing the same. Altogether the duration of the war, the resulting widespread carnage, and the demands placed on international commerce made diplomacy between belligerents and neutrals extremely important.

Diplomatic relations between the neutral and warring powers was a trying and unremitting process. In a memoir recounting his experience in the First World War, former US secretary of state Robert Lansing aptly noted, "The hoary old adage, 'Hindsight is better than foresight,' is constantly verified in the course of history but never more frequently or more convincingly than in the field of diplomacy, where presumption and hypothesis are unavoidable bases for action, and where the successful diplomat is generally the one who 'out guesses the other fellow,' and anticipates his opponent's next move."[2] This was certainly true in the first two years of the war, a period of uncertainty in the ongoing relationship between the United States and Great Britain. Throughout the conflict, officials in London and Washington developed policies that they hoped would protect their national interests. That task was not simple. Each side had to consider many domestic and international issues, some outside their control. To secure their own well-being and to preserve the delicate relationship that existed between their countries, US and British leaders navigated a political and economic labyrinth, walled in by issues such as ideology, overseas trade, international law, and public opinion, all demanding constant attention.

Many individuals and agencies worked throughout the early years of the conflict to manage the relationship between the neutral United States and the belligerents, but the key American participant was President Woodrow Wilson. When he was elected in 1912, he had hoped to focus his administration on domestic concerns and in the days before taking office allegedly declared, "It would be the irony of fate if my administration had to deal chiefly with foreign affairs."[3] Yet, his fate was to do just that.

Soon after the European nations went to war, Wilson announced that his country would remain neutral. Historians tend to agree that Wilson sincerely wanted to keep the United States out of the war; however, the president's management of American neutrality has spurred extensive debate among scholars. Revisionists' arguments, which emerged in the 1920s, focused on the role that economics played in Wilson's decision making between 1914 and 1917. During the interwar period, some authors asserted that the United States was pressed into the war by financial and armaments firms that hoped to make large profits off of the conflict.[4] Most revisionists discount this extreme assertion but agree that the expansion of Anglo-American trade made it very difficult for him to maintain a balanced approach to the belligerents.[5] Beginning in the 1950s, most historians began to minimize and even discount economics as a significant factor in Wilson's thinking. Instead many emphasize Wilson's interest in collective security and his desire to spread democracy across the globe.[6] Others argue that national security was the major objective behind Wilson's diplomacy.[7]

These more recent interpretations have addressed many important issues that clearly influenced the president during the period of American neutrality; however, to fully understand Wilson's approach to diplomacy in the early months of the war, historians need to reevaluate the significance of the US economy.

While this study examines many of the same events and issues addressed by these noteworthy scholars, it focuses on the paradox created by Wilson's idealistic aim to bring the belligerents to the peace table and his pragmatic goal of buttressing the US economy between August 1914 and December 1915. During this formative period, the quandary created by his effort to pursue both visionary and pragmatic objectives made his agenda untenable and convinced him to intentionally violate American neutrality.

Throughout the first 12 months of the war, Wilson made a sincere effort to remain neutral.[8] As an idealist, the president declared in early 1915 that at the heart of American neutrality was "sympathy for mankind. It is fairness, it is good will at bottom."[9] The president hoped that by adhering to higher principles and remaining neutral he could help all of humanity by convincing the warring parties to resolve their differences and develop a postwar world that was free of militarism.[10] Promoting this goal was a motivating factor behind the president's mediation efforts. More than once, the commander-in-chief and his personal advisor, Colonel Edward House, tried to encourage British and German diplomats to meet. On his missions to Europe, House traveled to London and Berlin in the hope of discovering common ground.

Wilson and House assumed that bringing about a conference required the White House to maintain an official position as an unbiased observer. Only then could the administration convince the belligerents that the United States would be a fair peace broker. For this reason, throughout much of the period, the Wilson administration tried to sustain neutrality by taking steps that went beyond the legal requirements placed on a neutral power.

At the same time, Wilson recognized that his country could benefit financially from the war. Evidence suggests that Wilson regularly considered the economic welfare of the United States. For much of his political career, Wilson emphasized the importance of commerce and asserted that the federal government needed to play a central role in its development. During his first presidential campaign, Wilson promoted a strong relationship between the business community and Washington. Speaking to the New York Economic Club on May 23, 1912, Wilson stated that the government must be involved in regulating and promoting business because "business underlies every part of our life; the foundation of our lives, of our spiritual lives included, is economic." Wilson also assumed that for the economy to expand, the US business community had to look overseas for new markets. In his 1912 acceptance speech at the Democratic National Convention, Wilson promoted tariff reform and the expansion of the US merchant marine. American companies, he stated, "have expanded to such a point that they will burst their jackets if they do not find a free outlet to the markets of the world . . . Our domestic markets no longer suffice." When the war began, US businesses and farmers were temporarily cut off from many overseas markets. This situation could have created serious problems for the US economy. But throughout the early months of the war, Wilson put his words into action by supporting policies designed to ensure that Americans would suffer little from the European conflict. Furthermore Wilson reasoned that there was a strong connection between republicanism and commercial growth. And like many of his predecessors, he assumed that trade and economic prosperity were directly related to and often a precursor to international harmony.[11]

Through Wilson's dualistic approach to diplomacy, he hoped that his country could save Europe from itself and garner the fiscal rewards available from the Old World conflict. The president believed that his objectives were compatible but failed to recognize that he could not achieve the idealistic and pragmatic aims simultaneously. Thus as the war progressed, Wilson's approach to foreign relations became increasingly difficult to maintain.

Despite Wilson's efforts to bring London and Berlin together, White House personnel never persuaded the warring parties to talk because they did not understand the casus belli of the European conflict. Wilson's staff approached mediation from a moralistic perspective, seeing the war as a battle for the future of the civilized world rather than a struggle to maintain the European balance of power. London's leaders were very successful at nurturing the president's idealism and using it to their advantage. While none of the belligerents wanted mediation until they could negotiate from a position of strength, Great Britain effectively played to Wilson's utopian worldview by portraying Germany as a militaristic autocracy that would continue the war until it dominated the continent. The Oval Office's desire to be a peacemaker and the belligerents' refusal to participate ultimately colored Washington's approach to the war, though Wilson's ambitious goal for the United States was not enough to single-handedly draw the country away from neutrality.

As with his mediation efforts, defending American commerce and remaining an unbiased neutral proved difficult. The Wilson administration had to confront the Allied blockade of the European coast, designed to prevent Germany from accessing war materiel, and the German decision to use submarines to attack trade ships around the British Isles. The Allied cordon interfered with neutral commerce on the open seas and spurred major controversies over US commercial rights and Britain's ability to prevent Germany from obtaining American-made goods. To defend their positions, both the United States and Great Britain appealed to international law, particularly wartime decisions regarding neutral shipping. On occasion, the United States and Great Britain worked to safeguard their interests by using precedents that reached back to decisions made before and during the American Civil War.

Wilson's confidence in the economic opportunities presented by the war bore fruit, but it also created problems for his administration. US businesses benefited greatly from the belligerents' demand for foreign-made goods. By late 1915, Britain became the chief international market for US agricultural and industrial products. His Majesty's Government was dependent on US munitions and financing to carry out its military campaigns and, because of the Allied blockade, American companies relied almost exclusively on the United Kingdom for their prosperity. The situation convinced the president that while the White House must continue protesting against London's naval policies, sustained economic development was subject to good relations with Britain. Protecting and expanding the American economy, however, inadvertently encumbered Wilson's ideological objectives. Stopping Anglo-American trade was a key factor in Germany's decision to use U-boats in the Atlantic. The resulting submarine crisis soured US–German relations and further complicated Wilson's mediation efforts.

Simultaneously internal divisions and personal agendas within the Wilson cabinet and American public opinion on ideological and economic issues influenced the president's impression of the war and the belligerents. Members of his staff could not agree on how to protect the country's interests during the first phase of neutrality, lasting from August 1914 through June 1915. The resulting policy disagreements provoked infighting over who should have the president's ear. House and Lansing, among others, favored a bold diplomatic stance that was particularly harsh to Germany, while Secretary of State William Jennings Bryan believed that the United States had to approach both London and Berlin with equal vigor, even relinquishing certain rights at sea to avoid American involvement in the war. This difference in viewpoints led to serious confrontations over the direction of national strategy and ultimately tore the administration apart.

As an elected official, Wilson knew the importance of public opinion. The United States was quite diverse—and not only in its ethnic origins. The opening salvos of August 1914 divided the American public between innate European loyalties as well as in its outlook toward foreign involvement and traditional isolation. Many US citizens argued that the war was strictly a foreign affair, the result of weak political systems embroiled in militarism while trying to protect the remnants of declining monarchies—none of which required American attention. Others felt that historical ties to the Old World required America to choose sides and, if necessary, intervene. Wilson had to consider the influence that such views could have on his political career, and he certainly knew that acquiescence on the existence of the Allied blockade or pressing Germany too hard on the use of submarines could impinge on his mediation efforts and the country's economic prosperity. Thus these diverse views forced the president to walk a fine line as he led the country.

In August 1914, Wilson intended to remain neutral; however, by the latter half of 1915 he could no longer claim this status. The foundering of the president's mediation efforts and the ongoing submarine crisis exacerbated Wilson's perception of Germany as a militaristic state. Over the same period, British diplomats catered to the president's idealism and made wise concessions to the United States that were often timed to coincide with heightened tension in American-German relations. Additionally, as the war continued, the Allies' dependence on US goods increased so much that even without full access to Germany, the United States experienced profound commercial growth. Thus along with the breakdown of Wilson's peace efforts and his increasingly negative impression of Berlin, Britain and the United States tightened their economic and political bonds to the point that US interests and UK interests became Anglo-American interests.

1

"An Awful Cataclysm"

July 1914–September 1914

> They don't want peace on the continent—the ruling classes do not. But they will want it presently and then our opportunity will come—your opportunity to play an important and historic part.
>
> —US Ambassador Walter Hines Page to President Wilson, August 2, 1914[1]

In the early months of the Great War the purview and direction of Anglo-American diplomacy was cloudy because the United States and Great Britain confronted a multitude of complex issues that muddled their relationship. Each state had to orchestrate strategies for protecting its own economic and political well-being. For the Wilson administration, safeguarding American interests meant declaring neutrality, calling for mediation among the belligerents, and trying to convince Great Britain to accept existing international accords that secured neutral commerce. Protecting US trade, however, was not simple because Britain's plan for conducting its war effort was not compatible with America's interests. Britain could not avoid interference with US exports because it was committed to preventing Germany from purchasing goods that would help its military campaign. The Royal Navy's decision to cut off German trade would become a serious issue of contention for Washington and the American people. Additionally, as Wilson soon discovered, his country's economic and ancestral associations with Europe prevented his office from steering clear of the conflict. Instead the president and his advisors found themselves deeply immersed in global affairs. The ties between the Old and New World led to confusion over how to pursue relations that achieved political and fiscal objectives while minimizing the risk of diplomatic confrontation.

In the spring of 1914, President Wilson sent his friend and confidant Colonel Edward House to Europe in an effort to diffuse the rising tension that was engulfing the continent. House, who had first met Wilson during his bid for the Democratic Party's 1912 presidential nomination, was the president's closest advisor. He preferred to remain outside the official cabinet but wielded enormous influence in Washington because Wilson trusted House's political judgment.[2] After traveling to Berlin, House informed the president that problems had reached a point where the European powers could not find a solution on their own. The colonel insisted that the situation demanded outside mediation. He thought he had already made a small "dent . . . [s]ufficient enough to start a discussion in London," but "[u]nless someone acting for you can bring about an understanding, there is some day to be an awful cataclysm. No one in Europe can do it. There is too much hatred, too many jealousies."[3] The colonel saw an opportunity for Wilson to become an influential international leader by mediating a resolution to the escalating European crisis. During the remaining days of his trip, House continued working to keep the water from boiling over, but he was fighting a losing battle.

House was not alone. The American ambassador to London, Walter Hines Page, believed that only an intervention by the United States could restore tranquility between the European countries. He communicated to the president that "they don't want peace on the continent—the ruling classes do not. But they will want it presently and then our opportunity will come—your opportunity to play an important and historic part."[4] With Wilson's approval, Page offered the services of the United States government to London in hope that it might accept American mediation. Page, however, was not an objective bystander. Not only did he wish for an Allied victory, he also believed that Britain was fighting to protect what he considered the civilized world from German militarism. Thus Page developed a close relationship with British statesmen, and throughout his tenure as ambassador he tried to persuade Wilson to support Britain.[5]

When the war came in August of 1914, Page told Wilson that it had occurred because of German and Russian aspirations. "It's the Slav and the German. Each wants his day, and neither has got beyond the stage of tooth and claw." While the conflict was not as simple as Page's derogatory statement suggests, the July Crisis, which could have been a regional conflict over control of the Balkans, blossomed into a world affair. After the assassination of Archduke Franz Ferdinand on June 28, Germany offered Vienna a "blank check" of support to deter Russia from aiding Serbia. The kaiser and his advisors assumed St. Petersburg was unprepared to go to war. Events immediately surrounding Austria-Hungary's July 28 declaration of war on Serbia, however, proved Germany wrong. When Russia mobilized its forces, Germany's fears that the 1894 Franco-Russian alliance would force Berlin into a two-front war convinced the German high command to mobilize against both Russia and France. France in turn mobilized with the misplaced belief that because of improved relations with Britain established through the 1904 Entente Cordiale and the 1912 naval accords, which shifted the Royal Navy to the North Sea and left France to guard the Mediterranean, Britain would come to its aid against Germany. Thus in the confusion of late summer the major powers on the European continent prepared for battle.[6]

On August 1, Germany declared war on Russia. The following day when German troops marched west on their way to take Paris, government officials in London realized that they had to respond considering Berlin's next move was undoubtedly a move into neutral Belgium. Prime Minister Henry Asquith's cabinet met to discuss their options. While they did not want a German victory to upset the balance of power on the continent, the majority of the cabinet opposed going to war simply to aid France. Neither the 1904 Anglo-French Entente nor the 1907 accord with Russia, which unofficially established the Triple Entente, included a binding commitment to send the British Army to France in the case of war with Germany and thus were not military alliances. Herbert Samuel, president of the Board of Trade, asserted that "we are not entitled to carry England into war for the sake of our goodwill to France, or for the sake of maintaining the strength of France or Russia against that of Germany or Austria."[7] To Samuel, and many others in the cabinet, the only reasons for war would be to prevent Germany from violating Belgium's neutrality and, more important, taking control of the eastern shore of the English Channel. The cabinet agreed that a German presence in Britain's home waters was unacceptable.[8]

On August 3, the day Germany officially declared war on France, the cabinet met again and decided to send a note to Berlin demanding that Belgium's neutrality be respected. The next day, British leaders learned that German troops were already marching across the country. Britain followed up with a second letter requiring Germany to withdraw by midnight, but Germany did not intend to pull its soldiers back. As a result, Whitehall decided to go to war and began preparations for sending the small British Expeditionary Force of four divisions to France.[9]

Wilson grew increasingly apprehensive as the events unfolded. He told House that "the pressure and anxiety of the last week have been the most nearly overwhelming that I have yet had to carry." The president assumed there must be a divine explanation for why the war started despite their efforts. God must have a reason for the onslaught, "we must face the situation in the confidence that Providence has deeper plans than we could have possibly laid ourselves."[10]

Wilson's interpretation of morality and the law, along with a desire to increase US prestige and economic prosperity guided his foreign policy. The son of a Presbyterian minister, Wilson was a devoutly religious man who claimed he had the responsibility to do God's work on earth. Writing during his undergraduate years at Princeton, Wilson expressed in an essay titled "Work Day Religion" that "[w]ith all this diligence and earnestness we should perform every act as an act which we shall someday be made to render a strict account, as an act done either in the service of God or that of the Devil."[11] Wilson's convictions moved him to follow a Calvinist moral code that he applied to men and states alike, a position he carried into the political arena.

From an early age, Wilson aspired to enter politics, trained himself to become strong in "the art of persuasion," and focused his studies in law and political science.[12] Making a connection between religion and politics, Wilson regarded the presidency as a pulpit from which he could direct national and world affairs. In 1912, Wilson asserted that because the United States was a world power the "[p]resident has, of necessity, become the guiding force in the affairs of the country."[13] Similar to Robert Lansing, Wilson was also a student of the law. Having taught the subject from 1892 to 1894 as a professor at Princeton, Wilson concluded that international law was always changing and was "a body of abstract principles founded upon long established custom."[14] On many occasions he used the law to protect American interests and often interpreted international precedents to favor the United States. His world-view influenced his conception of neutrality and, aptly regarded by his contemporaries as the "schoolmaster in politics," the president held the conviction that his approach to diplomacy was right and everyone else was wrong.[15]

Wilson's stress over the burgeoning war was compounded by the recent loss of his wife, Ellen, who had been diagnosed with Bright's disease in early spring and died on August 6. She was the most important person in his life. They met right before Wilson entered graduate school at Johns Hopkins University and were married almost immediately. After her death, Wilson stated that "[w]henever I tried to speak to those bound to me by affection and intimate sympathy it seemed as if a single word would open the flood-gates and I would be lost to all self-control."[16] He had depended on Ellen's emotional support and companionship and her passing left a major void in his life. For weeks afterward, Wilson wrote letters to friends expressing his sorrow. It was in his work that he found solace. In a letter to House on August 17, Wilson stated, "It seemed for a time as if I would never get my head above the flood that came upon me, but the absolute imperative character of the duties I have to perform had been my salvation." Writing days later, he added "my great safety lies in having my attention absolutely fixed elsewhere than upon myself."[17]

Considering the perception that he held of his own role in the world, and the grief he experienced over his wife's death, Wilson focused intently on promoting the United States as a mediator for the warring parties. Thus on August 4, he sent letters to all heads of state, including Tsar Nicholas II,

Emperor of Austria-Hungary Franz Josef I, German Kaiser Wilhelm II, King George V of England, and President Raymond Poincare of France, stating that the United States deemed it a "privilege and duty to offer its friendship and welcomed an opportunity to act in the interest of European peace, either now or at any other time that might be more suitable."[18]

That same day, Wilson announced his country's intention to remain neutral. The president and his cabinet reasoned that if the United States was to be a fair mediator it would have to be nonaligned. He believed his country could not officially back one belligerent or the other and expect the Europeans to allow him to broker a peace.

Maintaining neutrality was not simply a matter of diplomacy. The administration fully understood the traditional American view of distant wars. The public perceived the conflict as a foreign affair that was none of its business. For more than a century, US citizens had watched as armies wrecked the European continent. The wars of the French Revolution and Napoleonic era drained continental resources and devastated the populations of many powerful countries. In 1914, many Americans continued to heed George Washington's warning against entangling the United States in long-term alliances. During Washington's farewell address, he warned his people not to become embroiled in European political and military dealings. He feared that foreign alliances could draw the young country into conflicts that might damage if not halt its growth. Washington declared that "permanent, inveterate antipathies against particular nations, and passionate attachments for others, should be excluded; and that, in place of them, just and amicable feelings towards all should be cultivated." In the midst of the French Revolution, Washington realized that taking sides could tear the country apart and that allying with France or Britain could subjugate the United States to one or the other's wishes. He claimed that supporting one side over another could make the United States "in some degree a slave" to foreign influences. Americans, he argued, should focus on economic relations with Europe and avoid political alliances because there were very few similarities between US and European politics. The interests of countries such as Great Britain and France forced them into "frequent controversies" that Washington argued his country could and should avoid.[19]

Adhering to a policy of avoiding political alliances did not mean refraining from all interaction with the rest of the world.[20] Like Wilson, many Americans favored one belligerent over the other. According to the *New York Times*, more than 300,000 people filled Times Square on August 5 to read the "red-lettered" bulletins that the paper posted in its windows listing the declarations of war. Many in the crowd cheered when they learned of Britain's decision for war against Germany. Soon others shouted their approval after Berlin acted in kind.[21] The United States was a very diverse place with a multitude of cultures, languages, and ethnic backgrounds. Predictably it split over whom to support. According to the 1910 US Census, of the 101,115,000 people living in the United States, over 13,515,886 were born overseas. Of this number, 2,501,333 were born in Germany. Another 5,781,437 were native-born second-generation German-Americans, making them the largest immigrant group in the country, followed by 4,504,360 Irish-Americans; 2,541,649 Russian-Americans; 2,322,442 English-Americans; and 2,098,360 Italian-Americans.[22]

The Wilson administration feared that the multicultural nation could erupt in violence if it did not place US interests ahead of those of other countries. In an effort to ensure unity among native and nationalized citizens alike, Wilson took an additional step when he appealed to the American people on August 18. He asserted that Americans' actions and opinions could influence US involvement in the war more than any other factor and called on them to keep their country's interests at heart. "Every man who really loves America," the president wrote, "will act and speak in the true spirit of neutrality, which is the spirit of impartiality and fairness to all concerned." To respond differently would threaten the security of the country. Concluding his message, Wilson insisted, "The United States must be neutral in fact as well as in name during these days that are to try men's souls."[23]

Americans, he asserted, must do more than simply comply with the legal definition of neutrality. The president asked the people to remain loyal only to the United States and place all other affiliations and sympathies aside. Many citizens praised Wilson's call to maintain the spirit of neutrality—a message that was initially more than simple rhetoric. He and his cabinet worked to assure that the government abided by the pronouncement. This was especially true of Secretary of State William Jennings Bryan. The "Great Commoner," appointed to the position because of his lifelong work for the Democratic Party, was a pacifist. Sitting prominently on his desk was a paperweight that he had specially made to remind him and others that violence was not a solution to the world's problems. Bryan commissioned an artist to melt down a sword and reshape it in the form of a plowshare. Engraved on the face of his small monument to peace read "Nothing is final between friends" and the bible verse "They shall beat their swords into plowshares. Isaiah 2:4." To the secretary, very little, if anything, was worth the bloodshed and destruction that came with war. He believed that the best way to end confrontations was through talking and compromise.[24]

Like Wilson, Bryan hoped the United States could be a moral leader that used its resources to uplift the world. The secretary also wanted his country to avoid the entangling web of alliances and international relationships that might destroy what he perceived as American idealism. To do this, Bryan expected the United States to lead by example rather than by direct involvement overseas.[25] This mindset drove his view that the Oval Office should remain impartial. Only then could the government find a way to save the world from itself.

A week prior to Wilson's speech, Bryan acted to preserve American neutrality by opposing the issuance of bank loans to belligerent powers. On August 10, Bryan wrote the president that the French had contacted the Morgan Company of New York about a loan and J. P. Morgan wanted to know if the government had any objections. The secretary said he had spoken with State Department Counselor Lansing and the two found no legal objections to the loan. However, Bryan asserted that there was another concern they needed to consider. Approving international loans to belligerents could have a detrimental effect on American neutrality.

Bryan offered several other reasons why he opposed loaning money to belligerents. "Money," he argued, "is the worst of all contrabands because it commands everything else." Without funding, the warring states would have less capital available to purchase weapons and supplies. By denying loans, Bryan thought the administration might be able to shorten the conflict: "I know of nothing that would do more to prevent war than an international agreement that neutral nations would not loan to belligerents . . . could we not by our own example hasten the reaching of such an agreement? . . . [O]ur refusal to loan to any belligerent would naturally tend to hasten the conclusion of the war . . . the only way of testing our influence is to set an example and observe its effect."[26]

Lansing added that he feared that the warring parties might conclude the loans were a sign of sympathy toward the country that received the loan. Sympathy for one side or the other could challenge the Wilson administration's policies. If US investment houses offered loans to one government, the United States might feel forced to offer funds to all belligerents merely to seem fair minded. Additionally Bryan and the counselor claimed that if the government approved the loans, private citizens would advance money to the side they favored, which would impact America's neutrality. Finally they concluded that private corporations that loaned money might try to convince other Americans to support one of the belligerents. Bryan worried that financiers might use the press to create public support for the state to which they loaned the money because the security of their investment would be directly tied to the result of the war.

Defending his position, Bryan added that Lansing did not want the government to safeguard American companies from losing money. If the businesses decided to invest in foreign governments, they did so at their own risk. Bryan found no difference between an American going overseas to enlist in a belligerent army and a company investing overseas during a war. Both did so without US government protection.[27]

Wilson agreed with the secretary's argument. Loans were not, he argued, in line with the spirit of neutrality and therefore Washington should not support them. Several days later, Bryan replied to Morgan that the administration could not endorse a loan to the French or any other belligerent. He saw "no reason why loans should not be made to neutral governments, but in the judgment of this Government, loans by American bankers to any foreign nation which is at war is inconsistent with the true spirit of neutrality."[28] The purpose of the administration's decision was to distance the United States from the European conflict and prevent Washington from becoming too close to one or the other of the belligerents.

While the loan issue may have temporarily bolstered US neutrality, the diversity of the country's population was a serious factor in Anglo-American relations. Well versed in domestic politics, the president knew that conducting policy required the public's approval, which forced him to walk a narrow line between the demands of his pro-German and pro-Allied countrymen. American public opinion would remain an important factor in his decisions throughout the first phase of neutrality and convinced Wilson to take additional steps to uphold the country's neutrality. In turn, it would also affect British policy.

Because London did not want to cause an irreparable breach between the Allies and Washington, Britain too weighed the importance of American public opinion. One way to achieve this goal was to control the flow of information reaching the United States. As soon as the war began, Britain cut the transatlantic telegram cable that connected New York to the European continent. Consequently, after August 5, 1914, most of the news that reached the American public had to go through the British censors. In the early days of the war when people were still impressionable and formulating their opinions about the belligerents, this censorship tactic gave the Allies a decisive advantage.[29]

Great Britain was so concerned about developing a favorable American public opinion that it organized a division under the War Propaganda Bureau at Wellington House in London called the American Ministry of Information. The organization, which was so secret that many senior British officials did not know of its existence, was responsible for the distribution of books, pamphlets, speeches, private letters to prominent citizens, and any other form of manipulated materials sent to the United States.[30] Wellington House hired numerous prominent writers such as Sir Arthur Conan Doyle to offer advice and write much of the propaganda that ended up in the hands of American and British citizens. The main objective of the American Ministry of Information was to buttress the idea that Germany was the aggressor and that Britain was fighting to save civilization. It was successful at drawing people of influence to the British cause—not through bribery but through befriending them. The organization focused its attention on convincing ministers, politicians like Theodore Roosevelt, professors, newspapermen, and other influential people to disseminate Britain's case to fellow Americans.[31]

Along with the desire to stay out of European politics, Wilson maintained a watchful eye on his country's economic health. When he spoke to the press on August 3, the president assured Americans that the United States was not going to suffer from the war. He said that after talking to Secretary of the Treasury William McAdoo, he concluded that the country's fiscal position was in stable shape. "There was no cause for alarm," said the president, because "the bankers and businessmen of the country are cooperating with the Government with zeal and intelligence, and spirit which will make the outcome secure."[32] Wilson soon discovered, however, that he was wrong.

Industrial expansion and advances in communication had made the Atlantic barrier no more than a fantasy. Indeed diplomatic confrontation with the European powers was quickly becoming likely. Europe was America's most important trading destination and as US industry continued its rapid expansion in the latter half of the 1800s, the country exported more goods than ever before. In the 1890s, US companies produced enough steel to make America the third largest exporter of metal products in the world. The agricultural sector was also strong, exporting over one billion dollars' worth of commodities in 1914 alone.[33] In the years leading up to the war, 77 percent of all US exports went to the belligerents. By 1914 America's exports to Europe depended heavily on ties to Germany, to which it shipped goods valued at $344,794,276 in 1914, but more so the United Kingdom where the United States sent $594,271,868 worth of merchandise.[34] Additionally, before the outbreak of the war, investors around the globe purchased securities on the New York Stock Exchange (NYSE), making the stock market hum with foreign capital. Collectively these developments meant that the US economy was increasingly reliant on its connections to the European community.

In July 1914, saber rattling had brought havoc to the American economy. Foreign investors immediately began selling off US stocks. In the final week of the month, Europeans withdrew $45 million. The rapid sell-off of stocks forced officials to close the NYSE to prevent its total collapse. The doors of the NYSE remained sealed for nearly four and a half months, the longest shutdown in its lengthy history.[35] The crisis caused the American dollar to decline in value overnight, dropping from $4.86 to $7.00 to the British pound.[36]

Wilson quickly recognized the war's effect on the American economy. In a special address before Congress on September 4, the president discussed a significant drop in customs duties and explained that the decline could have a serious effect on the US Treasury and its ability to ensure the country's continued economic growth. He expressed the opinion that "[c]onditions have arisen which no man foresaw; they affect the whole world of commerce and economic production; and they must be faced and dealt with." Wilson further exclaimed that Washington "cannot too scrupulously or carefully safeguard a financial situation which is at best, while war continues in Europe, difficult and abnormal."[37] While this speech was an appeal for a tax increase, it clearly indicates that the president was concerned about and intended to protect America's financial position.

High ranking British officials understood the stresses that the conflict placed on the American economy and that such risks could in turn have a negative impact at home. The United States owed large sums to Britain and the war made repayment of these loans difficult. Addressing the problem, British Ambassador to the United States Cecil Spring-Rice claimed that if the United States could not meet its obligations, London might not have the funds available to conduct a long war. Therefore, he suggested, London must take steps to protect the US exports: "I gather this that unless [American] exports increase . . . there will probably be [a] crisis here in November."[38]

In 1914, the daunting economic challenge facing US and British diplomats was London's decision to cut off German trade. Britain understood that to strangle Germany into submission, it had to rely on a naval strategy that had the unfortunate consequence of impinging on neutral states' commercial rights at sea. Britain planned to use its naval force offensively to cut off enemy trade, creating an economic disaster in Germany similar to the one London feared could affect the United Kingdom if the tables were turned.[39] Attacking German commerce became a major objective for the Royal Navy in the 1910s. Prewar strategy for naval operations emphasized that the best way to deal with Germany was by preventing it from trading on the oceans.[40]

From that point forward, all naval decisions emphasized conducting a blockade to prevent Berlin from acquiring materiel that it could use in its war effort—including guns, explosives, munitions, military clothing and camp materials, armor plating, warships, any type of aircraft, and any other item used exclusively for the manufacture of weapons. In the days before the outbreak of the First World War, the navy stationed the Grand Fleet at Scapa Flow in northern Scotland. From this base, the Royal Navy was expected to prevent the German High Seas fleet from leaving the North Sea by establishing a defensive line from Scotland to Norway. Therefore, when the war began, Asquith's administration planned to use a maritime policy developed over the previous decade and had no intentions to change direction in the face of neutral opposition.[41]

On August 5, 1914, British officials sent all neutral governments a list of contraband items, creating a serious problem for the United States. If Washington accepted the list, it would be giving up the country's cherished right to trade freely and could threaten its neutral status. The day after Britain publicized the contraband items, Bryan ordered Page to contact British Foreign Secretary Edward Grey in hope of finding a solution to the commercial controversy. Bryan wanted Britain to accept the 1909 Declaration of London as the principal guideline for regulating international trade during the war. Developed at the February 1909 London Naval Conference, the declaration provided a set of rules for how belligerents could approach neutral trade and provided a clear explanation of what the signatories agreed constituted absolute contraband, conditional contraband, and what would remain on a free list, which included items such as cotton and rubber. On August 3, Germany had announced that it would follow a 1909 Prize Code that complied closely with the Declaration of London if Britain would do the same. This offer prompted Bryan to tell Page he should stress that the declaration would reduce misunderstandings between belligerents and nonaligned countries.

Britain did not offer a quick response. When the declaration had gone before Parliament for ratification in 1911, public concerns that the document might hinder the Royal Navy in a future conflict convinced the House of Lords to reject the treaty. Therefore 13 days after receiving the US request, Grey informed Bryan that he was not sure if the Declaration of London was an instrument his government could recognize. Delaying any definitive answer, the foreign secretary stated that he must first see what the other belligerents planned to do.[42]

Weeks later, the cabinet held a conference to decide what to do about the declaration. Asquith's cabinet included 23 members, but few had any real influence on Anglo-American relations. This inner circle included Grey, Chancellor of the Exchequer David Lloyd George, Secretary of State for War Lord Horatio Herbert Kitchener, First Lord of the Admiralty Winston Churchill, Home Secretary Reginald McKenna, and the prime minister himself. While all of them offered their input throughout the first months of the war, Grey had, as historian Ernest May claims, more "popular prestige" than anyone else. Even Asquith, who fellow cabinet members considered aloof during the many meetings they had together, gave Grey plenty of room to manage diplomacy with Washington.[43]

The meeting's participants, led by Grey, decided to accept certain parts of the declaration but not everything in it because the fixed set of rules would tie British hands and eliminate the flexibility needed to conduct the blockade. One concern was that article 35 of the declaration outlawed the doctrine of continuous voyage when applied to conditional contraband. In the end, the cabinet chose to accept the existing list of contraband but concluded that it must assure Britain's right to use the doctrine of continuous voyage if it was to cut off Germany's food supply. The decision still left a legal barrier to the blockade policy because foodstuffs were conditional contraband, and unless London could prove the food was destined for the armed forces, the Royal Navy could not legally confiscate it. To circumvent this problem, the cabinet accepted McKenna's assertion that the Imperial Government controlled the food supply in Germany. McKenna told the cabinet that he had "reliable reports" to support his claim and therefore Britain had the right to stop such shipments destined for the Central Powers. "There would be a presumption," he argued, "that all foodstuffs cosigned to Germany were contraband."[44]

Two days later, Assistant Undersecretary of State for Foreign Affairs Eyre Crowe made the cabinet's decision to remain steadfast when he told Page that Britain would accept the declaration in general but intended to make modifications "judge[d] indispensable to the efficient conduct of their naval operations." Crowe claimed that the Declaration of London was outdated and did not reflect the demands of modern warfare. In the August 20, 1914, Order in Council, Britain provided an updated contraband list and claimed the authority to search and seize neutral vessels on return voyages if they carried false manifests. Grey's office wanted to ensure that it closed as many loopholes as possible so that Britain could effectively cut off imports to Germany. It also claimed the right to confiscate conditional contraband traveling to Germany via a neutral port, a practice known as a "broken voyage." Doing so, Britain reopened a controversy with the United States that dated back to the War of 1812.[45]

Despite its initial protests, the Wilson administration concluded that defying the British pronouncement could threaten American neutrality. When asked about insuring US cargoes, Lansing told the director of the War Insurance Bureau, William C. Delanoy, that trying to help merchants circumvent the contraband list was a dangerous decision that might create problems for the White House. Lansing asserted that the government should not insure vessels carrying contraband goods to belligerent parties because such an action would be a breach of neutrality. War risk insurance was supposed to protect legitimate trade against the "ordinary risk of war." In Lansing's opinion, shippers who decided to carry contraband took the risks on themselves: "The best and most direct means of forestalling a charge that our Government is encouraging, fostering or participating in contraband trade through issuance of war risk insurance is to insert in the policies which its agency may issue a provision which makes it clear that the Government does not insure contraband articles or ships engaged in contraband trade, but leaves the individual involved to suffer the penalty imposed by international law, namely, the confiscation or destruction of contraband goods."[46]

Lansing reminded the director that Wilson had decided not to "encourage" loans to warring states and that insuring contraband would also threaten American neutrality. "How much closer," Lansing asked, "to a breach of neutrality would this Government approach if it were underwriting or insuring contraband trade with one of the belligerents." If the government intended to underwrite American cargoes, it could not accept a list of approved ports. He stated that the restricted destinations included most German harbors. Despite the heightened risk of sailing to these ports, refusing to insure ships headed to such places could appear to be "partiality upon the part of the Government of the United States, and again would imperil the neutrality of this Government . . . I cannot conceive how such a discrimination could be upheld or defended." Additionally he asserted that Washington should not have to regulate the country's commerce. As a neutral, the US government would not accept the responsibility of policing its own businessmen. If Britain wanted to enforce the list, *Britain* would have to assume the burden of regulating what it considered unneutral trade.[47]

Dealing with the blockade was not the only threat to American commerce that the Wilson administration faced in the first months of the war. Even before making an official declaration of neutrality, he and his cabinet discussed the weak state of the merchant marine. For decades, US industry had relied on foreign shipping to transport its cargoes around the globe. In the first months of the war, however, exports declined because Americans could not find adequate cargo space for their goods. American bottoms carried only 17 percent of the country's exports while Great Britain and Germany transported approximately 70 percent of the trade. Britain alone owned 45 percent of all cargo vessels that could carry 100 tons or more.[48] This was a major problem for the United States because the Allies had redirected their merchant vessels to support their war effort and since the majority of the world's cargo ships belonged to European companies, stockpiles of US goods began filling up loading docks with nowhere to go.[49]

Wilson realized that the country needed more domestically owned tonnage if it was to end the American dependence on foreign shipping. Building a merchant fleet, though, was not something the president could immediately accomplish, and he realized that the simplest solution was to purchase as many foreign vessels as possible. Wilson decided to sit down with several senators and draft the "free ships" bill, which would allow US companies to register foreign vessels in the United States.[50] After a long working weekend, led by Alabama Senator Oscar Underwood, the group proposed their bill in the legislature. The Foreign Registry Bill passed both houses of Congress on August 17.

Over the same period, McAdoo was also working on a piece of legislation that would allow for the government purchase of merchant ships to increase the number of vessels available to American businesses. McAdoo asserted that government-owned ships would provide US exporters with access to Central and South America. Writing to the president on August 16, McAdoo asserted that the vessels would allow the United States to "quickly establish business and political relations that will be of inestimable value to this country—perhaps for all time." He also believed that if the government augmented the number of ships available it could regulate shipping rates and keep them at fair levels for merchants. Plus, the federally owned vessels could act as a naval reserve if the country went to war.[51]

When the president approved McAdoo's plan he asked the secretary, "We'll have to fight for it, won't we?" When McAdoo responded, "We certainly shall," Wilson added, "Well, then let's fight." They were right; there was an enormous outpouring of opposition. Many Americans felt that the bill would provide the government with too much influence in the business world and threaten free enterprise. Others thought that it could place the United States at odds with the belligerents and endanger its neutrality. Opposition to the plan frustrated the president because he and McAdoo were trying to aid the business community by providing the ships that the private sector could not afford and at a time it desperately needed the help. The lack of support for the bill in Congress and from commercial leaders pushed the ship purchase measure to the back burner in the House of Representatives and it did not come up for discussion in the Senate until much later in the year.[52]

One of the first complaints about the lack of shipping came from Standard Oil. Like other companies, Standard Oil owned ships registered in different countries and sought to regain control of the vessels after the outbreak of the war. On August 18, the company's representative, William Libby, wrote Bryan, asking him about transferring a number of vessels from German registry to the United States. Libby stated that Standard Oil owned many ships registered to the Deutsch-Amerikanische Petroleum Gesellschaft Company and stressed that the vessels "are all American-owned" because Standard Oil controlled "the entire capital stock of the D. A. P. G." What he feared was that the belligerents would not agree that the transfers were legitimate. If Britain captured and detained its ships, Standard Oil would lose large sums of money while prize courts considered the ships' fates. Libby hoped Washington might "secure the assent of powers engaged in the present conflict" so that the belligerents would not capture ships transferred to the US flag that American companies owned before the war.[53]

In response to such requests, Bryan sat down with British Embassy Counselor Colville Barclay and discussed the transfer of ships to the United States. Bryan argued that American "trade was being completely strangled . . . that the United States, though neutral, were being ruined . . . all because it pleased others to settle their differences by force of arms." He wanted Britain to allow US companies to transfer their internationally registered vessels and purchase German merchant ships to alleviate the pressure on the country's commerce. Barclay disagreed with the secretary. He maintained that this would harm London's war effort because Germany would gain needed income and the ships would continue carrying valuable goods. When reflecting on his discussion with Bryan, Barclay concluded that Britain had no real choice but to allow the United States to purchase vessels. He told Grey that "arguments were quite useless" because it was "evident that the United States Government mean to buy some of the German ships . . . [and] any opposition on our part will be very badly received, and create a feeling of hostility, which might prove embarrassing."[54] Barclay argued that standing up to Washington on this issue was dangerous because it could damage diplomatic relations.

Grey agreed. He was already trying to find a way to explain that Britain would not comply with the Declaration of London, and adding another barrier to US trade might damage his country's image among the American people. After speaking with Page, Grey relayed a message to Barclay that London would "not press objection to Germany getting the money for the sale of the ships." The foreign secretary decided that good relations with the United States outweighed the financial benefits that Berlin might receive. Answering another of Page's questions, Grey stated that London felt that as long as the United States agreed not to use the vessels for trade with Germany it would have no objections: "Our real apprehension about the American purchase of the German ships was that they might run under the American flag with traffic of that sort." Britain wanted to ensure that the ships stayed off their normal trade routes. It did not want them used to supply Germany—through neutral or German ports—under the protection of the Stars and Stripes.[55]

Lansing forwarded the foreign secretary's telegram to Wilson and wrote that he found Grey's argument to be fair—that the British demands were appropriate considering the circumstances. There was, however, no reason, he added, to consent publicly to London's additional stipulations and risk German protests over a violation of US neutrality; American shipowners would avoid trading with Germany simply to avoid the risk of seizure by the British. In other words, owners would willingly comply without restrictions in order to protect their vessels from confiscation, which would prevent the United States from violating its neutrality.[56] This was a satisfactory suggestion to Wilson and he was pleased with the British decision, telling Lansing that he thought "the situation is clearing up in a very satisfactory way."[57]

Avoiding major confrontations with Germany and Britain may have played a part in Wilson's decision; however, the president's key objective was to expand the merchant fleet so US companies could export goods to new markets.[58] As previously mentioned, McAdoo and Wilson were working on a bill that called for the purchase of German vessels docked in US ports. On August 19, days prior to Britain's decision, the house and senate commerce committees approved McAdoo's and Wilson's ship purchase plan, which then had to pass a congressional vote.[59] Britain's pronouncement could make this goal easier to pursue.

Yet, unbeknown to the Foreign Office, British and French officials did not see eye to eye on the purchases of German vessels. French Ambassador to the United States Jean Jules Jusserand told Wilson that as long as Germany owned ships trapped in US ports, it had a financial burden to maintain them and that if Berlin sold the vessels, it would obtain "gold credit in New York which is of the greatest importance at this moment."[60] The French reaction worried Barclay because it was in stark contrast to London's announcement to Washington. Barclay commented that now that his government had made its opinion public, it was unable to work with Paris: "I am afraid we have tied our hands, and are now unable to support France in insisting on the U.S. gov. respecting treaty rights." Grey also asserted that Britain could not take back its response to the Wilson administration, pointing out that he "had already sent a telegram to Washington before this reached me."[61] The Paris announcement created a rift between the Allies and the United States because it ultimately prevented American businessmen from buying the German ships without risking their capture by the French.

In addition to the confrontations arising over commerce, American efforts to bring the belligerents together for peace talks continued. At his biweekly press conference on August 3, the president told the correspondents, "[T]his country could reap a great permanent glory out of the help she would be able to extend to other nations."[62] The United States could emerge as a world leader by molding a lasting peace that allowed American democracy to become the guiding model for other powers around the globe.

To be a mediator, the administration had to remain out of the fray across the Atlantic. Having returned from Europe in late July empty handed, House still had a desire to lead the conciliation effort for the president. On August 30, the colonel arrived at Wilson's summerhouse in Cornish, New Hampshire. Wilson was interested in House's travels across Europe and wanted to know what the various leaders were like. Demonstrating how out of touch he was with the causes of the war the president told House "it made him heartsick to think of how near we came to averting this great disaster." Wilson apparently blamed himself for not acting fast enough to stop the fighting before it started. He wondered if he should have sent House to meet with the leaders earlier, but his friend replied that it would not have mattered. Preventing the war was out of the hands of the Washington government and the only thing the administration could do now was continue pressing for mediation.[63]

The president was also very worried about the possible outcomes of the contest raging in Europe. He feared that if the war ended with a clear victor it would "turn back the clock across the Atlantic, especially if Germany won." House wrote in his diary that Wilson was unsympathetic toward Germany and that he argued it carried the chief burden for starting the conflict. When House explained that Kaiser Wilhelm II had built up his military to maintain peace, Wilson responded that the German leader was foolish "to create a powder magazine and risk someone's sropping [dropping] a spark into it."[64]

Wilson's pro-Allied position was quite clear and his comments to House demonstrate that privately he was not complying with his own "spirit of neutrality." Nevertheless, despite his personal antipathy toward Berlin, Wilson still believed that his views should not affect America's official neutrality or his chances to open talks. This approach became evident in late August and early September when the president deliberated over how to respond to Germany's march through Belgium en route to France. To subdue the Belgian population, Berlin authorized a strategy of *Shrecklichkeit* or frightfulness. The idea was to scare the population into submission by burning down houses and executing civilians accused of guerilla warfare.[65] On August 28, Bryan relayed a message to the White House—a telegram from the Belgian minister for foreign affairs, Jacques Davignon, informed Bryan that the German army had unjustly razed Antwerp and forced the city's residents to flee. According to the minister, the soldiers executed several city leaders and left the centuries-old community of 400,000 in a "heap of ashes." The atrocity, he asserted, was an "outrage on the rights of humanity." Despite Davignon's claims, Bryan felt that the United States should not respond immediately. He feared that if Washington investigated the matter, it could come into conflict with Berlin and probably not receive support from other neutrals: "I am so anxious that we shall avoid anything that can possibly bring us into collision with the belligerent powers that I am not sure that we should make any protest at all."[66]

Wilson agreed with Bryan, asserting that protesting German behavior might jeopardize efforts at mediation. He concurred that the government should act slowly on such matters. If the United States made a formal protest, it would "be in danger of becoming chronic critics of what was going forward." Additionally Wilson added that the "time for cleaning up all these matters will come when the war is over and the nations gather in sober council again." If he pressed issues that did not directly affect the United States, Wilson feared his government might not appear neutral. Thus, regardless of his perception of Germany, the president decided not to directly address Berlin's actions because doing so could restrict his chances of ending the war.[67]

Not everyone connected to the president welcomed Bryan's efforts to direct Washington's policy. Like Wilson and Bryan, House saw a great opportunity for the United States to play a leading role in world affairs, but he did not like Bryan. The colonel opposed Bryan's nomination for president in 1900 and claimed the secretary was still "wildly impracticable." As soon as House returned from Europe, he made clear that he viewed himself as the best candidate to be Wilson's spokesman to the foreign dignitaries. He worked to push Bryan out of a seat of prominence, warning against letting him make overtures to the European powers. He claimed that Bryan had no standing with their leaders: "They look upon him as purely visionary and it would lessen the weight of your influence if you desired to use it yourself. When you decided to do anything, it had best be done by you directly for they have the highest possible opinion and respect for you which Mr. Bryan unfortunately in no way shares."[68] He later added that Wilson should make sure that the American people realize it was the president's idea to press for mediation, not Bryan's: "I hate to harp on Mr. Bryan, but you cannot know as I do how he is thought of in this connection." House considered Bryan naïve, unsuited for the moment, and incapable of bringing together the warring parties. Arrogantly, House saw himself as the perfect person for the job. The Europeans, House insisted, knew that he held the president's confidence and therefore spoke directly yet unofficially for the White House.[69] Such personal attacks continued throughout the war as House and others vied for Wilson's ear. The animosity created enormous tension among members of the administration over the direction of American policy, and while Bryan continued to play a significant role in the early efforts at mediation, the secretary of state's influence slowly diminished in part because of House's ongoing efforts to undermine him.

In early September, House decided to send a letter to German Assistant Foreign Secretary Arthur Zimmermann emphasizing that Washington still wanted to help bring the fighting to a close. House and Wilson hoped they could convince the kaiser to be the first to call for a peace settlement. Taking a page from Theodore Roosevelt's playbook, House tried to flatter Wilhelm II by praising his success on the battlefield. The colonel wrote, "Now that His Majesty has so brilliantly shown the power of His army, would it not be consistent with His life long endeavor to maintain peace, to consent to overtures being made in that direction?"[70]

In private, Wilson again expressed his fear of a German victory. The president stated that if Germany triumphed, the United States would need to prepare to defend its "form of Government and American ideals." Wilson's comments point out that he was thinking about how the war's outcome might influence American national security.[71] However, regardless of his personal and confidential views, in 1914 Wilson did not act on this concern. At that point in the conflict, the president had not yet decided to expand the US armed forces nor had he chosen to actively aid the Allied war effort. The president still intended that his government would maintain absolute neutrality.

On the evening of September 3, Grey replied to Spring-Rice that he concurred with the president's statement that a German victory would bring militarism to the US doorstep. He also clarified to Spring-Rice that Britain should do everything it could to prevent tension with the United States. "Such a dispute would indeed be a crowning calamity as the president says & probably fatal to our chances for success."[72] This did not mean, however, that London was prepared to consider a negotiated solution to the war.

The president and his advisors soon discovered that neither side was ready for peace because both Berlin and London felt confident of victory. Germany was still perched along the Marne ready to strike Paris. At the same time, London controlled the seas and no victory on land had convinced its leaders that Berlin would overrun the continent.

On September 4, German forces were only 35 miles from Paris and expected victory in mere days. Imperial Army Chief of Staff Helmuth von Moltke gave orders to his forces to cross the Marne, advance toward the capital, and surround the French opposition. At the same time, French Marshal Joseph Joffre observed that his enemy's offensive had exposed the flank of the German forces east of Paris and he too ordered his troops to advance. Therefore, when the Allies and Central Powers contemplated peace talks, each side intended to discuss terms from a position of strength. The belligerents wanted to force their adversaries to the negotiating table while winning the war and were not inclined to take Wilson's mediation efforts seriously. France and Russia were particularly unwilling to discuss terms with the Germans. Having suffered more than 200,000 casualties in the month of August alone and having lost territory to Germany as well, France had no desire for peace. The losses actually spurred the country's desire to fight. In a letter to the French Foreign Ministry, Jusserand said that when Bryan suggested returning to the status quo antebellum, he had firmly replied that the French would accept such an arrangement only after the Germans "gave us back the lives of our dead ones." Like France, Russia had suffered serious losses on the eastern front. The Allies were not ready to end the war, and at St. Petersburg's behest France, Russia, and Britain signed the Pact of London on September 5, 1914, agreeing that none of them would sign a separate peace with Germany.[73]

High-ranking German and British leaders were also unwilling to negotiate, yet they understood the importance of maintaining a conversation with the United States concerning peace. Outright rejection of mediation could damage relations with the Wilson administration. Therefore, the belligerents continued to feign a desire to end the hostilities. In early September, US Ambassador to Germany James Gerard informed Washington that the Imperial Government was willing to confer, but with one important stipulation: Talks could occur only if all the other belligerents simultaneously agreed to meet.[74]

On September 9, Page told Grey the United States knew about Germany's willingness to discuss ending the hostilities. He warned the foreign secretary that if Britain did not consent to talks the Allies would appear like warmongers. Grey, however, was not willing to commit Britain to negotiations. After listening to Page, Grey had to address one of the many challenges he would face throughout the war: giving the impression that you are willing to discuss peace even though you are not. The solution was to claim that Britain, France, and Russia were fighting a just war and to make demands Germany could not accept. According to Grey, the war had revealed that Europe was "living on the brink of a precipice" and Germany had done irreparable damage to Belgium. As a result, "no peace can be concluded that will permit the continuance of or the recurrence of an armed brute power in central Europe which violates treaties to make war and in making war assaults the continuity of civilization." Britain wanted to prevent German domination of Europe, in effect ensuring the balance of power on the continent, and as Grey asserted, London had to right the "cruel wrong [that] had been done to Belgium." The foreign secretary added that he did not oppose mediation, but because of Britain's obligations, Germany would first have to agree to pay reparations for its occupation of Belgium. Page accepted the secretary's terms, although he realized Germany would be unwilling to comply with London's demands.[75]

Germany too changed its stance. By mid-September, the Battle of the Marne had bogged down and the Allies pushed their enemy back over ground it had fought for in previous weeks. Finding themselves in retreat, the Germans took up a defensive position to prevent any further loss of territory. Ordering his troops to dig in on September 14, German General Helmuth von Moltke turned the war from a mobile war into the stagnant trench war that would dominate the western front until 1918.[76]

Within days it became evident that peace talks would not take place. Germany was no longer on the offensive and the massive opposing armies had ground to a halt. This lethal standoff quickly changed Germany's tone about mediation. On September 16, Bryan wrote to Wilson that he had learned from German Chancellor Theobald von Bethmann-Hollweg that German officials had no desire to pursue peace. He informed Bryan that it was "up to the United States to 'get our enemies to make peace proposals.'" Germany no longer thought mediation appropriate because the Allies would interpret such a move as a sign of weakness.[77] Trying to dissuade his own government from pursuing mediation, Page let House know that in his opinion, London likewise was not interested in mediation at this point. The British still believed that victory was just over the horizon. "You needn't fool yourself," wrote the ambassador, "they are going to knock Germany out, and nothing will be allowed to stand in their way." Showing his pro-British attitude, Page added, "It'll be fought to the finish. Pray God don't let . . . The Peace Old-Women get the notion afloat that we can or ought to stop it before the Kaiser is put out of business."[78]

Nevertheless Wilson and House pressed on. Because of Wilson's and House's focused determination to end the war, they ignored the political and military realities in Europe. If they could not get the foreign leaders to meet, maybe they could convince the German and British ambassadors to sit down together. Two days after Bryan learned the discouraging news from Bethmann-Hollweg, House informed the president on September 18 that he was trying to persuade Spring-Rice and German Ambassador Johann Heinrich von Bernstorff to meet for lunch. House hoped that if he could convince the ambassadors to discuss the suggestion, the two countries might start talking. The colonel, however, asserted Washington needed to push the idea of peace while it still had a chance because Britain "dominates her allies. Later she may not."[79] London, however, was still not interested in a compromise with Berlin. Yet, it still had to entertain Washington's requests. Whitehall would only consider talks that required Germany's acceptance of dictated peace terms, but on September 19, Spring-Rice sent Wilson a paraphrase of a telegram he had received from Grey outlining Britain's view on negotiations. The foreign secretary wanted Wilson to believe that Britain was not opposed to opening a discussion.

Grey again made strong preconditions that Germany would have to accept, which included disarmament and reparations to Belgium. "[I]f Germany desires the mediation of the United States," the foreign secretary argued, "these facts must be considered in drawing up the conditions of peace. But we have no indication that Germany is prepared to consider them . . . and up to the present moment we have neither stated nor heard any conditions for peace." Grey made his stipulations as if Britain was negotiating from a position of strength and suggested that Germany should accept blame for the war.[80] By declaring that London still favored peace, Grey continued implying that it was acting honorably. But Germany had not lost the war, much less the battle, and was still capable of continuing the fight; it was *not* going to accept Britain's proposal.

Bryan slowly accepted that the war was going to be long. Britain's and Germany's stalling tactics aggravated the secretary of state and he could not fathom that all they seemed capable of doing was asserting that the war was not their fault. Bryan told Wilson that "continuing the war was just as grave as the responsibility for beginning it . . . The world looks to us," he wrote, "to lead the way and I know you deeply desire to render every possible assistance. Both sides seem to entertain the old idea that fear is the only basis upon which peace can rest." In a statement that revealed his distress, Bryan aptly concluded that if there was a clear winner, it would want to dictate terms to the other and that would "probably mean preparation for another war." Bryan suggested that the president should write a letter to the belligerents charging that their unwillingness to negotiate had prolonged the conflict. The fault lay with all parties, he argued. The secretary hoped Wilson could "appeal to them to meet and exchange their views as to the terms upon which permanent peace can be insured."[81]

Again Bryan's comments irritated House. He did not view the secretary as a polished diplomat and asserted that Bryan was incapable of understanding the complexities of the war. The colonel did not want Bryan to interfere with the White House's mediation efforts. Indeed, he wanted the secretary to stay out of American foreign policy all together. The secretary of state, House claimed, was useful only for delivering the official statements made by the president, not drafting them. To defend his case to Wilson, House relayed a message from Page suggesting that the Germans had angered the secretary and were simply trying to "save their mutton." Overstepping his authority, House asserted that the president should authorize him (House) to continue the efforts to organize a secret dialogue between the German and British ambassadors.[82]

It did not take long for the colonel to discover that even his furtive efforts were destined to fail. He joined Spring-Rice for lunch in New York on September 20 and learned that the ambassador did not feel the time was right for a meeting with Bernstorff. London wanted to delay any real discussion about peace. After talking to the French and Russian ambassadors, Spring-Rice agreed with them that Bernstorff was pressing for talks simply to "make mischief." Spring-Rice asserted that the German ambassador hoped to foster a division among the Allies by convincing one of them to support discussions while the others maintained militant stances. In response, he proposed that if the president asked House what the British position was on peace, the colonel should state that neither the ambassador nor Grey could offer a definitive answer because of Britain's obligations to its allies not to make a separate treaty.[83]

On September 21, House received a similar response from Bernstorff. House responded that the British did not feel they could meet without approval from all the Allies. Asserting that this was reasonable, Bernstorff added that talks were going to be difficult and that the present was probably the wrong time to sit down together. If the ambassadors were able to start a dialogue, they would have to deal with a "deep-rooted distrust" of each other. Finally, Bernstorff pointed to the reality of the situation. Neither side wanted to start the negotiations because the other belligerent would view the act as a sign of weakness, placing whoever initiated the discussions at a diplomatic disadvantage.[84]

When war broke out in August 1914, disagreements over mediation and neutral trade began to complicate the relationship between the United States and Great Britain. Wilson claimed that he could and should become a voice of reason in helping the warring states find a solution to their problems. The president immediately declared that his country would remain neutral because, as he asserted, the American people wanted to avoid European affairs and he wanted to lead the mediation effort to end the war. Wilson also called on Americans to conduct themselves in the spirit of neutrality, something he would prove unable to do himself. Yet he seems to have thought he had a balanced approach to the belligerents and in certain cases attempted to assure American neutrality by going beyond its legal definition found in international law. Demonstrating their resolve to maintain neutrality, the president and his staff deterred US companies from providing loans to all belligerents and opposed providing insurance for ships that carried contraband to Europe. Remaining isolated from the war, however, would become impossible. The United States relied on European markets and financing to ensure its economic growth, which meant that, unless the US business community was willing to accept a shrinking share of the global market or immediately secure new overseas customers, policies enacted by their most important trading partners would affect the country and make tension unavoidable. Because both Britain and Germany initially expected to win a quick and decisive victory, they paid only lip service to Wilson's mediation proposals and had no real desire to conclude the war without some form of reparation. The belligerents' reaction forced Wilson to postpone further efforts to initiate peace talks for several months. Additionally, the British government did not want to create problems with the United States, but it refused to accept the Declaration of London in full because the document included restrictions that would hinder the Royal Navy's ability to conduct economic warfare against Germany.

Throughout August and early September, there were hints about the future direction of Anglo-American relations and the eventual constrictions placed on diplomatic discourse. Concerns over the purchase of belligerent ships, initial discussions about the Declaration of London, the treatment of US trade on the seas, the warring states' apathy toward mediation, and developments on the battlefield all pointed to potential complications between the Allies and the United States. By the end of September 1914, Britain and the United States had more sticking points than solutions to the issues in their relationship and without some degree of compromise on both sides, the outlook for Anglo-American diplomacy had become dangerously uncertain.

2

"An Exceedingly Tender Spot"

October 1914–November 1914

[C]ertainly no administration ever tried more diligently or watchfully to preserve an attitude and pursue a line of conduct absolutely neutral.

—Wilson to Professor Hugo Münsterberg, November 10, 1914[1]

In announcing the August 20 Order in Council, Prime Minister Henry Asquith's administration had demonstrated that it had no intention of accepting the Declaration of London or any other international accord that interfered with its political and military objectives. Once the western front had developed into a near stalemate, however, British officials recognized that they would need more men and significantly larger quantities of materiel to win the war. Foreign Secretary Edward Grey realized his government would have to compromise with the United States if Britain was to assure a constant flow of goods across the Atlantic. At the same time, the Order in Council placed the United States in a difficult position. Wilson, it seems, did not believe that Britain would give in to American opposition. Nevertheless, being an astute politician, he knew that anything other than a bold stand against the August 20 decree might turn public opinion against him and the Democratic Party during the upcoming midterm elections. In the months of October and November 1914, Britain and the United States worked to find a middle ground regarding the Order in Council and sought to compromise on the adherence of the Declaration of London without alienating the American public.

When Counselor Robert Lansing first read the August 20 Order in Council, he was not pleased because he still hoped Britain would accept the Declaration of London. On September 26, Lansing wrote a draft response for the president in which he acknowledged that the Declaration of London had "not been ratified by any country represented at the [1909] conference" and thus accepted that Britain was not obligated to comply with an accord that Parliament had refused to accept. Yet he hoped London would reconsider the document "as a code of naval warfare for the present war" and withdraw its Order in Council. Lansing was interested in protecting his country's commerce and asserted that the articles in the Order in Council "strike at the very root of the indubitable right of neutrals to continue their industrial and commercial enterprises with the minimum inconvenience and confusion, which are inevitable consequences of a maritime war." Lansing complained that the order gave Britain too much power and interfered with "neutral trade between neutral ports."[2]

He also asserted that the Order was weak because Britain could not successfully cordon off the entire German coast. If the United States accepted the British policy, Lansing argued, the Wilson administration would be legitimizing a "paper blockade." The Order in Council would allow the Allied governments to sustain a trade barrier "without the necessity of maintaining it with an adequate naval force."[3] Drawing on the 1856 Declaration of Paris, the counselor noted that for a blockade to have legitimacy, the belligerent navy had to have the capability of shutting off maritime access to its enemy's coastline. In his opinion a permeable boundary was not a valid blockade. Therefore, if a navy could not prevent vessels from breaching the line and reaching enemy ports, the international community should not have to recognize the blockade.

Calling attention to the British policy toward foodstuffs bound for Germany, Lansing contended that the United States viewed them as conditional contraband. Britain, therefore, had the responsibility to prove the food was destined for the German government. Any changes to its status, he claimed, would violate American law and precedent set forth by the British themselves. Lansing claimed that during the Anglo-Chinese Opium Wars of the mid-1800s, London opposed France's attempt to classify rice as military material, thereby making it totally off limits to the enemy—or absolute contraband. Then Foreign Secretary Lord Granville George Leveson-Gower had declared that rice was not contraband unless destined for use by China's military. London, according to Lansing, employed a similar argument when it fought the Boers in South Africa. Preventing neutrals from sending food to belligerents, he concluded, would break with diplomatic tradition and infringe on US rights.[4]

Lansing's strongest argument was that his government could not accept Britain's changes to the Declaration of London because other states might view the acquiescence as "evidence of unfriendliness to them." He claimed that all the other warring parties accepted the treaty without modification. Complying with the alterations would put the US government in "a position where its neutrality and impartiality are doubtful or open to question."[5]

The following day, Lansing asked the president to approve his message to US Ambassador Walter Hines Page so it could go out in the next day's pouch. Lansing emphasized that Britain's modifications to the Declaration of London warranted the "unqualified refusal of this Government to acquiesce in its [Order in Council] legality and that our objections should be clearly and firmly stated." He added that Wilson might see similarities to the "obnoxious Orders in Council of the Napoleonic Wars," and that London's actions were sure to create resentment among the American people.[6]

Wanting advice, the president forwarded the letter to Colonel Edward House, who expressed concern that Lansing's instructions to Page were "undiplomatic." Referencing Lansing's point that Britain had not signed the 1909 Declaration of London in the first place, the colonel asserted that demanding compliance to it did not make sense. In his opinion, the matter needed further consideration and he advised Wilson, despite Lansing's protest, not to send the note. House wanted to take control of the debate personally and suggested that he meet privately with British Ambassador Cecil Spring-Rice to discuss the matter in more detail. To this proposition, House wrote in his diary that Wilson "expressed his warm approval."[7]

Per Wilson's request, the following morning Lansing submitted a new draft of the instructions for Page. The president handed the dispatch to House, who took it to his meeting with the British ambassador. The message shocked Spring-Rice. He complained that the problem would never have risen had the State Department spoken to him first. Spring-Rice asserted that for over a month, Lansing's office knew London's position, but no one had made it an issue. The note, he claimed, contained language that his government might perceive as controversial or threatening and added that "if that paper should get into the hands of the press, the headlines will indicate that war with Great Britain was inevitable, and he believed one of the greatest panics the country ever saw would ensue." Spring-Rice did not want the letter to create a public outcry against Britain and hoped to find a private way to solve any international differences. The two men, according to House, then "outlined" a new dispatch for Page.[8]

House later noted that he enjoyed the idea of meeting clandestinely with Spring-Rice, writing, "It caused me some amusement in thinking about the kind of diplomacy in which I was indulging." In circumventing Bryan and Lansing, the colonel claimed, he was building a better communication link between the countries and thereby preventing misunderstandings. House and Spring-Rice also decided to keep their discussions out of official channels. Doing so, they concluded, would offer them more flexibility to negotiate without causing an international incident.[9] House's actions were at the very least ignorant considering the president's desire to remain neutral. The colonel took his unofficial role for granted because he did not consider how other nation-states might perceive his dealings if they were made known. Regardless of his cavalier diplomacy, his intentions were clear. In talking with Spring-Rice, House hoped to prevent Anglo-American problems from becoming public.

The colonel did not keep his meeting a secret from Wilson. House wrote in his diary that he told the White House doorman to keep Lansing outside of the Oval Office until he finished telling Wilson about the conversation with Spring-Rice. House, with the president's consent, concluded that Lansing's latest draft to Page could not be sent and requested that the counselor revise the memorandum once more.[10]

After receiving Lansing's newest draft, the president toned down some of the language to reduce the risk of increasing tension between America and Britain. Wilson wrote that the United States was "greatly distressed" over London's decision to modify the Declaration of London. He approved of Lansing's warning that Washington hoped to avoid a formal protest against the Order in Council but wanted to demonstrate its dissatisfaction in a conciliatory manner. The administration, Wilson reiterated, was not threatening London; rather, it hoped to open up dialogue over the issue. To emphasize this point, he edited the end of the instructions to state, "In presenting the substance of this instruction to Sir Edward Grey you will assure him *of the earnest spirit of friendship in which it is sent. The President is anxious that he should realize that the terms of the Declaration of London represent the limit to which this Gov't could go with the approbation and support of its people.*" After revising the message, the president told Lansing to send it that afternoon.[11] When considered in conjunction with the president's other efforts to remain neutral, it appears likely that in working with House to soften the language of Lansing's instructions, Wilson did not intend his actions to aid the Allies.[12] Rather the new message was constructed to make American demands clear and at the same time avoid additional tension that could make mediation more difficult to initiate.

The president was successful. Following his meeting with House, Spring-Rice told Grey he had heard from a "secret source" that Washington planned to oppose the Order in Council. He made clear that the United States would have accepted the Declaration of London in its entirety, but not with the modifications. The ambassador then warned that if British officials did not change their policy, it might spark widespread protest.[13]

The American demands surprised Grey. Like Spring-Rice, he did not expect the Wilson administration to protest the move.[14] Once Page met with the foreign secretary, on September 29 he reported that Grey did not want to create problems, but emphasized that the declaration was "never ratified by the British Government." Defending his course of action, Grey argued that the Order in Council had modified the Declaration of London simply to deny food and war materiel to the enemy government. London, he claimed, did not intend to interfere with legitimate neutral trade. Grey concluded by informing Page that he was willing to initiate a discussion on the matter so they could reach a "satisfactory understanding."[15]

In midmorning on September 30, House and the president sat in the White House study and discussed the continuing problem. As they spoke, Wilson opened a copy of *A History of the American People* that he had written years before and read about how President James Madison had dealt with the beginning of the War of 1812. Wilson felt that he was in a similar situation. The War of 1812, he noted, had started over the British seizure of American merchant vessels. Wilson viewed Madison as a peace-loving man, yet popular feeling in the country made it impossible for him to avoid the conflict: "Madison and I are the only two Princeton men that have become President. The circumstances of the war of 1812 and now run parallel. I sincerely hope they will not go further."[16] Wilson's comments demonstrate the degree of stress that he felt and illustrate his belief that relations with Britain were in danger. Even though the president personally favored London over Berlin, he placed American interests before all others and knew that public opinion could force his hand against Britain.

While Wilson may not have intended his private comments to have an effect on international relations, they did. Once he left Wilson, House told Spring-Rice about his conversation with the president. The colonel wrote in his diary that the British ambassador was visibly concerned and planned to speak with Grey.[17] Upon hearing about Wilson's concerns the foreign secretary became increasingly anxious that the crisis could damage his country's image among the American people and told Spring-Rice that he wanted to sit down with Page.[18]

The following afternoon, Grey met with the American ambassador, informing him that the Foreign Office planned to compromise by formulating a new Order in Council that would "endeavor to meet our [American] wishes so far as that is possible." Grey said that his government would change the contraband list and that his office had received a guarantee from the Netherlands, which was neutral, that it would not "reexport" foodstuffs to the German government. London sought this agreement to appease US demands and allow Americans to ship food to the Netherlands with minimal British interference. Page emphasized that Whitehall wanted to alleviate the situation, stating that Grey's decision was an "important concession" to Washington.[19]

Grey immediately sent Spring-Rice a note that the Foreign Office would write the new Order in Council but added that the ambassador should tell Wilson that Parliament had not approved the treaty. He also advised that future discussions should not "mention the Declaration of London." According to Grey, Page suggested that the United States should be allowed to announce London's plan to revise the Order in Council. The ambassador hoped this development would "calm public opinion" in America and prevent additional damage to his government's image.[20]

Grey's decision to revise the Order in Council was a diplomatic victory for the United States; however, Lansing continued to press Whitehall to accept the Declaration of London. He tried to convince Spring-Rice that adhering to the 1909 agreement might prevent further complications between neutrals and belligerents. At the beginning of the war, Lansing had reminded the ambassador that every warring state except Britain considered the declaration an acceptable guideline for naval warfare. If recognized as valid, the "causes of controversy would be reduced as far as possible and neutrals as well as belligerents, would not be in doubt of the rules." Lansing was not ignorant of London's needs and suggested that the Foreign Office simply alter its list of contraband to suit modern combat. He pointed out that articles 23 and 25 of the defunct treaty allowed the Allies to add new items to the list when necessary, noting that "this right appears to be arbitrary except that notification must be given" and that absolute contraband had to be "exclusively used for war."[21]

Lansing liked the Declaration of London because such phrases were open to wide interpretation. He argued that, article one of the August 20 Order in Council was not a "modification of the Declaration but merely an act performed under its provisions." "Now the point I am driving at is just this. Do not the powers conferred upon a belligerent by Articles 23 and 25 furnish sufficient means to protect the interests of your Government without modifying the Declaration at all?" The counselor continued that he understood that Britain's main goal was to "apply the doctrine of 'continuous voyage' to certain articles now listed as conditional contraband, but which you consider munitions of war. If such articles can be treated as absolute contraband upon notice, what is the use in modifying the articles of the Declaration?"[22]

Lansing's suggestions could be interpreted as an effort to help the Allies.[23] However, the counselor's actions are more likely an attempt to convince the British to accept the Declaration of London without alteration. Lansing assumed that Britain had plenty of enforcement power under the treaty and that there was no reason to change it because neutrals would have a clear set of maritime laws to follow. He claimed that all the Foreign Office had to do was reclassify certain goods as contraband when necessary. This would prevent confrontations with neutral powers and protect American neutrality because the United States had already made known its willingness to accept existing international law. Lansing, therefore, did not oppose Britain's right to regulate neutral trade with its enemies. He simply hoped the British would accept the Declaration of London because it provided rules that everyone could accept.

Spring-Rice noted in his diary that Lansing also said there was a way to get around Britain's need to use the doctrine of continuous voyage. London could draw up agreements with European neutrals "to prevent [the] re-exportation of military supplies to the belligerent armies." The ambassador agreed that establishing such arrangements "would obviate the difficulty of a non-acceptance of the Declaration by the Allies." Spring-Rice added that the arrangement with Holland not to export goods to Germany made sense and that "if she [Holland] does not take these measures then it is a fair case for the application of the doctrine that was applied by the United States to Nassau in the Civil War."[24]

Grey considered the ideas but continued working on the new Order in Council, which took into account some of Lansing's recommendations.[25] In drafting a new Order in Council, the Foreign Office weighed the impact that its decisions might have on American business and politics. Writing in his memoir, Grey claimed that his goal was to "secure the maximum of blockade that could be enforced without a rupture with the United States."[26] London did not want the American public to turn against Britain. Therefore, Grey endeavored to formulate a policy that achieved Britain's war aims but damaged the American economy as little as possible. The secretary knew that the US fiscal position was beginning to rebound by mid-October, to the point that America no longer needed to borrow money from other countries. Grey understood, however, that the new Order in Council could still have a negative effect on the US public's opinion of Britain. Additionally, he did not want business leaders across the country to pressure Washington into making pronouncements or adopting policies that endangered Anglo-American relations.[27]

On October 10, Grey told Spring-Rice that he had completed a draft of the new Order in Council and wanted to give a copy to Washington. By sending it unofficially, he hoped to receive feedback from the United States and make any necessary changes before its public pronouncement. Grey knew that once the order was available for everyone to read, changing it would be much more difficult. In the draft sent to Page, Grey upheld Britain's right to the "application of continuous voyage in respect of goods consigned to neutral ports" if conditional contraband did not carry a record showing its final destination. In other words, if the ship's papers did not indicate the ultimate buyer of the goods, they were subject to confiscation. Britain also updated the list of absolute contraband by including petroleum, motors, and raw materials such as copper and rubber, which were used in the production of munitions. To offer some degree of compromise, however, Britain chose to keep certain items that were vital to the German army and to the American economy, including cotton, on the free list.[28]

It did not take long for Grey to grow impatient. Within a week, he asked Spring-Rice to find out if Washington found the document acceptable. He had provided a compromise and hoped for a rapid response because he wanted to "issue a list of contraband of war that will not meet with objections from the United States government." According to Grey, all other negotiations were on hold until the president made a decision about the Order in Council. Until Wilson accepted the "new proclamation," Britain could not craft arrangements with the Netherlands to prevent exports from reaching Germany. Additionally, the secretary noted that London was in a difficult position because it might have to "choose between a dispute with [the] United States Government or giving up all attempts to prevent Germany from getting free supplies for her army." Grey emphasized that he recognized the importance of international trade to America and pointed out that the Foreign Office had temporarily ceased its detentions of foodstuffs headed through the Netherlands even though it knew the goods would ultimately head "up the Rhine."[29]

In a letter to Wilson, Spring-Rice defended his government's policy, stating that it was going to do everything possible to prevent the disruptions of "neutral trade." To gain Wilson's approval, Spring-Rice reminded the president that nearly sixty years before, the United States had found itself in a similar position in its struggle to win the American Civil War. Spring-Rice asserted that when Washington told Britain to end its trade with the Confederacy, London acquiesced. Concerned about the US reaction, Spring-Rice stated that he did not expect Washington to violate its neutrality, but he did hope the United States would abide by a principle that American statesmen had insisted on and "successfully asserted against ourselves" in the past.[30]

The Order in Council divided Wilson's cabinet. Lansing argued that the changes were "even more objectionable" than the original document because Britain would have the power to declare that a neutral country was aiding the enemy and therefore subject to laws regulating the confiscation of belligerent ships and cargoes.[31] He still hoped Britain would accept the Declaration of London without modification and told Wilson that if he approved of his objections, the president should send them to Page as soon as possible because Grey wanted to get America's impression. But the administration did not offer an immediate response.[32] Page wanted the United States to accept Britain's position without protest and emphasized to Bryan that the issue caused unnecessary tension. According to the ambassador, Britain had accepted all the US demands and had done everything it could to satisfy Washington, other than allowing it to ship war materials to Germany. Page did not like the American position because its policy protected a minority of shippers and threatened to generate problems with

Britain. The government, he claimed, was splitting hairs. Trying to appeal to Wilson's desire to mediate an end to the war, Page asserted that in London the crisis seemed "academic and of the smallest practical consequence compared with the grave danger we [might] incur of shutting ourselves off from a position to be of some service to civilization and to the peace of the world."[33] From the beginning of the war, Page opposed the idea of using the Declaration of London. He accepted Grey's assertion that the document threatened the British war effort and wanted Wilson to approve London's point of view without debate. Refusal by Washington, he feared, might provoke a major diplomatic crisis.[34]

The ambassador's comments did not sit well with the president. Wilson was becoming irritated with Page and immediately replied that he did not see the issue as purely academic. He charged that the ambassador was out of touch with American public opinion. Asserting that Page was not keeping the welfare of the United States at heart, the president added, "Contact with opinion on this side of the water would materially alter your view." Wilson understood the importance of maintaining the current debate because of its effect on the US population. The president emphasized that he had to consider the influence that his policies might have on Americans' perception of the administration and argued that abiding by the Order in Council would fulfill Britain's demands while "touching opinion on this side [of] the water in an exceedingly tender spot."[35]

The president did not appreciate interference with American trade and stated to Page that he had an obligation to defend his country's neutral rights. More important, Wilson feared that German-Americans would view his acquiescence to Britain's policy as a breach of US neutrality. Wise to the connection between international affairs and domestic politics, Wilson certainly wanted to maintain national unity to prevent political problems at home. If he accepted an arrangement that seemed pro-British without at least putting up a fight, the public might turn against him and his administration in the upcoming midterm elections, weakening Wilson's and his political party's control in Washington.[36]

Trying one last time to convince Britain to accept the Declaration of London, Wilson sent a letter to Page in which he asserted the edict was an adulterated version of the Declaration of London that "would not be satisfactory to other belligerents, who have accepted the Declaration upon the condition that it is accepted by all the belligerent powers." The president affirmed Britain's right to use economic warfare against its enemies but wanted London to accept the declaration because it would be internationally recognized and provide a guide for neutral states to follow. Wilson continued by pointing out that the new Order in Council "extends the list of contraband," something that Britain could do under the Declaration of

London, "hence it was needless to modify the Declaration itself." Finally the president complained that London had actually expanded the doctrine of continuous voyage by declaring the Royal Navy's right to stop conditional as well as absolute contraband headed through neutral ports if a cargo's recipient was listed as "To Order" or if the receiver was unknown. Wilson was particularly bothered by article 4 of the new Order in Council, which read, "[I]t shall lie upon the owners of the goods to prove that their destination was innocent." Wilson disagreed and insisted that article 4 "introduces a new doctrine into naval warfare and imposes upon neutral commerce a restriction, which appears without precedent." Wilson did not like the article because it gave Britain the authority to seize American cargoes headed to neutral ports even if Britain was uncertain whether the goods were destined to legitimate neutral customers or not. In closing, the president added that it was "inconsistent to declare a nation to be neutral and treat it as an enemy."[37]

The following day, Grey contacted Spring-Rice and reemphasized that Britain could not simply accept the Declaration of London because it would "in effect bind us to carry out every detail of an instrument which we have never ratified and to which objection has been taken in Parliament." Nevertheless Britain did not want it to generate animosity. Grey wanted Spring-Rice to explain to Wilson that the new Order in Council followed most of the Declaration of London. The only real differences were its list of contraband and its preservation of the "doctrine of continuous voyage, which I believe up to and even during the discussion of the Declaration of London every authority in the United States upheld."[38]

Grey recognized Wilson's concerns and did not want to cause his administration undue harm; yet the foreign secretary had to protect British interests. With this in mind, Grey suggested a compromise that might preserve American neutrality and achieve London's military objectives. He told Spring-Rice he hoped that if Washington was not going to accept the legitimacy of the new directive, it would at least not publically challenge it. The US government should simply reserve the right to protest individual cargo seizures and not the decree "in principle." The only alternative was the "withdrawal of the Proclamation," which he claimed would certainly stimulate more tension between the two governments.[39]

On October 20, the British ambassador approached Lansing, then acting secretary of state while Bryan was campaigning for the Democratic Party in the Midwest, to convince him that Britain was bending over backward to satisfy the United States. He claimed that his country had withdrawn its first Order in Council at America's request and that the decision was hurting Britain's ability to prevent Germany from receiving contraband through neutral countries. He wanted Lansing to see the British side of the situation and understand the issue's importance to its war effort. Spring-Rice added that if London did not have the power to block neutral trade with Germany, its efforts to shorten the conflict would fail.[40]

To defend Britain's decision, Spring-Rice harked back to history. During the American Civil War, the Confederacy tried to purchase British goods via Mexico. This resulted in a US Supreme Court decision stating that the legal status of the vessel should be judged based on its final destination. The ambassador was correctly pointing out that the United States had adopted the doctrine of continuous voyage itself, a move that "raised no objection" with the British government. He added that the "doctrine of continuous transport and continuous voyage was in fact known as the American doctrine and went by that name in the Law Books. It seemed strange that the American Government was now insisting on the abandonment of this doctrine by the British Government as a sine qua non."[41]

Despite Grey's and the ambassador's arguments, Lansing maintained that the only document all governments should use as a basis for discussion was the Declaration of London. His stance irritated Spring-Rice, who reported to Grey that he was unsure that he had convinced Lansing of the British position. Venting his frustration about Lansing, the ambassador added, "You will see the difficulty of negotiating with a subordinate who has the lawyer's instinct to make his good case, and of being unable to address myself directly, except by letter, to the person who has the real authority."[42]

Despite Spring-Rice's impression of Lansing, the Foreign Office had made a dent in the acting secretary's resistance. In addition to his conversation with Spring-Rice, Lansing received a letter on October 20 from Page, who stressed that London was not going to change its policy: "The Declaration of London will not be accepted by Sir Edward Grey without amendment: First . . . Parliament declined to ratify it; and second, for the reason that the Declaration of London itself forbids additions to [the] contraband list of such articles as rubber and iron ore which now seem necessary for the manufacture of war materials." Page added that Grey would not change his mind: "All hope of his acceptance of the Declaration of London as a whole therefore is finally ended."[43] The ambassador's comments demonstrated his affinity toward Britain, but also made London's position clear—it was not going to approve of a policy that might severely hinder its ability to defeat Germany.

After his conversation with Spring-Rice and reading the letter from Page, Lansing concluded that the two governments were at an impasse. Being well versed in maritime and international law, he understood that precedent guided legal affairs among countries. US actions in the American Civil War did support the British case and the long history of foreign affairs showed that neither belligerents nor neutrals could expect their principles of behavior to rule international relations on a consistent basis. The debate over the Declaration of London was no exception.[44] Lansing had pressured the British ambassador in the hope of obtaining as much as he could for the United States but accepted that London would not budge.

Later that same afternoon, Lansing explained to Wilson that the British were not going to compromise on the Declaration of London and that further negotiation was futile. "It seems to me," Lansing wrote, "that in view of the rigid attitude of the British Government further attempts to obtain an agreement on the Declaration of London are useless. We must, therefore, stand on the rules of international law which have been generally accepted without the Declaration." Lansing was obviously disappointed adding that "[i]t is to be regretted that in spite of all that has been done, the purpose of the negotiation has failed."[45]

Wilson and Lansing apparently believed that the United States did not have international law on its side and seeing no viable option decided they had to concede.[46] Defending the administration's decision to give in to Britain on the Order in Council, Lansing wrote to Chair of the Senate Foreign Relations Committee William J. Stone on January 8, 1915: "There is no Hague convention which deals with absolute or conditional contraband, and, as the declaration of London is not in force, the rules of international law only apply. As to the articles to be regarded as contraband, there is no general agreement between nations."[47] Lansing went on to point out that the United States had used similar practices during the American Civil War and was right in claiming that "the record of the United States in the past is not free from criticism. When neutral, this Government has stood for a restricted list of absolute and conditional contraband. As a belligerent, we have contended for a liberal list, going to our conception of the necessities of the case."[48] Asserting that international law favored Britain, Lansing wrote, "The Government therefore cannot consistently protest against the application of rules which it has followed in the past, unless they have not been practiced as heretofore."[49]

Even if international law had supported the American case, Lansing argued that pressing the argument further was futile because the British navy ruled the seas: "History shows that whenever a country has possessed that superiority our trade has been interrupted and the few articles essential to the prosecution of the war have been allowed to reach his enemy from this country."[50] Regardless of the administration's protests, Lansing, who certainly would not have presented this argument without Wilson's approval, claimed that continued pressure from Washington would not alleviate the blockade's effect on neutral trade.

Assuming that international law favored Britain was certainly not the only reason that Wilson accepted the Order in Council. If he chose to keep pressing Britain, Wilson had few choices available. He could have resorted to more drastic measures such as a trade embargo, severing diplomatic relations, or simply ignoring the new Order in Council and risking a confrontation at sea. It seems, however, that Wilson either did not recognize these options or more likely reasoned that such actions might endanger neutrality and the profits made by the US business community. In his *A History of the American People*, the president stressed that in the past, US efforts to force British compliance to American policies had failed dismally. When discussing Thomas Jefferson's Embargo Act, he wrote that the "closing year of his [Jefferson's] presidency was darkened and distressed by its effects . . . America's own trade was ruined. Ships rotted at the wharves,—the ships which had but yesterday carried the commerce of the world." He realized that the Embargo Act had hurt the United States much more than it hurt Britain.[51] The circumstance of 1914 may have been quite different, but a failed embargo would have been political suicide. Additionally when Wilson's capitulation is considered in combination with his desire to mediate an end to the war, forcing Britain's hand might have created additional barriers to the administration's effort to initiate peace talks. The president and Lansing, therefore, accepted Britain's decision to reject the Declaration of London because they must not have recognized a workable alternative.

Ultimately the president decided to rely on existing international law and announced that the United States would protest British interference with American trade on a case-by-case basis without formally protesting the Order in Council. Wilson and his advisors assumed that their decision would still assure American rights. On October 22, Lansing sent a message declaring that the administration "feels obliged to withdraw its suggestion that the Declaration of London be adopted as a temporary code of naval warfare to be observed by belligerents and neutrals during the present war." Lansing added that the US government expected combatants to comply with international law "irrespective of the provisions of the Declaration of London; and that this government [United States] reserves to itself the right to enter a protest or demand in each case in which those rights and duties so defined are violated or their free exercise interfered with by authorities of His Britannic Majesty's Government."[52]

On October 28, Page wrote to Wilson that Washington's decision to acquiesce and accept the Order in Council had positive effects in London. Almost immediately, Britain released all but one American vessel stopped by the Royal Navy.[53] By abandoning its effort to seek British compliance with the Declaration of London the United States had not breeched its neutrality. The decision certainly favored the Allies; however, the Wilson administration had not intervened in the war against Germany nor had it given up its right to protest or its efforts to protect American economic interests. In the last quarter of 1914 they found themselves continuing discussions over the transfer of belligerent ships to American companies and the blockade's impact on the US cotton industry. Additionally, Wilson faced a threat to his authority resulting from growing opposition among the American people to his decision making. The challenges persisted as both states continued searching for a middle ground yet tried to maintain the most important elements of their foreign policies.

Despite negotiations in August concerning the US purchase of German merchant vessels, Washington and many of the country's shippers were still uncertain whether the Allies would recognize the transfers. France's and Britain's differing positions sparked uncertainty as to the amount of risk that American businesses would assume in purchasing belligerent ships. By the middle of October, the US Treasury Department had received many letters from merchants who wanted to know if the government would protect their investments against seizure by the Royal and French navies.[54]

Assistant Secretary of the Treasury and head of the Bureau of War Risk Insurance A. J. Peters told Lansing that his bureau classified vessels based on their purchase date. He noted that it had approved insurance on vessels that were American owned before the war started because they were under the protection of the US government. Ships owned by belligerents and sold to Americans after the outbreak of hostilities, however, were not insured because the administration had not yet taken an official position on the status of these ships. Peters wanted to know if Washington intended to insure them. Over the previous few months, the assistant secretary had received numerous letters from shipowners who feared that if the government did not offer them some defense against capture, "they will be unable to use their vessel and their investment will have gone for naught." Peters added that the government needed to make its position known. If it did not, there was no reason to "grant American registry to foreign-built ships." If the government chose to insure them against capture, the United States would have to "be prepared to insist on its protection of these vessels . . . and might be called upon to pay the loss or damages for detention."[55] Lansing considered the matter and informed the president that insuring former belligerent ships could provoke an international incident. In making such a decision, the government would in effect take the position that it would protest the capture of such vessels.[56]

The question of US registry of foreign ships came up almost immediately when the British navy stopped the *Brindilla* and turned it over to the prize court in Halifax, Nova Scotia, on October 18.[57] The matter was complicated because at the beginning of the war, the *Brindilla* was registered to a German subsidiary of Standard Oil. After the war started, the company transferred the ship's registry to its parent corporation, changing the vessel's name in the process. Considering it ultimately belonged to Standard Oil, the Bureau of War Risk Insurance had insured the vessel for a voyage to Egypt. Lansing pointed out to the president that "this case is, therefore, a transfer of flag rather than a transfer of ownership." In the acting secretary's opinion, London's actions were not acceptable and the administration must immediately protest.[58]

Days later, the prize court in Halifax released the *Brindilla*. According to Grey, the government concluded that the "voyage . . . was bona fide and that unless there is reason to suppose she was intending not to go to Alexandria but to supply the enemy, she should be released." After examining the case, Grey told Spring-Rice that Britain was not planning to question the "transfer of the flag" for the vessel. Detaining neutral vessels, however, was essential to the war effort and Britain would continue searching American ships if their destinations were suspect. Yet Grey did not want to bring about unnecessary tension by causing fear among shippers that London would automatically confiscate their goods if they were "detained."[59]

Grey's comments demonstrated that his government did not oppose the transfer of the flag. Nevertheless, this case did not settle the matter because the United States was still not clear about how the Allies viewed US purchases of German-owned ships. On October 26, Lansing responded to Peters' inquiry about insuring former belligerent merchant vessels. In an ambiguous statement certainly intended to shield the White House from repercussions resulting from ship transfers, Lansing asserted that the United States was only required to follow existing precedent. He added that "under international law, as it has been understood and practiced in this country in the past, the bona fide, unreserved, unconditional private transfer of ownership of belligerent merchant vessels in neutral ports to nationals of neutral counties is in general valid, but the transaction is nevertheless open to great suspicion, and for that reason it may be expected to be scrutinized by the belligerents." In other words, American owners had the power to transfer such ships, but they had to be prepared to deal with the opposition of the belligerents. Lansing warned that it was the owners' responsibility to ensure that the transactions were legitimate and that their ships did not aid the warring states from which they were transferred. If the ship did not carry the proper documentation to prove that the transfer was legitimate, the "vessel [was] liable to condemnation."[60]

Consequently, Lansing's statement did not resolve the matter of ship ownership and Washington found itself still trying to figure out how to address the issue in late November when Wilson was drafting his State of the Union address to include a promotion of his shipping bill, which

Congress still refused to pass. On November 23, Wilson told Lansing that France's and Britain's diverging views on purchasing German vessels frustrated him and that he sought advice on how each government might react to buying ships owned by the North German Lloyd Hamburg-American Company interred in US ports.[61]

Lansing concluded that buying German ships was a touchy topic and thought Americans had the legal right to do so, yet Paris and London might not agree. He replied later that afternoon that he could not predict French and British governments' attitudes toward the purchase of such ships, but if the country vigilantly differentiated between the "transfer of flag and the transfer of ownership," Washington should not have much difficulty. Simply transferring the registry of a ship should not be a problem if American companies and their subsidiaries already owned the vessels. Therefore he did not think that officials in London or Paris would oppose these transfers. As an example, Lansing pointed out that the *Brindilla*'s registry was changed in this manner and that the prize court released it.[62]

The transfer of ownership from an enemy state was a different matter. Lansing had not discussed that subject with French Ambassador Jean Jules Jusserand for a while, but Lansing said "the last time we did so he [Jusserand] was most emphatic in his opposition." Lansing told Wilson that France's "official utterances" made clear its opposition to the sale of German merchant liners to neutrals because "it is always done for the purpose of avoiding the consequences of belligerency." Jusserand argued that belligerents changed ownership of their ships solely to avoid capture. The ambassador viewed the transfer of ownership as tantamount to "giving aid to the enemy" and therefore, Lansing argued, France might regard the ships as "liable to condemnation as prize[s]." Spring-Rice, on the other hand, "has been far less definite than his colleague in expression of his views." Lansing speculated this was the case because London did not want to provoke a confrontation with France and would support Paris if its navy confiscated such a ship.[63] As a result of the Allies vague and conflicting declarations, the United States struggled with the legality of purchasing German vessels to expand its merchant marine. Not until several months later (see Chapter 6) did Britain offer a new position on the transfer of ships and even then its answer was not definitive.

While Lansing evaluated the belligerents' position on shipping, the State Department found itself dealing with merchants' fears that London intended to include cotton on its new list of contraband. The outbreak of the war had already placed a serious strain on the cotton industry. Within the first few months, cotton was selling at 6.5 to 7 cents per pound, which was half its prewar value. At that price the South could lose $500 million on the vital cash crop and have a glut of nearly 6,000,000 bales.[64] Placing cotton on the contraband list could exacerbate this problem. Concerned, the president of the Galveston Cotton Exchange, I. H. Kemper, notified the State Department, on October 24, that he had learned in newspapers that the British viewed shipments of cotton to Scandinavian nations with "suspicion of being intended ultimately for German use," and that they might "divert" the cargoes.[65] Even the president of the New York Chamber of Commerce, Seth Low, complained that American shippers "are in a serious predicament owing to the uncertainty regarding Great Britain's attitude towards shipments of cotton to neutral European countries." Britain's silence was driving many transport and insurance companies to abstain from taking risks unless they knew the British position.[66]

Lansing informed Page that Americans were irritated because Britain had not announced its position on the cotton trade. He suggested to the ambassador that a statement from London would alleviate "public opinion which is imputing selfish motives to Great Britain on assumption that cotton shipments, at least those destined for belligerent countries, will be prevented by the British Government." Because of the growing number of protests in the United States, Lansing wanted Page to stress that Britain should make public its policy as soon as possible.[67]

The Foreign Office did not plan to place cotton on the absolute contraband list. Even though Germany used it to make uniforms and in the manufacture of ammunition, Britain understood the effect that a ban would have on the southern cotton industry and on Anglo-American relations. Grey stated that "includ[ing] cotton would certainly provoke a challenge from the United States and would impair the prospect of her agreeing to a list that included copper and rubber."[68] Not recognizing the limitations that Wilson had placed on his own policy because of a desire to lead mediation, the foreign secretary added that he feared that if Britain stopped cotton, the United States might respond by "convoying merchant ships possibly to the enemy, certainly to neutral, ports." He wrote in his memoir that if Washington decided to use the convoys to protect cotton, the shipments would "not have been limited to cotton." The navy would have to allow the ships to reach their destinations because the alternative was "to stop the convoys by firing on the American ships of war that accompanied them; this meant war with the United States."[69] This was not probable because Wilson certainly had no intentions to jeopardize his mediation efforts by challenging the British at sea. Nevertheless, not knowing US intentions, Grey had to consider the worst-case scenario and chose to compromise rather than risk a falling out.

In a further complication, Spring-Rice informed Grey in late October that the US midterm elections were coming up in the next few weeks and that he thought it unlikely that Wilson would retain control over both houses of Congress. "At the present moment as you know," the ambassador wrote, "he [Wilson] controls both [the House of Representatives and Senate] and it is very rare that a President succeeds in maintaining his hold during the second half of his term." The ambassador claimed that US public opinion was "very sensitive" to the shifts in international relations. German-Americans and others who supported the expansion of the merchant marine, he asserted, constituted a large electorate that could threaten the president's power. Spring-Rice warned that all that was necessary to turn the American population against Britain was a simple incident like the recent detention of US oil tankers destined for the European continent.[70] Thus, he wanted the British government to do what it could to prevent pro-German politicians from gaining seats on Capitol Hill.

In the sixty-third Congress, Democrats held a majority in the Senate—51 seats to 44.[71] Additionally, the Democratic Party commanded 291 seats in the House while the Republicans held only 134. One region of the country that was essential to the president's control in Washington was the South. The president knew the consequences of losing seats in the South, where the Democrats had a substantial.[72] Because of the declining price of cotton caused by the war, southern Representatives and Senators had put forth plans that they hoped would save their states from economic disaster and pleaded to fellow congressional members for financial aid. On October 21, Georgia Representative Dudley M. Hughes dramatically claimed that "[t]he European war, like lightning from a cloudless sky, a thunderbolt from the blue heavens, broke over the world and absolutely closed at once temporarily the prevailing foreign demand for two-thirds of the cotton of the United States." Hughes requested that his colleagues approve an emergency "relief measure" that would bail out southern farmers through direct loans. He complained that the secretary of the treasury's efforts to assuage the crisis by funneling "[g]overnment deposits in national banks" to planters were not working because some of the banks were "hoarding currency and keeping it out of circulation." If Congress did not approve the bill, he believed it would "allow a consuming fire to destroy your neighbor's house, thereby endangering your own; and you do this when you have control over the water which can easily extinguish the flame."[73] Southern congressmen understood how closely their political careers were tied to the financial success of their constituents. Consequently, saving the cotton South became a major issue by mid-October.[74]

From the first days of the war, southern congressional members received letters from farmers protesting what they perceived as inadequate aid and threatened to shift their political allegiances. In a message to Senator John H. Bankhead of Alabama, cotton grower Jackson M. Young declared that people needed the government to decide how to help them as soon as possible. Emphasizing the war's effect on his sharecroppers, Young described the plight of Henry Stone, who sold a 497-pound bale and, after expenses, made only $8.05 for his hard work. He added that the lack of support from Washington made Stone regret voting for a Democrat. The man swore that he "would see the whole lot of you in h-ll before he would ever again quit his work to vote a Democratic ticket."[75]

Young himself was upset with leaders of the Wilson administration, asserting that they had done nothing for the South: "[T]hey all seem to find many difficulties in the way of helping the farmers directly. They seem to forget that when they were asked to go to the aid of the stranded millionaires in Europe, they found absolutely no difficulty in appropriating money to be GIVEN to them." Young went on to assert that he knew Congress was debating the issue of the cotton crop, but that its inaction ignited problems. Congress, he argued, seemed to have "a diarrhea of plans and a constipation of action." Young was by no means alone in his demand for action by the government. Like other senators, Bankhead received numerous letters from his constituents requesting government aid.[76]

In late September, House complained in his diary that the president was not paying close enough attention to the "European Conflict" and that he seemed "more interested in domestic affairs."[77] Wilson was right to focus on US politics. While the colonel's statement demonstrates that *he* saw a divide between domestic and foreign affairs, maintaining control over Congress was very important to Wilson. He entered the presidency with the intention of focusing on domestic policy and a weakening of the Democratic majority in Congress might derail his agenda. Additionally it seems Wilson understood that a loss in the elections could make it more difficult to maintain US neutrality because a different Congress might approve policies that he did not interpret as neutral.

Grey too recognized that the cotton crisis could cause problems for the president and Anglo-American relations. In his memoir, the foreign secretary wrote that he realized that "to include cotton [on the contraband list] would certainly provoke a challenge from the United States." Thus when Page went to Grey on October 26 seeking an assurance that London would not place cotton on the absolute contraband list, the secretary made clear that his government did not view cotton as contraband.[78] Spring-Rice reaffirmed the decision later that afternoon when he relayed a message from Grey directly to Lansing. In the letter, Grey noted that cotton was not on the British contraband lists. Cotton was "in the free list and will remain there."[79]

The British decision relieved some of the mounting pressure that Wilson felt bearing down on his shoulders. At a press conference, on October 26, he reported that the situation over the sale of cotton was ending. He cited the British verdict to the newspapers and argued that because US merchants could ship cotton to Germany they should feel some relief. He nevertheless recognized that London's announcement might not solve the matter, adding, "The only way to restore the cotton situation is to stop the war."[80]

For Wilson, however, the political damage was done. When Britain finally published the second Order in Council on October 29, it was true to its word in protecting the southern staple's status, but the announcement came too late. Because of national diversity, satisfying the entire population was impossible. Wilson took it personally when many people went to the polls on Tuesday, November 3, and voted against his party. Although the Democrats preserved their majority, the Republican Party earned 1,150,765 more votes nationwide than in the 1912 election. Even in the South, the Democrats received 306,158 fewer votes than two years earlier. Around the country, Wilson's party lost 58 congressional seats, including one in the South to Republican Representative James Jefferson Britt of North Carolina. Among states where the Democrats retained control, the margin of victory was smaller than the previous election as well.[81]

In a visit to the White House on November 4, 1914, House went to the president's study, as he did on numerous occasions, to discuss the current issues of the day. According to House, Wilson stated that he was quite distressed over the midterm elections. He was tired and felt rejected by the American people. Wilson told his friend that he wondered if it was worth his effort to work as hard as he had the previous two years. To him, the Republican victories were a direct attack on his administration. Despite House's consoling, Wilson argued "people are not so stupid not to know that to vote against a democratic ticket is to vote indirectly against me." Wilson apparently feared that the election results would ruin his prestige at home and across the Atlantic and argued that the Europeans' first impression would be that he had suffered a defeat.[82]

Like the administration, the Foreign Office was interested in the election results. In a message to Grey, Spring-Rice remarked that, although it appeared the president would retain a majority in both houses, the results had hurt him.[83] The consequence of the Republican surge was that Wilson would have a harder time assuring success for his policies in 1915, and the numbers demonstrated that the sixty-fourth Congress would reflect the changing position of the American people. The ambassador stated that some attributed the shift to the rising voice of the German-American population, which was growing frustrated with the president's policies. It viewed Washington's relationship with London as unneutral and too cozy for a government that claimed it wanted to remain above the fray.[84]

From the beginning of the war, Spring-Rice maintained a constant eye on German efforts to promote their cause in the United States. He wrote that Germany had numerous agents throughout the country who were trying to sway opinion by spreading deceit in the newspapers and lectures. The ambassador told Grey that the main "press agents [of] the German Government" were Herman Ridder and Harvard Professor Hugo Münsterberg and that these men were spreading lies about Britain. Ridder reportedly received $2 million to purchase an American newspaper.[85] Spring-Rice later added that many German-Americans teaching in US universities were energetically speaking out in favor of Germany. He vented to the foreign secretary that "[t]he king of Wurtemburg used to say 'Huren und Professoren Kann man immer fur Geld kriegen' [One can always get whores and professors for money] and no doubt the professors have earned their salaries."[86]

Not long after the election, Wilson received the first of a series of letters from Münsterberg. On November 6, the psychology professor wrote the president that the German-American population opposed his diplomatic efforts. Just as Lansing and Wilson feared, German-Americans disliked the White House's decision to give up on the Declaration of London. German-Americans viewed the action as pro-British, believing that the government did not aggressively protect American neutrality. Münsterberg maintained that the consequence of Wilson's policy was that the German-Americans came out in force against the president on November 3. They overwhelmingly voted Republican, Münsterberg claimed, because they wanted Congressmen in office who would not favor Great Britain, something they believed the administration had done when it did not stand up for US trade.[87]

The professor's letter disturbed Wilson. He wrote to Münsterberg several days later expressing that he was doing everything in his power to walk the tightrope between pro-German and pro-British camps while also ensuring the interests of his own country. Wilson claimed that the professor's accusations were unfounded and that the administration had gone to great measures to maintain neutrality: "[C]ertainly no administration ever tried more diligently or watchfully to preserve an attitude and pursue a line of conduct absolutely neutral." Not only did the president attempt to defend his record, he expressed interest in improving on any challenged element of his policies if it meant assuaging the public that voted against his party. Wilson communicated to Münsterberg that he would appreciate it if the professor would point out any "unneutral acts" conducted by the White House so he could correct them.[88]

The professor's response to Wilson clearly suggests that some citizens considered the president's actions unneutral. However, Wilson's comments to Münsterberg and his private correspondences with House and Lansing related to the Declaration of London, the cotton crisis, and merchant shipping suggest that he believed he was protecting American neutrality and interests. The way that a number of Americans reacted to Wilson's decisions is understandable. From the beginning of the war the administration did favor the Allies over the Central Powers. Nevertheless, sympathy for one side is not the same as overt support, and while the president's diplomacy often resulted in, as Ernest May asserts, "benevolent neutrality," in no case had the president violated American neutrality to this point in the war.[89]

3

"We Are at Peace with the World"

October 1914–December 1914

> [W]e are at peace with the world . . . we are, indeed, a true friend to the world, because we threaten none.
>
> —Wilson, Annual Address to Congress, December 8, 1914[1]

In part because of growing economic connections, Anglo-American relations remained in flux. The British Army was desperately low on military supplies and found itself more reliant than ever before on the United States to fill orders for munitions and other necessary supplies. The Allies' growing dependence on foreign materials, therefore, required them to continue to appease the United States. Britain's distress offered Wilson an opportunity to strengthen the US economy. However, while the president welcomed the possibility of improving his country's fiscal position, there were certain steps he still refused to take because they apparently threatened his views on neutrality. Consequently, between October and December 1914, Wilson made decisions that hindered Britain's war efforts. As autumn gave way to winter, the two governments continued deliberating over neutral rights at sea and found that there were certain measures that neither side could take to protect their own interest.

Great Britain recognized that the American economy was recovering rapidly from its initial problems. US merchants sold enough goods to the Allies and to Germany that London analysts reversed British Ambassador Cecil Spring-Rice's September prediction that the country might be in a state of fiscal crisis by November. Foreign Office advisors reported in mid-October that within a month's time America would again be able to pay its debts to European banks.[2] British officials also knew that the Allies were becoming dependent on American industry. Early in the war, British Army commanders realized that domestic production could not supply the huge quantities of ammunition needed by their divisions in France. As the war became a stalemate, the army needed more heavy artillery and massive quantities of shells to conduct assaults on enemy trenches. Supplies of such equipment, however, did not meet the battlefield demands. As early as October 13, 1914, Secretary of State for War Herbert Kitchener contacted Field Marshal John French, the commander of the British Expeditionary Force, to tell him about the shortages. "The supply of ammunition gives me great anxiety . . . Do not think we are keeping munitions back. All we can gather is being sent, but at [the] present rate of expenditure we are certain before long to run short, and then to produce more than a small daily allowance per gun will be impossible." When the Cabinet Committee on Munitions met on October 21, 1914, it discovered that as early as June 1915 it would be able to acquire only 781,000 rifles from British firms, 400,000 short of what was needed.[3] This predicament made maintaining workable relations imperative.

British officials were not the only ones to recognize the developing bond. Members of the New York banking community argued that the Allies purchased so much that they could not envision continued long-term economic growth for the United States unless the belligerents found new ways to finance the goods. State Department Counselor Robert Lansing informed the president that one financial firm had received "cabled instructions for the payment of more than $50,000,000 for American goods and that the volume of this business is increasing." As a result of dwindling cash reserves, some foreign government representatives and US companies recommended that banks provide "temporary credits for these purchases" to assure European nations' "buying power."[4]

If the United States did not act quickly, American banks and companies would lose out. To stimulate trade, bankers argued that they needed to offer short-term credits to foreign governments, both neutral and belligerent. Lansing observed that while American financiers wanted to stimulate US trade, he assumed they would follow the White House's existing policy. He told Wilson that "[s]uch purchases would necessarily be limited to the legal capacity of the particular bank and, as these warrants are bearer warrants without interest, they could not and would not be subject to public issue." Such acts would prevent direct governmental involvement and protect neutrality because neither the government nor the public would be investing in such loans.[5]

Wilson appreciated the connection between belligerent purchases and national prosperity. With the president's consent, Lansing met with William Straight, a partner at J. P. Morgan and Company, at the Metropolitan Club across the street from the White House. During the meeting Lansing explained the president's position on the financing of US exports. Wilson recognized a distinct difference between issuing government bonds for sale on the open market and allowing foreign governments to negotiate credits directly with American companies. If the government offered bonds, Wilson asserted, it would drain American gold reserves and directly affect the American people. He also reasoned that if people purchased the bonds, they were in effect loaning their personal savings to the belligerents and helping to finance the war. Justifying the president's decision, Lansing added, "The acceptance of Treasury notes or other evidences of debt in payment for articles purchased in this country is merely a means of facilitating trade by a system of credits which will avoid the clumsy and impractical method of cash payments. As trade with belligerents is legitimate and proper it is desirable that obstacles, such an [as] interference with and arrangement of credits or easy method of exchange, should be removed."[6]

The president made his decision to protect the American economy. As historian Arthur Link asserts, Wilson's position on credits was intended to help "keep the channels of exchange open during these months of expanding foreign trade." Wilson's position complied with the international laws of neutrality and was not initially opposed by the Allies or the Central Powers, which were both seeking loans in the United States.[7] However, the president's decision opened the door to new problems. The policy certainly helped to prolong the war because it provided the belligerents—especially Britain—with access to private funds. The Allies and the Central Powers could now finance and purchase more of the materiel necessary to keep their armies in the field, which in turn provided the hope of a victory, and as long as any of the warring states thought they could win, there was no possibility of peace talks.

Even if it had wanted to support British policy, Washington was not in a position to stop the sale of contraband to Germany. As Spring-Rice emphasized to Foreign Secretary Edward Grey, the Wilson administration was under great pressure to protect the country's exporters and "it [was] very difficult for the State department to oppose them."[8] Business with Germany was minimal compared to the traffic with Britain and France, but Americans perceived interference with their economic pursuits as an assault on free trade.

Many US businesses continued selling enormous quantities of contraband to European neutrals that reexported the goods across their borders into German territory. From October through December, London increased its efforts to thwart the traffic of such products by preventing US shipments from reaching neutrals that, according to Britain, had purchased a greater amount than they could themselves consume. Spring-Rice told Grey that he could not understand the constant complaining his embassy received from the State Department. He argued that Britain was fighting for survival while Americans were protesting in the "interest of the [*sic*] Standard Oil, the richest corporation in the world, and of the Copper Syndicate, which had already in the growing trade in munitions of war an increasing market in this country."[9] Lansing replied that he grasped the situation but stressed that his government had to protect American interests. Britain, however, could not stand aside and allow supplies to reach its enemies. Calling neutral countries the "backdoors to Germany," the ambassador expressed his hope that the trade that traversed Denmark, Norway, Sweden, and Italy to the Central Powers could be halted. Doing so, however, would be a delicate matter.[10]

The American position angered Spring-Rice. He professed to Grey his bewilderment that the United States could declare neutrality in a war that, the ambassador argued, was to protect the civilized world. He told Grey, "An American who is really neutral in this fight is not a real American if, as they boast, that expression means citizens of a country brought up in and for liberty." When Washington mounted its protests against the Royal Navy's interference, Britain could "face [the complaints] with the confidence in the justice of our cause." Regardless of Spring-Rice's bombastic statements, he knew that London could not ignore the protests. It would have to respond skillfully and in a manner that did not convert its most important arsenal into an enemy. Britain, the ambassador stressed, must tread lightly because any "slip or mistake" could be detrimental, and "we must be quite sure of our ground."[11]

On Friday, November 6, Grey instructed Spring-Rice to inform the American press, in an unofficial manner, that his government knew large quantities of contraband goods, including copper, were heading through Italian ports "on their way to Germany." Grey emphasized that this copper was used to make ammunition and some shipments stopped by the Royal Navy were destined for German arms manufacturer Krupp Company. As of October 25, the British had confiscated 7,700 tons of copper passing through the Straits of Gibraltar. The foreign secretary claimed that the enormous amount traversing Italy was not all for domestic consumption and that the excess gave Britain "no alternative . . . but to stop contraband trade in copper with Germany through Italy." In an effort to forestall American fears, Grey concluded the note by mentioning that Britain did not want to harm the US economy and intended to purchase all the copper it had detained prior to October 29.[12]

When Britain issued its second Order in Council, it had placed copper on the absolute contraband list. This move angered American businessmen who demanded that the government needed to protect them. After returning to Washington from the campaign trail, Secretary William Jennings Bryan received numerous letters from companies protesting the British decision. The president of the Perth Amboy Board of Trade in New Jersey

John Pfeiffer, argued that the United States exported 1.2 billion pounds of copper annually and that only a small percentage was used for military purposes. According to Pfeiffer, over one million Americans depended on the copper trade and, if the good remained on the contraband list, "it is probable that in a brief time it will become necessary to close refining plants entirely." Pfeiffer claimed that making copper unqualified contraband would affect states across the country. Refineries in the East and mines in the West would feel the impact.[13]

The Wilson administration took these complaints seriously. The reduction of such an important export could hurt public support for the president. In a letter to Spring-Rice, Lansing argued that if neutrals reexported US merchandise to Germany, Britain should take up the matter with the neutral nations, not the American shippers. It was not the responsibility of the vessel's owner to prevent cargoes from reaching the Central Powers: "The treatment which such goods may receive after delivery to the consignees in a neutral country is a matter between the belligerent government investigating the shipment and the neutral government concerned, for which a *bona fide* [Lansing's italics] shipper should not be made to suffer." Accordingly Lansing concluded that Britain should stop detaining American ships bound for neutral countries.[14]

Frustrated, the British press came out against the US effort to protect copper shipments destined for Europe. Newspapermen echoed the sentiment of the British population, which was aggravated about the attitude of the United States toward Germany's access to foreign copper. In a snide attack on US business interests, the British paper *Punch* printed a short poem: "So while we pray for Prussia's fall / And look to your stout arm to whop her, We mean to answer every call / She makes on us for copper."[15]

In his memoir, Grey reiterated the importance of preventing the delivery of copper to the Central Powers via neutral countries: "Was the British Navy to let copper pass under its very guns to a Swede who was importing it for the German Government and going to send it straight to Germany to be made into munitions to kill British soldiers?"[16] In messages to Spring-Rice and to the British ambassador to Italy J. Rennell Rodd, Grey stated that the Royal Navy would detain every shipment not consigned to the Italian government. To assuage the situation, the Foreign Office would permit low-grade copper, which was unsuited for the manufacture of munitions, to reach Italian firms, if they could guarantee that the copper was solely for domestic use.[17]

Impeding the passage of contraband to their adversaries was not the only way the British hoped to hinder Germany. As part of its war effort, Britain restricted the exportation of certain goods from its colonies to neutrals. London wanted to ensure that it had plenty of rubber, wool, and other commodities needed by the armed forces and sought to prevent neutrals from using them to manufacture items for the Central Powers. The problem this policy possessed for Anglo-American diplomatic relations was that the embargoes placed a strain on American firms that were dependent on such raw materials. Goodyear Tire and Rubber Company Chairman Paul W. Litchfield contacted Secretary of Commerce William C. Redfield on October 27, informing him that the ban on the importation of rubber from British colonies in Southeast Asia would greatly harm the corporation's sales. Litchfield declared that his company imported approximately $1,000,000 in "crude rubber" per month and already had contracts for finished products lined up through July 1915. He pointed out that "crude rubber is not contraband," and that the only reason for the embargo was to prevent the rubber from reaching Germany. Litchfield stressed that the rubber the company purchased was used in Ohio and Canada and that Goodyear would "be subject to serious loss" if the government could not convince Britain to change its policy.[18]

This was not an isolated incident. Lansing received numerous letters from American companies like Goodyear that needed raw goods from British and French colonies. They requested that the State Department try to end the restrictions to preserve their profits. Through Ambassador Walter Hines Page, Lansing contacted the British government to ask what steps were necessary for US industry to have free access to such commodities. Page informed Lansing that London would lift the restrictions only if neutral governments guaranteed "no such articles and manufactures thereof will be exported from the neutral country [to the Central Powers]."[19]

Grey did not want a confrontation with Washington. He and his staff knew that the rising tide of German-American protests and the Allies' dependence on US industry meant that Britain must be careful. Spring-Rice asserted that Britain was already losing ground in the United States because German sympathizers had become more influential and could bring pressure on the US government. Wilson apparently concurred. The president, according to Spring-Rice, believed that while many Americans favored the Allies, the German-American population adamantly supported the kaiser. Spring-Rice wrote that Wilson worried "the methods of the Germans here [in the United States] were having an extremely exasperating effect upon American public opinion and that this Government was in some danger of having to face a violent racial division which has hitherto been avoided on this Continent." The president feared that if a domestic crisis erupted, it would be difficult for his administration to maintain peace at home. Wilson's statements strengthen the idea that he favored the Allies but implied the necessity of neutrality. Wrapping up the letter, Spring-Rice reiterated this assertion stating that the German-American population played an important part in the recent elections and that they had opposed the Wilson administration. The ambassador argued that German-Americans might force Wilson to make an "ex-parte statement" concerning his position on contraband.[20]

Grey did not want German-American pressure to influence the White House, especially because of the Allies' growing dependence on US industry. To fill the demand for weapons, Britain sent numerous agents to negotiate with American companies. By November, agents were swarming over the United States, brokering deals and often creating complications since some of them were not official representatives for the British government. Nevertheless, sanctioned buyers arranged for the purchase of the 400,000 guns from two large companies in the United States: Remington and Winchester.[21] This demand for munitions escalated throughout the war, increasing the Allies dependence on the United States and influencing Grey's diplomatic approach toward Washington.

In addition to its growing reliance on American business, Britain's policy was colored by the fact that the conflict remained in a deadlock. On October 29, Page wrote Wilson about a conversation he had with two "associates" of Sir John French, then at the battlefront. French, Page stated, thought the fighting would reach a stalemate by the following summer. The war, however, had already reached a point where neither side could effectively breech the no-man's-land that separated the miles of trenches across Western Europe.[22] On October 31, 1914, the German army attacked the Allied lines at Ypres in Belgium. The battle that followed took the lives of many men without a decisive victory for either side. Lasting until November 22, when the German commanders concluded that continuing the offensive was futile, the Battle of Ypres ended only after amassing over 100,000 casualties. The war was taking a major toll on the armies that marched into the fire in early August. Estimates suggest that the French alone had lost nearly 306,000 men since the fighting began.[23] The armies needed more supplies and men if they were going to renew the attack and end the impasse. Thus, the war of attrition became a war of production and this meant, for Britain, an increasing reliance on the United States.

The assumption that the war's outcome depended on production of war material meant that Britain also needed to further stem the flow of supplies to its enemies. Grey told Spring-Rice, on December 1, that he knew German purchasing agents had worked in Denmark and were "importing numerous quantities of contraband . . . obviously for German use." Foreseeing future shortages in Germany, he asserted that American merchants would do everything they could to take advantage of rising prices by shipping additional goods to Britain's enemies.[24]

His prediction was quickly borne out. As the Royal Navy halted increasing numbers of vessels, it discovered that shippers hid contraband on board their cargo liners. Grey learned that, on occasion, businesses attempted to trick the British by mislabeling shipments of rubber headed for European neutrals as "gum." Writing to Spring-Rice, he declared that "no doubt there will be several similar cases of fraud in the future."[25] The British were also confronting the consequences of their decision not to declare cotton as absolute contraband. Ingenious and cunning businessmen at major southern ports including New Orleans, Mobile, and Savannah used cotton shipments to smuggle copper to Germany. The copper was loaded in the bottom of a ship's hold and concealed with cotton stacked on top, making it very difficult for inspectors to discover the smuggled goods on the high seas.[26]

The alternative to confrontation with Washington over contraband was to devise two new strategies that protected trade and prevented the US government from making a stand that might jeopardize Britain's war aims. The first plan was to establish a compromise with the United States in which both countries would monitor their own merchants' activities. Second, Britain planned to work with neutral countries bordering Germany to prevent the reexportation of US goods. Together or separately, Britain anticipated that the programs would alleviate the growing Anglo-American tension.

On November 18, US Commercial Attaché Chandler Anderson sat down with Grey and discussed ways to reduce British interference with American trade. Grey offered the United States access to wool and rubber if the American government would ensure that neither of them reached Germany. At first, Anderson thought doing so might be difficult because it would require the United States to interfere with American trade by establishing legislation that limited neutral rights; but he concluded that his government might make agreements with individual "traders" instead. Grey and Anderson considered this a workable solution. In the course of negotiation, Anderson tried once more to convince Grey to leave US copper exports alone. Grey replied that the British government regarded copper "not only as much absolute contraband as gunpowder, but by far the most important article of absolute contraband on the list. His Majesty's Government had evidence that copper was selling in Germany for three times more than it fetched anywhere else, and that the German Government had practically commandeered all copper for military use." Because Germany desperately sought copper, Britain planned to exacerbate the problem by stopping any copper shipment "[proved] to be going to Germany." In the end, the foreign secretary asserted that Britain could not risk copper reaching German hands and that it was the responsibility of shippers to ensure that they did not carry smuggled goods across the ocean. As a concession, Grey offered an alternative: Instead of placing the burden of inspecting ships on the US government, the Asquith ministry could set up "depots" in Britain where all goods headed for the continent could be inspected before proceeding onward.[27]

Within weeks, Anderson and Grey worked out an acceptable bargain. Through the proposed "working arrangement," Britain approved the export of wool and rubber to the United States in exchange for an American guarantee that it would prevent smuggling. On December 6, Page relayed the proposal to Bryan, explaining that the Foreign Office wanted US assistance in preventing "fraudulent trade through American ports" and asked that the Wilson administration stop supporting merchants' complaints that Britain had "no right to detain copper merely because it is destined to enemy territory."[28]

Page had already stressed his interest in a compromise. On November 30, he wrote the president that the United States had to resolve its problems over contraband. Trying to convince Wilson of his position, the ambassador asserted that because the British had to handle the entire subject without help from Washington, vessel owners could expect holdups to continue or get worse. The failure of the United States to take an active role in policing its commercial fleet, Page asserted, had spread frustration across the Atlantic: "Depression hangs over everybody as a London fog."[29]

Unfortunately, the "working arrangement" called for something that the US government was still unwilling to do. When Lansing replied that the arrangement was unacceptable, British leaders were surprised. They did not think he understood the "real spirit of the proposal," adding that the Wilson administration "[seemed] to brush aside so lightly" how far London was willing to go to give the United States access to rubber.[30]

Foreign Office officials were apparently not clear about the American position. Safeguarding neutral trade was a matter of principle, not just dollars and cents. Lansing told Spring-Rice that the US government would not interfere with the country's trade because the "export of contraband is legitimate." Washington claimed it did not have the authority to step in. As far as Lansing was concerned, Americans had the right to deal with whomever they chose. Merchants, not the government, had the responsibility to ensure that they were conducting legal trade. Lansing claimed that the burden of stopping such traffic was solely Britain's to bear.[31] Consequently, the "working arrangement" failed because Britain did not recognize the importance that American businesses placed on government noninterference. Lansing wanted the Allies to realize that his country's long-standing commitment to freedom of the seas prevented Washington from restricting US international trade. Additionally, the White House realized the impact that such an agreement might have on public opinion. Wilson and his staff assumed that accepting London's compromise would seem unneutral to German-Americans and Germany, putting the administration in a difficult predicament.

Since stopping American merchandise at the source was not the only way to thwart exports to Germany, Grey's department addressed its dilemma from a different angle—that of circumventing Washington. His government tried to convince neutrals bordering the Central Powers that they should no longer allow German agents to purchase surplus for Germany. In November, British and French representatives met with the Dutch minister for foreign affairs hoping to modify an existing agreement between the countries by tightening restrictions on exports to London's enemy. They wanted a set of "uniform revised rules concerning the trade in contraband" that would prevent any goods beneficial to the German military from leaving the Netherlands. To guarantee this outcome, the British stipulated that the Dutch government must be the official receiver of all imports. If not, Britain asserted that it was "prepared to accept, in form still to be agreed, the guarantee of The Hague Trading Committee as to their home consumption." Britain had to have proof that any contraband goods shipped to the committee had a bill of lading that designated the domestic purchaser.[32]

To insure that Germany did not receive contraband, on November 23, the Dutch agreed to establish the Netherlands Overseas Trust (NOT). Run by banking and shipping leaders, the NOT would be the consignee for all goods entering the country except imports destined for government use. In turn, the NOT signed agreements with Dutch importers who guaranteed that the products they purchased were for domestic use only. By January, the Foreign Office had an acceptable agreement. US Consul-General at Rotterdam Soren Listoe informed Bryan that the Dutch Government had established the NOT to "act as an intermediary for Netherlands Merchants or trading companies, with the view to enable the unmolested conveyance from oversea [*sic*] of merchandise which has been declared contraband." The company would make sure that merchants followed all regulations concerning the sale of contraband and "maintain[ed] absolute neutrality." Britain eventually secured commitments from other neutrals not to reexport goods to Germany and convinced several, including Sweden in early 1916, to organize their own overseas trusts on the Dutch model.[33]

The advantage of this system was that it allowed Britain to regulate the contraband trade without involving the US government. The strategy was essential to the British war effort because it protected commerce between neutrals and evaded the American challenge to continuous voyage, eliminating a significant issue of contention between Washington and London.

Since the trusts did not directly interfere with the international transactions of US businesses, merchants had no room to protest. Nevertheless, the overseas trusts were not enough to end all British interference with neutral commerce. Britain continued detaining vessels it thought were carrying absolute contraband to Germany, which generated additional tension between the Atlantic states.

In a November 11 letter to Spring-Rice, Grey explained Britain's conviction that several German ships docked in the United States were preparing to sail and that Berlin planned to use them in "belligerent operations" in the Pacific Ocean. Spring-Rice warned Wilson of the "extremely serious consequences which such a contingency would entail." Grey warned that if the vessels left the US ports, British popular sentiment would force his government to hold the United States accountable.[34] Later that afternoon, Spring-Rice replied that German activities in the United States had angered the president. Wilson understood the danger and noted that if the German ships caused problems for British shipping, it would infuriate American citizens as well. The ambassador added that the president was "aware that if the German ships do get out and prey on commerce, public opinion will be stirred up especially if [Britain has] shown our wish to help [the] commercial situation . . . and your conciliatory attitude with regard to contraband." The president was certain that German-Americans were against him. He asserted that they were trying to build a third political party, which according to Spring-Rice, Wilson thought was "directed against him."[35]

The pressures of the executive office were wearing on the president's nerves and patience. After his wife died, he felt alone and often wished that he could step out of his own skin, if for only a moment. Wilson's conviction that it was his duty to end the crisis in Europe and assure US neutrality remained a constant weight on his shoulders. House stated that the president confided in him many times about the stress that came with the highest office in the land. On the evening of November 13, House and his wife Loulie went out for dinner and to see a play. When they returned to their apartment afterward, the colonel discovered that the White House had called to say the president planned to come over at six the following morning. House quickly cancelled his appointments for the following day and, after cleaning his home, finally went to bed "well after midnight."

When the president arrived, he was not alone. He brought with him his daughter Margaret and his personal doctor, Rear Admiral Cary T. Grayson. After breakfast, they traveled to the Piping Rock Club outside the city to play a round of golf. Wilson, Grayson, and Gordon Auchincloss, Grayson's son-in-law, hit the links while House waited in the clubhouse. After dinner that evening, when most of the guests had left, the president and House continued to talk about philosophical matters, including life after death.

Afterward, the two men took a walk through the city. They strolled along until a crowd recognized them and they slipped into the Waldorf Astoria hotel to elude the public. Wilson and House stepped into an elevator and headed up. Then they secretly exited the building from the other side. According to House, the president seemed to enjoy the affair and told his friend that he wished he could simply get lost in the crowd. House recalled, "I suggested the next time he came I would have some whiskers for him. He thought that a great idea, but later said it would cause a terrible scandal if it were found out. He left me in doubt as to whether he wanted the whiskers or not."[36]

The pressure of being president was beginning to weigh heavily on the widower. He explained to House that he yearned for his misery to end and wished that someone would "kill him" while they were out walking that night. "His eyes were moist when he spoke of not wanting to live longer, and of not being fit to do the work he had in hand." Nevertheless the president said he would continue doing the best he could as long as he was alive. House wrote, in his diary, that this was not the first time Wilson mentioned the stress he felt.[37]

In the midst of his frustration, Wilson received another letter from Professor Hugo Münsterberg. The professor outlined several concerns that "German sympathizers" had about the actions of the government. According to Münsterberg, Germany did not doubt Wilson's declaration of neutrality, but German-Americans did. They distrusted the State Department because it had taken steps that seemed concessions to Britain's demands, which were the main reason so many German-Americans had voted against the administration. In particular, Münsterberg wanted to emphasize three issues. The first, he wrote, was that the United States did not censor British telegrams, but it censored all wireless news. This was a major issue for Münsterberg since Germany had to send most of its messages to America via wireless communication after Britain cut the telegraph cables connecting Germany to the United States. Second, he argued that German and Austrian passengers on American and neutral ships were "detained and searched," which he saw as a violation of an American policy that extended as far back as the War of 1812. Finally, Münsterberg declared that German-Americans opposed the Wilson administration's approach to the contraband issue. The United States, he claimed, had willingly allowed London to violate the Hague Convention and international law concerning the shipment of goods to belligerents. In accepting Britain's policy on the sale of conditional contraband to neutral states, the United States appeared to support the Entente's strategy to starve the German people: "The nation by reversing its own policy thus seriously handicaps Germany and Austria in their fight for existence."[38]

Münsterberg stated that these were only examples and that the sentiments of the German- and Irish-American populations were best summed up in an excerpt of a letter written by George Sylvester Viereck, the editor of a pro-German newspaper, the *Fatherland*. According to Viereck, "We permit English warships to nose about in our harbors; we permit them to search our ships. In 1812 we went to war for smaller reasons . . . It is time to reassert our declaration of independence. German-American citizens feel, rightly or wrongly, that the administration is hostile to them, because its interpretation of neutrality had been at all points disadvantageous to Germany." Münsterberg denounced the administration's decisions to drop its disapproval of private loans to belligerents and allow companies to sell ammunition overseas, actions that he claimed were advantageous only to Britain and France and that would ultimately prolong the war.[39]

The professor's comments greatly disturbed the president and after several weeks of deliberation, he sent the letter to Lansing. He told Lansing that Münsterberg's message summed up how the German-American population viewed his administration and that he and his staff should consider the issues carefully because at first glance, they seemed "very plausible indeed."[40] Lansing read Münsterberg's letter and tried to reassure the president that the charges were false. He concluded that Münsterberg must be working for the German government and that the impact that the administration's policies had on US citizens was a domestic matter, "not subject to discussion with a foreigner." Münsterberg's agenda, Lansing insisted, was to divide the American people. The professor was trying to stress to German-Americans that they were German first and that they needed to unite against the White House to force Wilson into "showing special favors to Germany and Austria."[41]

Lansing refutation of Münsterberg's accusations clearly illustrates his interpretation of neutrality and the one accepted by the administration. In response to the allegation that the United States was not strictly neutral, Lansing argued that "if one belligerent had by good fortune superiority in the matter of geographical location or of military or naval power," the United States could not force it to change because that would appear to be bias in favor of the weaker power. Lansing correctly asserted that it was not the United States fault that Britain dominated the seas: "Whether one belligerent or the other is successful, is not a matter of concern to a neutral government and it cannot vary the rules or change its policy because of a particular triumph or defeat by either during the progress of the war." He defended the administration's policies concerning the sale of munitions and loans to belligerents, noting that international law did not prevent the sale of munitions during a war. In his opinion, sales of contraband goods were "mere matters of trade." If Britain did not control the shipping lanes to

Europe, "[t]he manufacturer, unless particularly sentimental, would sell to one belligerent as readily as he would the other." Consequently he deduced that the conditions of the war allowed the United States to remain neutral and conduct business conducive to the Entente cause without intentionally supporting victory by either side.[42] Wilson was impressed by Lansing's comments, which seem to have further bolstered the former's belief that his policies toward the belligerents were actually neutral.[43]

Despite his stress over the complexity of relations with Great Britain and the animosity of his own German-American constituency, the president did not want his personal sympathy for London to influence the course he pursued in "upholding" neutrality. He continued taking steps that did not overtly support either side. As Lansing pointed out in his message, the United States was well within its rights to make loans to the belligerents and sell war material—neither of which had sparked official protests by the German government. The administration believed that it had not breached its official neutrality and the United States did not bear the responsibility of putting pressure on Britain to allow Germany equal access to trade routes across the Atlantic. The war itself, not American policy, was the reason that Germany could not conduct business with American companies.

In addition to managing US trade relations, the president reasoned that he could ensure America's unaligned position by managing domestic policy, including the idea of preparedness. In 1914 and for much of 1915, Wilson opposed building up the military. However, many members of his staff did not. Men including Assistant Secretary of the Navy Franklin D. Roosevelt, Secretary of War Lindley Garrison, and House favored an expansion of the armed forces. As early as April 1914, House wanted to strengthen and expand the size of the US military. Charles Seymour, the editor of House's papers, asserts House believed that, backed by a powerful fighting force, the Wilson administration's "moral influence" would have a greater impact in world affairs. House had not given up on the idea in November when he spoke to former Army Chief of Staff General Leonard Wood. Wood, a career soldier who managed the occupation of Cuba after the Spanish-Cuban-American War, was an ardent proponent of military preparedness. Over the decade preceding the outbreak of the war, he gave many speeches across the country to promote the idea of a large professional military and continued to promote his cause when he took command of the army's Eastern Department in April 1914. The two concurred that the country must be ready if it suddenly found itself at war.[44]

On November 4, House argued to Wilson that they needed to consider building up the reserve army. House concluded that they should start increasing the military's size slowly to prepare the United States in the event of a German victory. Wilson disagreed. Perhaps still reflecting on the midterm elections, the president feared that Americans would object. He added that even if Germany did win, it would be so weak that the United States would have plenty of time to organize later. Countering, House argued that strengthening the army would ensure that the country was powerful enough that other countries would not be tempted to attack. If the government started enlarging the armed forces after a German triumph, it would amount to a declaration of war. Nevertheless, to House's frustration, Wilson disapproved. "The President" he wrote, "does not seem to fully grasp the importance of such matters."[45] Unlike House, Wilson was sensitive to the domestic political realm. Actions that might suggest that his office was preparing to enter the conflict on either side could turn the American public against him, threatening his political future and hampering mediation.

Undeterred, the colonel tried to rouse support for his plan. On Sunday, November 8, he chose not to attend church with the president and instead went to talk to Bryan. House wanted to know how the secretary of state felt about expanding the army. To his dismay, Bryan adamantly opposed any increase in the reserve. He rightly assumed that there was very little chance a foreign power would invade the United States and, like the president, he believed that even if Germany won the war, Washington would have ample time to prepare for an attack. Bryan's assertion irritated House. In his diary, he vented his anger, stating that Bryan "talked as innocently as my grandchild, Jane Tucker . . . He spoke with great feeling and I fear he may give trouble." The conversation convinced House that as long as Bryan remained secretary of state, he would have difficulty influencing American policy and reinforced House's desire to push the secretary out of the administration, or at least into a subordinate role.[46]

Changing the subject, House asked Bryan what legislation he felt the White House should try to pass in the near future. The secretary wanted a national primary law and a rule prohibiting a second presidential term. House then used this information against Bryan in a conversation with Wilson later that day. The colonel explained that Bryan was "unreasonable" about the army and that the secretary was probably trying to get the second term bill passed for selfish reasons. He thought they should allow Bryan to pursue the "primary bill" because it might keep him out of the way. Knowing that the bill would consume his time, House wrote in his diary that Bryan would be "tangled in it as a fly in molasses."[47]

Weeks later, on his way through New York, the president stopped to have breakfast with House. The colonel again argued that the US military was unprepared for future conflicts and reasserted that Bryan was an "impractical" man on the issue. Despite his growing distaste for Bryan, Wilson supported the secretary's view of neutrality. The president concluded that raising the strength of the military could create more problems than solutions. When House denoted that the country needed a large reserve force, Wilson replied, "Yes, but not a large army."[48] In the conversations on preparedness that House and Wilson had during November, the president's opinions were quite clear. He did not want to arouse suspicions overseas that Washington was preparing for combat or choosing sides.

Deterring the expansion of the military was not the only gesture the president made to ensure American neutrality, nor was it the only one that divided the administration. In early November, it came to the attention of the White House that several American companies wanted to sell submarines to Great Britain. These companies had already made offers to Britain for existing vessels and were in the process of constructing others. During a secret meeting with British First Sea Lord Admiral John Fisher on October 28, Charles Schwab, the owner of Bethlehem Steel, agreed to build the Royal Navy twenty submarines for a price of $10,000,000. Concerned about how the White House might react, Schwab's attorney James Hayden approached Lansing on November 5. As historian Gaddis Smith points out, there is no record of the conversation; however, Lansing's subsequent letters to Bryan and Wilson suggest that the counselor approved of the sale and judged that selling unassembled submarines was not a violation of strict US neutrality.[49] After returning from the campaign trail, Bryan contacted Lansing on November 12 because he was concerned about the effect that such sales could have on the United States. Lansing replied that selling a completed submarine "would, I think, be in violation of our neutral duty." According to international law "no war vessel of any sort should be allowed to leave our ports, which has been constructed for a belligerent government, in such a condition that it could be utilized for offensive operations without entering the port of the purchaser." The seemingly clear-cut law nonetheless offered US companies a loophole. While it was not acceptable to deal in completed vessels that were ready for "offensive operations," selling individual parts or disassembled submarines was a different matter. He pointed out to the secretary that the rule did not include the "sale of material for warships however completely prepared for assembling." Separate parts did not amount to a warship. If the submarine parts were sent in separate ships, "certainly no question could be raised." Therefore such transactions would not constitute an infringement of American neutrality.[50]

Bryan thought that Lansing was splitting hairs and he immediately contacted Wilson with his opposing view. "I fear," stated Bryan, "that we would be 'skating on thin ice' if we adopted the rule suggested." Asserting that while the sale of unassembled submarines was within US rights, he thought it would be a very complicated process to convince the public or Germany that selling parts was different from selling completed submarines.[51]

In a late November note to the president, Lansing explained that he had contacted the Joint State and Navy Neutrality Board on the matter and that it had seen no legal barriers to the sale of the submarines. Lansing added that there were also no laws providing penalties for either the federal government or American manufacturers.[52]

Wilson replied several days later that he had "given the matter serious thought" and had concluded that selling submarines may be legal, but it was in opposition to the "'*spirit*' of the '*Alabama* decision'" during the Civil War.[53] He was considering a precedent set more than a half century earlier that involved the CSS *Alabama*, a sloop-of-war built for the Confederacy in a British shipyard and completed in 1862. When the commerce raider was launched, it was not fitted for combat, though all parties knew its ultimate purpose. Charles Frances Adams, President Abraham Lincoln's minister to Britain—who knew that the vessel was designed to carry cannons—protested to the British government in an unsuccessful attempt to prevent its departure.[54] Once at sea, the Confederate Navy recommissioned the ship as the *Alabama* and it wreaked havoc on American merchant trade until June 1864, when the USS *Kearsarge* sank the vessel near France. Confederate estimates suggest that the *Alabama* damaged or captured more than sixty ships, collectively worth millions of dollars.[55] Theoretically, Britain had not broken any domestic or international law when it permitted the Confederacy to take delivery on the *Alabama* because the ship had no weapons when it left Liverpool. But it had violated the spirit of the law. In the aftermath of the Civil War, the United States took its case before a tribunal in Geneva, Switzerland, which concluded that Britain had to take responsibility for the destruction caused by the CSS *Alabama*, the CSS *Florida*, and the CSS *Shenandoah*. As a result, Britain had to pay the United States $15.5 million in reparations.[56]

Bryan's argument won the day and the United States refused to sell submarines to the belligerents. Lansing therefore contacted American manufacturers and told them the government's position. He wrote Hayden to retract his earlier approval and explain that Wilson and Bryan were "opposed to the sale of submarines or of their component parts by American manufacturers to belligerents, as being contrary to the strict neutrality which this government seeks to preserve in the present war, and that it will take all legal means to prevent the exportation of such craft and manufactured parts."[57]

The Foreign Office did not stop trying to convince Wilson that the sale of submarine parts should continue. Even after telling Lansing that he would accept the government's position, Schwab advised Grey that during the Russo-Japanese War, Japan legally received submarine parts. Therefore, a precedent existed to which the president could refer if desired. When Spring-Rice brought this to Bryan's attention, the secretary insisted that the Russo-Japanese War example did not apply because the "parts were sold to a third party and [the] question did not arise till export had taken place." Additionally Bryan reiterated Wilson's view of the *Alabama* decision arguing that "[under] the *Alabama* award it seemed to [the] President [that the] case might lie against [the] United States Government for damages and he did not wish to run the risk."[58]

The decision suggests that Wilson hoped to assure neutrality because it went against his private desire for a British victory. The course of action complicated the British war effort and Lansing had to explain the American position to Spring-Rice when they sat down to discuss the matter on December 3. He maintained that he did not see a problem, but that Bryan and Wilson had decided selling submarines was not wise. Lansing argued that they feared that the American public would not see a difference between selling submarines and selling their many parts: "International law was a thing [the] public would not understand."[59]

Wilson reaffirmed his desire to remain neutral and out of the war when he stood before Congress on December 8, 1914, and gave his annual State of the Union address. In his message, the president promoted several items of his agenda, including the shipping bill and the state of national defense. Wilson asserted that the only sane power left in the world was the United States and that it had the responsibility as a neutral country to find a way to end the fighting. Washington had worked hard to maintain peace in the world, but "circumstances of the whole age have been altered by war." According to the president, because of the struggle raging across the Atlantic, the governments of Europe would soon "need our help and our manifold services as they have never before." Wilson stated that US mediation was not possible if the government actively aided one belligerent over the other. As long as the United States did not transcend the legal boundaries of neutrality, Wilson expected that his administration would be the saving grace of civilization.[60]

Wilson again stressed his desire to protect America's economic future. One way, he asserted, to lessen the conflict's effect on US interests and prevent further problems with Europe was to redirect the focus of US trade. To that point, the president took the opportunity to promote the shipping bill that he helped formulate in the first days of August. Wilson said the war prevented the belligerent countries from servicing their world markets. The loss of European imports meant that states in Latin America and elsewhere would need American goods, and the United States had an opportunity to supply these markets. Yet he asserted that the country was not ready to do so because it did not have enough shipping to carry US merchandise throughout the Western Hemisphere: "We have grossly erred in the way in which we have stunted and hindered the development of our merchant marine. And now, when we need ships, we have not got them."[61]

Since the beginning of the war, Wilson sought to use federal funds to create a government-owned merchant fleet. For that reason, he wanted Congress to support the shipping bill. Congress needed to look forward and pass the bill even before it was "altogether profitable to open" the Latin American markets or "ask private capital to open them at a venture." With government aid, the administration could keep shipping costs low—even to small and unexplored markets. Federal support, Wilson deduced, would stimulate trade in such areas and help develop them into lucrative regions. Once the markets became profitable, the government could turn the ships over to private interests.[62]

In a last-minute addition to the address, Wilson included a section on national defense. Because it was an increasingly important issue within public circles, he wanted to discuss the idea of preparedness. He agreed that the United States was not in a position to go to war on a "brief notice." Nevertheless to assuage fears that the country would be at the mercy of an attacker, Wilson asserted that Americans had always risen to challenges in the past. The point he wanted to emphasize, however, was that preparedness could cause problems for the United States. He did not want to affect US neutrality or his plan to mediate an end to the war. Wilson reminded the Congress that "we are at peace with the world . . . we are, indeed, a true friend to the world, because we threaten none." Hence he did not see a reason to raise alarm by knocking the rust off the country's sword.[63]

Wilson did, however, argue that the country might ensure its domestic security by buttressing the National Guard. The United States, declared the president, had never depended on a standing army. Instead, it relied on citizen soldiers—Americans who volunteered to train for combat but maintained their civilian roles in society. To that end, he asserted that Congress needed to approve the development of a stronger National Guard. He did not see this as an aggressive move because the National Guard had one purpose: to protect the homeland. It was not an offensive weapon, like the army or navy, and in his opinion, would not endanger America's standing with the belligerents.[64]

The president's speech suggests that he believed he was still acting in a neutral manner. Wilson certainly intended the address to reemphasize to the American people and to the world that he planned to remain unaligned and protect the US economy. He insisted that his government was destined to play an important role in the history of the world and Wilson did not want to threaten its, or his, opportunity for glory. As the war continued, however, the president would discover that American neutrality and the quest for economic prosperity were increasingly difficult to reconcile.

The importance of the munitions trade had become clear by late 1914. Allied munitions needs placed Britain in a difficult position. The British government had to assure a constant flow of weapons to its men in the field, but it would not reverse its maritime policies because it still wanted to keep goods out of German hands. The problem spurred the Foreign Office to explore ways to pacify US citizens and prevent contraband from reaching the Central Powers—including the working arrangement and the establishment of the NOT. Britain soon discovered, however, that negotiations with the US government could not convince Wilson to regulate his own country's trade if the result hindered his political interests or the American economy. The working arrangement, proposed by Britain, required the United States to intervene to its own detriment. The Foreign Office therefore, had to find a way to circumvent the United States government by reaching agreements with other neutrals along Germany's border. Assuring that the Netherlands and other European states would not sell surplus goods to the Allies' enemies would help Britain regulate US exports without open interference. The outcome of deliberations over the working arrangement influenced Anglo-American diplomatic relations for the rest of the neutrality period. Britain took away from the experience an understanding that in the future, all trade policies needed to avoid direct US government involvement.

At the same time, Wilson took steps to protect his country's neutrality. He quietly assured that the government would not stand in the way of *private* credits to belligerents, deterred the sale of submarines, and opposed House's suggestion to increase the size and strength of the US military. All of these efforts were made by the president to protect American commercial interests and simultaneously prevent the impression that he was taking sides.

The decisions made in London and Washington created a viable—though delicate—diplomatic path to resolve their differences. While both countries continued working to protect their economic and political interests, it is plausible to deduce that they also discovered the limitations faced by their counterparts and understood that they would have to work within certain constraints if they were to continue cordial relations.

4

"As a Friend to All of Them"

December 1914–January 1915

> All must confess failure . . . now when the cup of sorrow is overflowing . . . it would seem to be this nation's duty as the leading exponent of Christianity and as the foremost advocate of world-wide peace, to approach the warring nations again and earnestly urge them to consent to a conference.
>
> —Secretary of State William Jennings Bryan to Wilson, December 1, 1914[1]

In late 1914 and early 1915, Congress deliberated over legislation that could disrupt Anglo-American relations. Many Americans believed that selling weapons to the Allies was an unneutral act and members of the House and Senate presented bills to stop the munitions trade in the hope of forcing a quick end to the war. Wilson opposed the munitions bills. He concluded that according to international law the United States had the right to sell weapons and ammunition to the warring parties and feared that if passed, the legislation could harm his administration's renewed effort to initiate mediation. Congress was also discussing the shipping bill. The legislation faced major opposition on Capitol Hill because many Americans believed that it would lead to excessive government interference in US trade.

Britain viewed both issues with concern. If it could not purchase war materiel in the United States, the Allies might lose the war. If the shipping bill passed, the presence of US government-owned merchant vessels would threaten the existence of the blockade because stopping federal property at sea could violate US sovereignty and turn the American people against Britain. The predicament forced Britain to maneuver cautiously concerning the detention of American merchant ships and Wilson's push for peace talks.

The timing of a renewed mediation effort divided the Wilson administration. Days before the State of the Union speech, Secretary of State William Jennings Bryan wrote the president that maintaining neutrality had proven to be a very difficult task. Questions continued to arise over the matter and Bryan felt that the administration owed it to the rest of the neutral world and the warring states to broker an end to the conflict. He argued that "as a friend to all of them," the United States needed to find a "peaceful settlement of their differences." The secretary claimed the belligerents were incapable of rational thinking because "[t]heir feelings are so deeply stirred that they take council of their anger rather than of their sober judgment; they cannot consider the question with calmness and their pride will not allow them to ask for mediation—the offer must come from us." Bryan added that America had a moral obligation to end the war and asserted that the Europeans states were "Christian nations" that should be able to come to terms. "All must confess failure . . . now when the cup of sorrow is overflowing . . . it would seem to be this nation's duty," Bryan pleaded, "as the leading exponent of Christianity and as the foremost advocate of world-wide peace, to approach the warring nations again and earnestly urge them to consent to a conference."[2]

The president and Colonel Edward House disagreed. Wilson and House not only thought that mediation would be futile at the moment, they considered Bryan naïve and assumed that he did not understand the complexities of foreign policy. Bryan's note exacerbated Wilson's growing distaste for him. The president appreciated his views on maintaining neutrality but did not want the secretary involved in any important mediation discussions. Because, as House and Wilson concluded, Bryan had overstepped his bounds, Wilson thought him "unsuited for the office of Secretary of State." According to House, they "thought that [Bryan] had served his usefulness as Secretary of State, and that it would be a good thing for the administration and for the country if he would pleasantly take himself out of the Cabinet."[3]

Ironically, less than two weeks later, House and Wilson changed their minds about pursuing mediation. They saw a ray of hope in a letter from German Undersecretary of State for Foreign Affairs Arthur Zimmermann. The missive, written on December 3, was a private reply to a message House wrote almost three months before. Zimmermann argued that because of the "zeal of our opponents . . . [the] question of mediation has yet reached the stage for action." Trying to blame the conflict on Britain and France, he asserted that the Allies were escalating the war by "summoning all the forces at their disposal, including Japanese and other colored races." Mediation, however, was not off the table. The undersecretary asserted that his government might consider negotiations if the Allies initiated the talks.[4]

When House's letter reached Berlin in late October, the Germans were not ready to stop fighting and assumed that any US-led discussion would be prejudiced against them. German Chancellor Theobald von Bethmann-Hollweg wrote that he saw "a certain danger in an American mediation move because it would probably lead to an international congress, and our position in such a congress—two great powers against three—would be an unfavorable one . . . And from the American side we would have to expect Mr. Wilson's and Mr. Bryan's known do-good tendencies and the injection of a lot of questions (disarmament, arbitration, and world peace) which, the more utopian they are, the more they make practical negotiations difficult." Nevertheless the German government could not reject the White House peace proposition, since the alternative was for the world to conclude that Germany favored war over peace.[5] Not knowing Germany's true intentions, Zimmermann's message encouraged House and Wilson. When House met the president for dinner in Washington on December 16, Wilson suggested that the colonel prepare to go overseas in hope of starting peace discussions.[6]

They decided that the first step was to meet with German Ambassador Johann Heinrich von Bernstorff to confirm Germany's interest in peace. The following afternoon, House sat down with the ambassador over lunch and discussed the letter. Bernstorff suggested the colonel should travel to Berlin. House stated in his diary that Bernstorff asserted that "if I [House] could get the Allies to consent to parleys, I would find the Germans willing" to do the same. House then warned Bernstorff that he knew Britain and France opposed any peace terms that did not include reparations for Belgium and disarmament. Bernstorff replied that he did not think "there would be any obstacle in that direction."[7]

Bernstorff's answer convinced House that he should pursue the matter with British Ambassador Cecil Spring-Rice. The colonel tried to pressure the British by stressing that a refusal to talk would place the Allies in a "bad light."[8] House's effort created a major problem for Great Britain because the Allies, like the Germans, were not interested in peace negotiations. The French were opposed to American mediation from the start. When Georges Clemenceau (former and future prime minister) of France received word of Wilson's proposal he opposed the suggestion. He claimed that only the belligerents could initiate peace talks. In his diary, Lord Francis Leveson Bertie, the British ambassador to France, recorded that Clemenceau told him that he "pooh-poohs American intervention."[9]

House noted on December 20 that he found himself running all over Washington. That morning he met with the German ambassador, who was very anxious because he had received information suggesting that Japan would send troops to Europe. Bernstorff told the colonel that if the Allies took this step, "all peace negotiations were ended as far as Germany was concerned." House promised to look into the matter, but secretly claimed that the Allies had every right to bring Japanese troops to the western front. Despite his argument, House did not expect Japan would send soldiers, but if it did, the move might make the Germans even more "anxious for peace."

Soon thereafter, he received word that Spring-Rice wanted to see him. Since he was leaving for New York that afternoon, he met with him immediately. Not surprisingly, the ambassador gave House an answer filled with stipulations. Foreign Secretary Edward Grey agreed to British participation in peace negotiations, but only if Germany agreed to compensate Belgium and accept a plan for disarmament. Spring-Rice, however, admitted that this was the personal view of the secretary and not an official position.[10]

When House returned to the White House with the news, the president was "elated." He became so focused on the prospect of mediation that after Bryan interrupted the meeting with a phone call to discuss patronage for a fellow Democrat, he laughed about the secretary's persistence and then slammed his hand on the table exclaiming "damn . . . he must relieve himself of such unimportant and futile talks at a time when the great world tragedy was upmost in [Wilson's] mind." The president and House developed tunnel vision concerning mediation, so much so that Wilson asked him if he could go to Europe as early as the following Saturday.[11]

The White House's determination to press for mediation greatly complicated the already tricky Anglo-American relationship. British and American diplomats found themselves participating in a balancing act as they juggled three major issues: mediation, armament sales, and shipping. For the United States, maintaining neutrality was a necessity if it was to lead the belligerents toward peace. Therefore, as part of its public diplomacy, the Wilson administration had previously asserted its right to protest on a case-by-case basis against continued British interference with American trade while simultaneously defending its legal right to sell munitions to any government it chose. Britain understood that it had to feign interest in mediation and compromise on US shipping if it was to assure American acquiescence to the Order in Council of October and guarantee a constant flow of materiel to its armed forces. Consequently, the months of December 1914 and January 1915 became a complex period during the first phase of American neutrality.

In the latter months of 1914, American exports increased to neutral countries across Europe. Spring-Rice reported to the Foreign Office that in October alone, US companies shipped 22 tons of copper to Italy, six times the country's normal monthly consumption.[12] On December 11, the ambassador wrote that US merchants recently shipped £250,000 worth of goods from New York to Sweden. This was a threefold increase over previous weeks. The ambassador reported similar numbers for consignments to other countries.[13] With such staggering numbers, Britain assumed that huge quantities of goods were still reaching Germany and that it had to continue detaining ships headed to neutral ports.

In a message from Grey, Bryan learned that the Royal Navy detained the *Alfred Nobel*, an American vessel, and placed it before a prize court because the cargo included wheat and meat consigned "to order." The foreign secretary claimed that German representatives had secretly approached US shippers in hope that they would "lend their [the shippers] names so as to appear to be the legitimate owners of the cargo." He pointed out that the *Alfred Nobel* was not an isolated case. The Royal Navy searched and detained other vessels—including the *Björnson* and *Fridland*—for carrying goods to an unnamed purchaser. Grey argued that the phrase "to order" was intended to hide the ultimate destination of the merchandise and raised a red flag for the British.[14]

Because of such actions, Bryan decided that the time was right for another protest against Britain's detention of American cargoes. On December 17, the same day Wilson and House received word from Bernstorff that the colonel would be welcomed in Berlin to discuss mediation, Bryan suggested that the president send London a protest message. Unaware of the president's negotiations with the belligerents, the secretary sought to put America's views in a "definite form." In doing so, Washington could defend US trade and, more important, let every state know that the government had done everything it could to reduce the "hardships imposed upon neutral countries." Bryan recommended that American Ambassador Walter Hines Page should address the seizure of US ships and protest the British decision "to uphold a policy which would starve the enemy largely at the expense of neutrals." Finally the secretary challenged the contraband list by asserting that the "doctrine of contraband" needed limits, "which the present course of Great Britain appears to transcend."[15]

Bryan's timing weakened his standing with the oval office. Wilson, according to House, immediately picked up his pencil and began editing. After making a number of corrections to the first page, he quit, stating, "It is not right to impose such a task on me . . . They have not written good and understandable English, much less writing it in a way to avoid offense." Wilson undoubtedly did not want to reduce the chance of convincing Britain to enter negotiations on ending the war. He also knew that the protest was necessary to protect American trade and neutrality. In disgust, he sent the document back to Bryan, demanding a revised copy with a more conciliatory tone.[16]

In a private conversation on Friday afternoon, House told Spring-Rice that the president had returned the message to the State Department because Bryan "did not understand the delicate phrasing of important diplomatic messages." Viewing himself and his statesmanship as superior to that of Bryan and his office, House did not want the State Department to influence US policy. He assumed that pressuring Britain at that juncture could hinder his mediation efforts and added that his comments should remain secret. Regardless of his arrogant attitude and efforts to assuage Anglo-American relations, House did stress that Wilson wanted the ships released as quickly as possible.[17]

The following Monday, Spring-Rice sent Wilson two letters he had received from Grey. They dealt with prize courts and commercial telegrams. The foreign secretary expressed sympathy concerning the seizure of ships, but in an effort to justify Britain's actions, he mentioned that during the American Civil War, US prize courts decided over three hundred cases, only one of which had been "disputed in England." In the telegrams that followed, Grey stated there were seven neutral ships in the prize court but that Britain had already released around twenty others. He also defended his government by stating that the court's decisions took time and that once it reached a verdict, any cargo deemed contraband would be paid for or released.[18] Wilson replied in a way that suggested he did not want the issue to overshadow mediation efforts, telling Spring-Rice that he believed such issues "will work themselves out."[19]

In another trade-related affair, the vast number of purchasing agents trying to buy weapons for the Allies convinced Great Britain to streamline the process. The challenge was to make acquisitions simpler without causing a rift with Wilson. Grey soon found this easier than expected. In mid-December, he received a message from J. P. Morgan, who offered his company as the "sole channel through whom all orders are placed in the United States." Using Morgan's company appealed to Britain because it was the major private financial institution in the United States. Additionally, it had branches in London and Paris but no ties to Germany. The foreign secretary decided to send a message to Spring-Rice asking him to find out how the administration would react to an arrangement between Britain and the Morgan Company. In a second letter, Grey told the ambassador that the accord with Morgan was purely commercial and did not relate to finance. His biggest concern was to avoid "embarrass[ing], the Administration or predispos[ing] radical elements in American politics against us or lead[ing] to protest in Congress." Ultimately Washington did not see any dangers of such an arrangement with a US company, and Morgan began a long and lucrative relationship with London.[20]

Grey's reasoning was valid, especially his fear of creating an uproar in Congress. Any arrangement that stirred "radical elements in American politics" could disrupt the flow of munitions from US firms. The Foreign Office was well aware of the ongoing debate over the sale of weapons to the belligerents. Many Americans opposed the armament trade because munitions sales might prolong the war. On December 7, 1914, the US Senate asked the Department of Commerce secretary William C. Redfield to inform it of the quantity of materiel the country had already exported to the Allies. Redfield replied nine days later that in the first two months of the war, American munitions exports to Britain alone grew from $19,111 in August to $700,699 in September. When France, Canada, and Japan were included, the numbers were much higher, jumping from $154,080 in August to $1,452,740 in September. This was a drastic increase over the fiscal year that ended in June 1914. During that 12-month period, the country sold a total of $2,657,106 in munitions, of which only $29,167 went to Germany.[21]

Throughout the first year of the war, the State Department received numerous complaints from pacifist and German-American groups about the munitions trade. They argued that selling weapons to the Allies prolonged the conflict and demonstrated the nonneutral stance of the Wilson administration. As early as August 26, the president of the National German-American Alliance in Massachusetts protested against the sale of Colt machine guns to Canada.[22] Such statements demanded a response from the government and in October, Counselor Robert Lansing announced that "for a private individual to sell to a belligerent any product of the United States is neither unlawful or unneutral, nor within the power of the President to prevent or control."[23]

Lansing's disclaimer did not deter further complaints. German-Americans made their feelings known at meetings where they argued correctly that Wilson's approach to neutrality, in reality, benefitted Britain. On November 24, 1914, Dr. Charles Hexamer, president of the National Alliance, a German-American political society, attacked what he called the "lick-spittle policy" of the United States. He sent a protest to the White House declaring, "You cannot imagine, Mr. President, with what chagrin and bitterness it fills the Americans of German descent to see the resources of this great country . . . placed at the disposal of enemies who . . . have proclaimed it their avowed purpose to crush our ancestral home."[24] Within weeks German-American Congressmen Henry Vollmer of Iowa and Richard Barthold of Missouri submitted bills to the House of Representatives to stop the sale of munitions to the belligerents. Bills in the senate soon followed. The first, sponsored by Senator Gilbert Hitchcock of Nebraska, echoed Vollmer's HR 377 in its call for ending arms sales to the belligerents. The other, presented by Senator John Works of California, went further by proposing an end to all exports, including "food, clothing, or other necessities which would serve to prolong the European conflict."[25]

The British government was apprehensive about the bills and made numerous calls to Page, Bryan, and Lansing. Grey talked to Page on December 13 and emphasized that he saw a distinct difference between the sale of submarine parts and the sale of munitions. He added that if the bill passed, it would go against the precedent set after the *Alabama* decision.[26] Trying to convince the State Department that the bills must be opposed, Spring-Rice expressed to Lansing that such legislation would not be neutral. He claimed that stopping arms sales would aid Germany over Britain. Writing to Grey, the ambassador stated, "I asked him if [the] United States Government wished to penalise the Power which prepares for peace in its contest with the Power which prepared for war."[27]

Adding to Whitehall's concern, on December 28, British Army leaders admitted at a cabinet meeting that the war was deadlocked and that troop increases alone were not enough to break the German lines. The army was considering various new technologies intended to break the stalemate and protect advancing troops, such as an armored steamroller that could flatten the barbed wire in no-man's-land, rockets with grappling hooks that would become entangled in the wire (the soldiers in the British trench could then pull on attached ropes and rip out the wire), bulletproof shields, and smoke grenades.[28] The number of unique inventions under consideration by the army suggests the military's eagerness to break the stalemate.

Any disruption to the shipments of arms from America would exacerbate the problems that the British Expeditionary Force faced in northern France. On December 31, Chancellor of the Exchequer David Lloyd George wrote to Prime Minister Henry Asquith expressing his frustration over the War Department's inability to acquire an adequate supply of urgently needed weapons. He told the prime minister, "I am uneasy about our prospects of the war unless the Government takes some decisive means to grip the situation." The chancellor criticized military commanders for underestimating the number of guns needed for the war. "The immense manufacturing resources of the country had not been organised for cannon, rifles, or ammunition and America was not even explored . . . Rifles not yet satisfactory owing to [Major-General Stanley] Von Donop's stupidity."[29] Lloyd George might have exaggerated the lack of "exploration" of the United States, but his complaint is understandable. The War Office was not managing purchases effectively, and Britain was badly in need of an efficient system to assure a constant supply of weapons. If any of the bills forbidding munitions exports passed through Congress, the Allies might find themselves at the mercy of the Central Powers.

According to article 7 of the 1907 Hague Convention Respecting the Rights and Duties of Neutral Powers and Persons in Case of War on Land, the United States was well within its rights to continue or end munitions sales to the belligerents—as long as both sides were treated equally.[30] Considering these rights and duties of neutrals, Wilson's pro-Allied sympathies could have been a motivating factor behind his decision to continue munitions sales; however, this is not clear from the internal conversations and memos of his administration. What is evident is that the White House viewed the legislation before Congress as a threat to the American economy and US-led peace talks. The president apparently believed Bryan's assertion that cutting off the sale of munitions aided one belligerent to the detriment of the other. Ending arms exports, Wilson reasoned, would have created tension that might have hampered his mediation efforts because Britain would lose its most important external source of supplies and therefore have no reason to work with the United States. Wilson and his advisors assumed that Britain would not view the United States as an impartial mediator because banning the sale of munitions would seem pro-German. In explaining Washington's position, Bryan told Spring-Rice that he "observed that certain nations had made greater preparations than others and that the bill would put a premium on preparedness for war and consequently on those principles of militarism to which the United States had always opposed."[31]

Over the next several weeks, the administration defended its stand against an embargo. On January 5, 1915, Bryan told Chairman of the Senate Foreign Relations Committee William J. Stone that if the munitions bills were approved, they would "be tantamount to an alliance with Germany."[32] By this statement, he was not implying that the United States would break its neutrality; rather, he feared that his government would influence the direction of the war.

Over the same period, House continued to push for mediation. When he arrived in Washington on the evening of December 23 he went straight to the White House. Once there, Wilson bombarded him with questions about the possibility of opening peace negotiations. The president wanted Spring-Rice to send Grey another telegram concerning Bernstorff's proposal. Around 9:45 p.m., the colonel met Spring-Rice at their usual rendezvous in the home of Assistant Secretary of State Billy Phillips. The British ambassador told House that Grey knew Anglo-German negotiations would be difficult because a major barrier was the "re-establishment of [Belgian] independence." Spring-Rice's comment seems to have been a ploy. Because of the military deadlock, Britain and France were not ready to end the conflict. Knowing Allied objectives, Grey's goal was to mislead the US government by appearing willing to talk, while ensuring that House failed to bring Britain and Germany together. Complicating matters further, Grey asserted that the only way to assure a long-term peace was for Germany to change its political structure. Appealing to Wilson's idealism, Grey said he wanted to see Germany shift toward democracy. The alternative, he claimed, was for Britain to continue fighting until Belgium was free from German occupation "even if we had to fight alone."[33]

Neither Britain nor the United States wanted to show its hand too quickly, and both tried to manipulate the situation. Grey lied to House by stating that he had not discussed the idea of peace with France or Russia. Because the Allies had agreed not to pursue peace separately, the foreign secretary had the advantage of arguing that he had to consult with all members of the alliance. Spring-Rice then asked House what he thought a settlement might entail. Realizing that any specific claims could derail his mission, House put him off, saying it was not time to get into such matters. He added only that he did not believe a settlement would mean the fighting would stop immediately or even after discussions had begun.[34]

After his meeting with Spring-Rice, House returned to the White House where Wilson was waiting. The two men concluded that they should delay speaking to Bernstorff until Grey heard from France and Russia. A positive answer from France and Russia would enable House to place pressure on the German ambassador. House could tell him he was heading to London to put the peace process in motion, but he did not want to get there only to discover that Germany had repudiated Bernstorff's statement. Finally, after 11:00 in the evening, they called it a night.[35]

The next day, Bryan sent Wilson a revised version of his instructions to Page. The secretary stated that he and Lansing had tried to soften the language but again argued that Britain was making a mistake by requiring such harsh restrictions on shipping: "She is unnecessarily arousing resentment among those interested in neutral trade." By protesting Britain's naval policies, the secretary concluded that he could assure America's neutrality. When the president examined the revised draft of the State Department's letter, he still claimed it might anger Britain's leaders. As with a munitions embargo he feared that a harsh public protest might cause unnecessary tension at a time when his hope for peace talks was very high. He immediately made additional changes and sent the draft back to Bryan's office, which amended it once again.[36]

The day after Christmas, Wilson examined the message titled the "Second Redraft of Instruction to American Ambassador at London" and altered it one more time before approving the final version to send Page. The communiqué, now with softer wording, formally complained about the number of American cargoes seized by the Royal Navy. Britain had exceeded the "manifest necessity" of a belligerent by infringing on the rights of US citizens, and merchants were frustrated by its decision to impose its "own rules on neutral cargos." The letter did not dispute the navy's power to search and detain neutral vessels at sea, but the State Department stressed that the United States needed a definitive set of rules to further its commercial interests: "We feel that we are abundantly justified in asking for information as to the manner in which the British

Government proposes to carry out the policy which they have adopted, in order that we may determine the steps necessary to protect our citizens, engaged in foreign trade." The message concluded by warning that if the existing conditions did not change, Anglo-American relations would sour: "Already it is becoming more and more the subject of public criticism and complaint. There is an increasing belief, doubtless not entirely unjustified, that the present British policy toward American trade is responsible for the depression in certain industries which depend upon European markets."[37] The number of drafts and the conciliatory form of the last version reveal that Wilson was cautiously balancing his public and private conversations with the belligerents.

Wilson's efforts were almost thwarted when the press got wind of the message. On December 29, 1914, the American "demands" appeared in many newspapers, including the *New York Times* and *Washington Post*. The media immediately bombarded the president with questions about the "note of protest." Throughout the affair, Wilson maintained a pacific tone. He told journalists that British policy did hinder American shipping, but when Britain discovered it was "in the wrong, damages have eventually been paid." Downplaying the State Department note, he emphasized that it was not the first protest. Wilson told the press that the administration had made numerous unpublicized protests in individual cases, adding, "If we made public everything that we do, you wouldn't have space for anything else." The message, he claimed, was in no way intended as a threat: "There is nothing of that kind in the note." Talking down to the newsmen, he emphasized that they were making judgments based on speculation because "the text of the note was not published." It was simply a matter of "the rules of international law." To take the heat off his office and London, Wilson blamed a minority of American shippers for many of the problems that arose between the United States and Britain. He pointed out that some merchants hid contraband under other cargoes in hope that they could slip past British searches. "[S]o long as there are *any* instances of this kind, suspicion is cast upon every shipment."[38]

When Spring-Rice and House met that evening, the ambassador expressed his frustration over the leakage of the note to the press. House tried to calm him down, telling him the president was unhappy as well. Nevertheless, Spring-Rice continued to complain. He attacked Bryan's department for its failure to keep the message secret and threatened to "absent himself from the Department in the future." The ambassador was so upset that House finally decided that talking further was useless and went back to the White House.[39] The following day, House received a new letter from Spring-Rice. The ambassador said he had seen the official note that Washington had sent to Page and believed it "very fair." Because

Spring-Rice termed the note as "just and courteous and firm," House concluded that he had "gotten in good humor again."[40]

When Grey received the official draft from Page, he knew that responding was a delicate matter. If he reacted harshly or placed the blame on the United States, he risked stirring up the American people at a time when such a crisis could severely harm the war effort. Luckily, Grey had a strong ally in Page. In his memoir, the foreign secretary wrote that Page came to him and said, "'I have now read the despatch [*sic*], but I do not agree with it; let us now consider how it should be answered!'" Grey seemed surprised yet pleased that the diplomat chose to help his office respond.[41] Together, they formulated a statement that defended British actions by pointing to the rapid expansion of US trade since the beginning of the war. Coincidence or not, two days before sending the Foreign Office reply, Page wired Bryan a note stating he had just learned that London wanted "to avoid trouble about copper shipments" and had proposed to purchase the entire wartime "output" of major American manufacturers. Such an offer was intended to eliminate one of the biggest problems for US industry at such a critical moment.[42]

In Britain's "preliminary" rejoinder, sent on January 7, 1915, Grey asserted that his country's naval policy had not interfered with neutral trade to the extent that the United States claimed. According to his statistics, in 1914 the United States exported more than double its 1913 levels to countries like Italy, Norway, and Sweden. In the case of Denmark, exports leaving New York had risen from $558,000 to $7,101,000. Disputing the State Department's charges, he said, "I can not [*sic*] believe that, with such figures before them and in such cases as those just mentioned, the Government of the United States would question the propriety of the action of His Majesty's Government in taking suspected cargoes to a prize court, and we are convinced that it can not [*sic*] be in accord with the wish either of the Government or the people of the United States to strain the international code in favor of private interests."[43]

As for the detention of neutral vessels, he pointed out that Britain had not seized a large number of merchant ships headed to Europe. Of the 773 vessels that left the United States between August 1914 and the beginning of January 1915, only 45 "had consignments of cargoes placed in prize court." And when the Royal Navy stopped US ships, he claimed its actions were justified because some Americans tried to hide illegal goods. Grey ended his message by stressing that Britain did not want to obstruct neutral trade except in the case of contraband destined for Germany. Additionally, the British government planned to offer an explanation in each case where it detained an American vessel and to arbitrate any differences in order to ensure that Britain did not "interfere with the normal importation and use by the neutral countries of goods from the United States."[44]

Lansing informed the president that Grey's letter seemed "conciliatory and that the presentation of the British case is adroit though transparently illogical . . . to one familiar to the facts." Lansing said that Grey's response was intended to reduce American frustration but did not "give any assurance that trade conditions with neutral countries will be relieved." In other words, he realized that Britain's response was a disingenuous effort to soothe public opinion and that it had no intention of changing its existing policy. He advised the White House not to answer immediately. Instead, it should wait until the Foreign Office sent an official response.[45] Wilson agreed. Replying to a journalist who wanted to know if newspapers were correct when they reported that the note did not please the administration, the president responded, "I saw an article headed 'Note Unsatisfactory to Wilson,' or something like that. I thought of writing to the editor and asking him how he found out. He didn't ask me, and nobody had asked me, and I have not expressed an opinion, because I have not studied the note yet. It is merely preliminary anyway."[46]

Later that evening, Bryan sent Page a message declaring that the White House "appreciate[d] the friendly spirit" of Grey's letter and that the two countries saw eye to eye on the "principles of international law." To prevent any immediate discussion, Bryan ended the communication by stating that Washington intended to delay an official response until it received "the further reply of the British Government." Consequently the United States temporarily dismissed the dispatch, thus preventing any controversy with London.[47]

With the note temporarily out of public conversation, Spring-Rice informed Grey a week later that at that moment, the biggest concerns he observed in the United States were the transfer of German vessels to the American flag and the congressional battle over the sale of munitions. The limited number of ships available caused freight rates to rise, which heightened tension over access to international markets, particularly in the South because the region was preparing its cotton crop for sale. According to the ambassador, in some cases rates increased "as much as 300%." Spring-Rice told Grey that this was why Wilson wanted the shipping bill passed. He added that the administration assumed a shortage of ships placed the United States at a great competitive disadvantage and, "whether reasonable or not, a large body of public opinion demands the purchase of ships either by the Government or by the private individual." Describing the president's desire to purchase German vessels, Spring-Rice noted, "He is absolutely bent on it and as you know his character is rather more than obstinate."[48]

The ambassador stressed that Grey had to face a "very real commercial grievance," and that he had to decide how to alleviate the situation. If Britain acquiesced to the US government's purchases of German ocean liners, Grey faced a dilemma because the moment that the navy "touch[ed] an American merchant ship you interfere with State property." Yet government ownership would mean government control, which could help Britain prevent contraband from reaching Germany. The ambassador put forward a suggestion that the London government accept the transfer of German ships to the United States as long as they were not used to supply the Central Powers.[49]

At the same time Spring-Rice sent this note, Anglo-American relations took a turn for the worse. For several months, the transfer controversy had remained quietly in the background, but it became a major issue in the new year when American businessman Edward Breitung bought the *Dacia*, a cargo vessel of the Hamburg-America Line interned in Port Arthur, Texas. Breitung claimed that he could not find a British vessel to purchase and decided that his only option was to buy a German ship to carry cotton to Europe.[50] On January 4, the Department of Commerce approved the transfer of the *Dacia* to US registry. By sending the *Dacia* to Europe, Breitung planned to test the British and French position, which in late 1914 vaguely suggested that Americans could purchase German ships. After leaving a meeting with Commissioner of Navigation Eugene Chamberlin, Breitung's attorney, Henry S. Hooker, stated to the press, "If the *Dacia* as an American vessel is permitted by the powers under the Declaration of London of February, 1909, to carry Southern Cotton to Europe, a solution of the cotton export problem will have been made."[51]

Breitung's decision created a quandary for the Allies and for Wilson. When the British public heard about the transaction, it erupted in anger against the United States. Many in Britain asserted that if Washington supported the purchase of German ships, it must favor the Entente's enemies and was certainly not neutral. For Wilson, such a perception could irreversibly tarnish the White House's image in London and torpedo his mediation efforts. As for the Foreign Office, it recognized the *Dacia* affair for what it was—an effort to challenge the British Order in Council. Additionally, if the Royal Navy allowed the ship to travel to Europe without interference it would set a precedent for future purchases.[52]

Because of the controversy, Bryan asked Spring-Rice for his opinion. Spring-Rice replied that he believed his government would not capture the vessel unless it was used to aid Germany.[53] The following day, Bryan replied that the *Dacia* was going to leave Port Arthur, Texas, on January 15 and that the vessel's "shipment of cotton in this case is in good faith." He hoped the Royal Navy would allow it to pass.[54]

The British cabinet split on how to deal with the predicament. Acting Foreign Secretary Lord Richard Haldane prematurely informed Page that London would not interfere with the ship as long as it was involved in trade with South America on coastal voyages. Grey and others disagreed with Haldane's position—the *Dacia* case could open the floodgates for additional purchases of German ships and, in a worst-case scenario, if the shipping bill was enacted, the US government could buy every German vessel in American waters. If state ownership protected the fleet, the Allies would be unable to detain federal property without major repercussions.[55]

The type of cargo made Britain's decision even more complicated. If it seized the *Dacia*, loaded with American-grown cotton, it could reignite a smoldering fire by angering southern farmers. Late in the evening of January 15, Page telegraphed Bryan that Britain "has no wish to obstruct the cotton trade" and therefore it planned to purchase the *Dacia*'s entire consignment by "paying the price which had been arranged by contract with the German buyers."[56] The future of the *Dacia* was another matter. The next day, Spring-Rice added that Grey declared the situation was "clearly a case of transfer in order to avoid capture" and warned that the navy would seize the ship and bring it before the prize court. This decision would prevent cotton merchants from losing money, yet it illustrated that London did not intend to allow Americans to weaken the blockade.[57]

When Bryan walked into his office the next morning, a new message from Page greeted him that expressed a gloomy future for American neutrality. The *Dacia* case had forced Britain to oppose the purchases of German vessels, even if they were used to ship goods to British ports. "The chief weapon that England has against any enemy," he claimed, "is her navy and that the navy may damage an enemy in two ways: by fighting and by economic pressure." In the current conflict, economic pressure was as important as combat, which meant keeping German merchant vessels "off the seas." Page added that America's standing had been hurt because many people in Britain perceived the transfer of the *Dacia* and the official US protest as evidence that German propaganda was working across the Atlantic. Britons looked at the *Dacia* affair as "proof of our unfriendliness." Concerned that the situation could worsen, Page asserted that "popular feeling will, I fear, run as high as it ran over the Trent affair; and a very large part of the English opinion will regard us as enemies." The British government still had a positive view of the United States, but maintaining such sentiment would become difficult "if a whirlwind of anti-American feeling swept over the Kingdom and over the Allies."[58]

Hostile public perception in Britain further threatened Wilson's efforts at mediation. Grey claimed to Page that many Englishmen believed that German-Americans remained loyal to Germany and were using propaganda to weaken Britain's economic stranglehold on the Central Powers. German-American efforts, the foreign secretary noted, to purchase merchant ships and to pass legislation preventing the sale of war materiel convinced many Britons that Germany had a hold on the American government and people. Relaying Grey's message to the president, Page warned, "These are reasons why anything that comes out of the United States arouses suspicion."[59]

Grey's concerns about Britain's access to American arms continued because legislation like HR 377 was still before Congress and German-Americans vociferously praised the embargo as a way to end the war quickly. Unknown to Grey, the bills themselves were not attracting much support in Congress since neither of the belligerents, much less the United States, claimed that international law prevented the sale of munitions. In December, Bryan received word that the German government recognized the United States had a legal right to make and sell weapons and ammunition to countries at war.[60] Additionally, many congressmen recognized the effect that HR 377 and others could have on the American economy. In mid-December, Spring-Rice reported to Grey that he did not think any such bill would pass, at least in the current session, because little time remained prior to recess, and a number of senators, including Henry Cabot Lodge of Massachusetts, opposed the legislation.[61] Most importantly, the White House continued to fight the legislation. When Grey asked Spring-Rice, on December 17, about the president's views on munitions sales, the ambassador replied that Wilson adamantly opposed any restrictions. The legislation lost further momentum after Bryan spoke to Congress on January 20, 1915. He claimed that "[t]here is no power in the Executive to prevent the sale of ammunition to the belligerents." Even though Bryan was incorrect considering that article 9 of the 1907 Hague Convention clarifies that prohibition is legal as long as it is conducted impartially, there is precedent that defends the neutral right to sell war materiel. He pointed out that in previous wars, European nations openly sold weapons to belligerents. Germany sold munitions to the both parties during the Russo-Japanese War. Strengthening his case, he noted that in late 1914 the German ambassador declared that "the adversaries of Germany in the present war are, in the opinion of the Imperial Government, authorized to 'draw on the United States contraband of war and especially arms worth billions of marks.'" Therefore, Bryan correctly asserted that the United States was simply following established international law concerning the sale of munitions to belligerents and was not violating neutrality.[62]

Despite their limited support in Congress the bills energized German-American organizations. Spring-Rice observed that the increased level of German-American activities concerned Wilson and his advisors because it might divide the American people. He stated that members of the president's cabinet thought the propaganda campaign was organized by a "foreign element" that had the "avowed object of pursuing national and un-American objects on American soil."[63]

In early February, Spring-Rice expressed to Grey that despite a common culture and the president's personal desire for an Allied victory, Wilson still intended to comply with international laws that defined the duties of neutrals. The ambassador added that remaining neutral might be difficult because German organizations in the United States continued to "pressure" congressmen. He also reminded Grey that, like other politicians, Wilson wanted to be reelected "and that a very large body of organized voters have warned him that they will spare no effort to defeat him unless he does their bidding." Spring-Rice claimed that most Americans preferred peace but that for a large number of them the war was injuring their personal and commercial interests. As a result, Spring-Rice argued that the war still divided the American people: "[I] am sure you are not misled by the statements to the effect that 80 or 90% of the American people wish success to the Allies." His comments demonstrate that he did not view American policies as pro-Allied and that Britain's leaders still feared that their decisions could alienate the American public, forcing the president to establish policies detrimental to the Allies.[64]

Together, the *Dacia* case and munitions bills threatened to upset the balance of Anglo-American relations. Grey became so concerned that he finally drafted a personal note to Wilson. The letter laid out all the complaints Britain had about the United States since the beginning of the war. Grey began his list by attacking Wilson's and Bryan's efforts to assure US neutrality. According to the foreign secretary, Washington acted unfairly when it prevented the Allies from taking out loans and purchasing submarine parts in the United States. Additionally, the British could not understand how Wilson could support the purchase of German merchant vessels or stand by while congressmen, supported by German-American organizations, pushed for legislation to outlaw the sale of weapons. Only German sympathizers, Grey asserted, supported cutting off the flow of munitions and simultaneously working to maintain open channels of trade to London's enemies. Grey went further, stating that many people in Britain and France believed that the Wilson administration was "insensibly drifting" toward Germany.[65]

As Grey penned his letter, Wilson and Bryan were formulating one for him. After reading the foreign secretary's concerns, Wilson hammered out a revised version of his own message and sent it to Page the following day. The dispatch, officially signed by Bryan, stated that the president "regret[ted]" that American neutrality was in question. He defended American policy and Breitung's legal right to purchase the *Dacia*. Wilson claimed that the British public was misinformed and that many of the problems resulted from the unfair treatment of US trade. He expected Page to deliver the letter as an official message, but the ambassador decided instead to relay its contents to Grey during a conversation, which he hoped would prevent it from being regarded as a formal dispatch and causing a confrontation.[66]

In the end, on the advice of Page, the Foreign Office asked the French navy to capture the *Dacia* and bring it into port. This approach ensured that the vessel did not reach its destination while avoiding further complications with American merchants and the US government.[67] The Allied collaboration effectively concluded the crisis, as Grey wrote in his memoir, "without a murmur in America."[68]

The *Dacia* case may have ended on a quiet note, but it heightened fears in Congress that purchasing belligerent ships could provoke a war with Britain. In a note to Theodore Roosevelt, Senator Elihu Root declared, "We shall find ourselves with government owned ships afloat . . . which are liable to be fired on and sunk."[69] Wilson hoped the ship purchase bill would free the United States from its reliance on the foreign carrying trade, but he discovered that powerful business interests opposed a government-owned merchant fleet. Businessman Henry Lee Higginson told the president on January 27 that "[y]ou would hardly believe how fear of the shipping bill unsettles people's minds and takes away their courage." Passage of the bill, Higginson asserted, could injure private companies because government ownership would mean unfair competition. As a result, investors would not want to risk losing money, which would hinder economic growth: "If it does not breed a war, it will breed unpleasant disputes and again agitate people so that they will not go on with their industries."[70] Wilson replied that he recognized that the measure "does make it possible to do very foolish things," but he believed the government would "be very slow to do anything that involves such dangers." Others realized that even though the current president might act with caution, he would not be president forever. Future leaders might not be as vigilant. Former Harvard University president Charles William Eliot warned, "Suppose that another Roosevelt should become President of the United States!"[71]

In early 1915, Senator Lodge added an amendment to the shipping bill that would prohibit the government from buying German vessels, but Wilson refused to accept any changes to the original proposal: the United States had the right to buy belligerent vessels. If Congress modified the proposition, he claimed it would weaken America's international position and, as with the munitions bill, threaten US neutrality. In responding to Eliot, Wilson defended his policy by claiming, "My difficulty in this whole matter has been this: Our rights as neutrals in the matter of the purchase of ships from citizens of belligerent countries is, I believe, susceptible of clear establishment in any impartial tribunal. Just now, the United States stands as the chief custodian of neutral rights and I do not think that any branch of the Government should say anything officially that would seem to be equivalent to even a temporary renunciation of those rights."[72] Thus Wilson asserted that if he gave in to German-Americans and pacifists over the arms embargo, Britain would view him as pro-German.

Theodore Roosevelt wrote to Spring-Rice on February 5 that his government should use caution in its relationship with the United States. He argued the Wilson administration was taking every step it could to avoid entering the war. Roosevelt warned that Britain should not interfere with American rights because it might provoke Washington to protect them. The former president added that he understood why the British felt "great contempt for the Wilson-Bryan Administration," because it was "truckling to the German vote." Roosevelt noted that he believed that the Washington government could not be "kicked into a war . . . it is just weak and timid, but [it is] shifty creatures of the Wilson-Bryan type who are most apt to be responsible for a country drifting into war."[73]

Grey and Spring-Rice were concerned about the impact that German-Americans could have on Wilson's policies. In a series of letters, the latter claimed that "nearly one third of the total number of voters in this country" were of German ancestry. Such a high number convinced Spring-Rice that they could have powerful leverage in Washington and that Wilson felt he had no choice but to listen to them, even at the expense of Britain.[74]

Grey and Spring-Rice soon learned that they had little to fear about the shipping bill. The ambassador claimed that after hearing Senators Lodge and Root denounced it, many congressmen accepted the assertion that building a government-controlled merchant marine was an "un-neutral act."[75] In his argument against the legislation, Senator Asle J. Gronna of North Dakota wrote that American exports were on the rise even though surplus goods could not reach America's regular customers in Germany and Russia. He asserted that the president presented the shipping bill to Congress as an "emergency measure," but Gronna claimed that purchasing interned German ships was a bad idea. The senator emphasized that Britain and France had already declared the vessels subject to seizure and argued that the United States had enough ships available in the coastal trade for international business. Finally, showing his dislike for Wilson, Gronna remarked, "[If] it were to take the President as long to name the members of the shipping board as it took to name the members of the Federal Reserve Board, or as long as it apparently is going to take to name the members of the Federal Trade Commission, this measure could not by any stretch of the imagination be called an emergency measure."[76]

On February 18, 1915, Senator Hitchcock decided to amend the shipping bill by tying it to an arms embargo in hope of getting both to pass. When the measure came to the floor, Republicans, wise to his motives, filibustered the legislation and thwarted a vote before Congress ended its session on March 4, 1915, and effectively ended the debate.[77] Observing the dispute, Spring-Rice happily reported that the bill seemed destined to fail. Writing to Grey he said, "We owe a great debt of gratitude to these Senators who acted entirely in the interest of peace."[78]

The failure of the bill was significant because without additional ships, the United States was unable to transport goods to potential Latin American markets. US companies had to continue relying on the British shipping and selling their goods to places on existing UK trade routes—especially the British Isles. Consequently, Americans could not enter as many new overseas markets as Wilson had hoped. This situation certainly favored the Allies. By preventing government interference in business, Congress and the shipping interests allowed Britain to retain the controlling share of merchant vessels available for conducting international trade. Additionally, Congress's decision unintentionally permitted Britain to control the spread of American trade and drew the United States closer to its side.

The munitions controversy also faded into the background as it too was filibustered on Capitol Hill. After Bryan's exchange with Senator Stone, the effort to end the sale of weapons to the belligerents floundered and did not reemerge until late 1915 when it again faced opposition. Under the Hague Convention of 1907, the United States could have ended the sale of munitions to all belligerents. Considering that the president favored the Allies, it is likely that he understood that cutting off munitions to Britain would hinder its ability to negotiate from a position of strength, which London deemed was necessary for mediation. However, this is not clear from the evidence. What is apparent is that Wilson and Bryan recognized that the United States could legally sell munitions to any nation that could purchase and collect them. Unlike Wilson's reluctant acquiescence to Britain over the Declaration of London, he insisted that ending the munitions trade was an act that was within his control and intervening would therefore be perceived as unneutral. The decision was a defining moment in the war because it did not have the effect that the Wilson administration expressed that it wanted. Considering Britain's mastery on the seas, only the Allies could take delivery of American weapons, meaning that the president's policies would have the same noteworthy effect on Anglo-American commercial relations as the Republican blockage of the shipping bill—bring the United States still nearer to the Allies.

In the midst of the shipping debates and controversy over the sale of munitions, Wilson and House continued to pursue their private efforts to bring Britain and Germany to the negotiating table. The letters House received from Zimmermann and Grey in December offered a false hope that the two countries were close to a compromise. The president's and his closest advisor's unwavering desire to bring about mediation blinded them from seeing the duplicity of the British and German governments. House sent a new message to the German foreign minister on January 5 stating that over the past several weeks he had conversations with Spring-Rice and Bernstorff that convinced him that negotiations were possible. He explained that Wilson wanted him to open informal discussions in Europe so that no one had to make any official commitments. Before he traveled to Europe, however, House wanted an assurance from Zimmermann that he was reading the situation correctly.[79]

While waiting for a reply, Wilson received messages from Grey who tried to deter the administration from pressing for a conference. Without saying no to talks, the foreign secretary argued that Germany's overtures for peace were insincere. Americans coming back from the continent, he claimed, reported that the German government did not support Bernstorff's comments about concessions for Belgium.[80] The following day, Wilson received even more troubling news from US Commercial Attaché Chandler Anderson, who had recently returned from London. Anderson told the president that the night before he sailed home, Grey called him to his office and "emphatically" stated that the time was not right to start a dialogue with Germany "or even the discussion of possible terms of peace." The Allies, Anderson told the president, had demands not subject to compromise. In addition to reparations for Belgium, Anderson said, Britain wanted to be able to reduce its "naval expenditures," which he implied to mean the "elimination of the German fleet." France wanted to retake Alsace-Loraine, which it lost after the Franco-Prussian War in 1871, and Russia "would desire Constantinople, and the Dardanelles." Grey also emphasized that the Allies had an accord not to pursue a separate peace; unless Germany accepted all of their ultimatums, talks could not occur. The foreign secretary knew Germany would not agree to the demands and that the Allies would not accept peace if Germany was not defeated in the field. Grey therefore wanted Wilson to understand the futility of any mission to Europe.[81]

Too impatient to wait for a reply from Zimmermann and despite Grey's caveat, Wilson and House's misguided view of European affairs influenced their approach to the belligerents. The president and House met in his study before dinner on January 12 and decided that regardless of the signs that Britain and Germany were not interested in peace talks, the latter needed to go to Europe at the end of the month. House thought he had done everything he could in the United States and that "we were now traveling in a circle" in dealing with the German and British ambassadors. The administration, he argued, might actually be "losing ground" and was not in "as close touch with the Allies as we had been."[82] The following afternoon, House began making plans for his trip across the Atlantic. After lunch with the president, he sat down with Spring-Rice, French Ambassador Jean Jules Jusserand, and Russian Ambassador George Bakhameteff. The conversation started out uneasily when Jusserand and Bakhameteff condemned the Germans and asserted that they could not be trusted. In their opinion, House's trip to Europe would fail. House defended his decision and played to their sensibilities by arguing that, if nothing else, he could at least discover how "utterly unreliable and treacherous the Germans were by exposing their false pretenses of peace to the world."[83]

House then met with Bryan. While they drove to Bryan's home, the colonel told him about his meeting with the ambassadors and his upcoming voyage. Bryan was not pleased that House was going because he planned to take the trip himself. House then said that the president thought he should go because he could speak unofficially and would not attract a lot of attention. The two continued to debate until they reached the secretary's residence, but House ended the discussion, believing it "footless."[84]

That evening the colonel headed back to the White House for dinner. He later wrote that Wilson was pleased with his efforts and remarked that, considering the results of House's meetings with the three ambassadors, they might as well bypass them. House then told the president about Bryan's frustration. Bryan's assertion that he should lead the mediation efforts angered the president. Making an irrational statement, Wilson claimed that he thought the secretary would prefer war if he could not personally establish the peace. Immediately regretful of his comment, the president retracted it but added that Bryan was obsessed with the idea of bringing about an end to the conflict himself and that he would "allow the secretary to resign from the Cabinet before he would let him undertake such a delicate mission, for which he felt he was so unfitted."[85]

Two weeks later, Wilson was still excited about the possibility of mediation. House noted that when he arrived in Washington on January 24, Wilson was anxious to start talking about the upcoming trip. House wrote that the president had high hopes and certainly thought the mission could succeed. Planning the trip, they talked for over an hour, even "delaying dinner ten or fifteen minutes, which is a most unusual thing for the President to do."[86] Later that evening, Wilson emphasized that he wanted Grey to know that the colonel spoke for the United States: "Let him know that while you are abroad I expect to act directly through you and eliminate all intermediaries."[87] The president was not deterred even after receiving a disturbing message from US Ambassador James Gerard in Berlin days before House was to set sail. Gerard informed Wilson that Zimmermann had given him a list that showed numerous munitions orders placed by the Allies for American goods. The German undersecretary was upset that the United States continued to sell Britain weapons and warned that Washington's actions were dangerous, adding that if trouble arose "there *were five hundred thousand trained Germans in America who would join the Irish and start a revolution.*" Gerard closed the letter by stating his belief that Zimmermann's comment seemed "ridiculous" but that "it would not surprise me to see this maddened Nation in arms go to lengths however extreme."[88]

Neither British warnings nor German warnings deterred the president. Wilson's approach to mediation blinded him from realizing that peace talks would not happen in the near future. The president had taken the view that the belligerents were irrational and needed the United States to intercede on their behalf and because of his earnest desire to mediate an end to the war, Wilson did not recognize the reality of the situation. Even when Grey and Zimmermann finally explained their actual positions on mediation, the president ignored their warnings and decided that he would have to push them toward peace talks. Thus Wilson and House continued preparing for the trip, and on January 30 House boarded the *Lusitania* and headed to Europe on schedule.[89]

The period from December 1914 to January 1915 was extremely important in defining wartime Anglo-American relations. Congressional decisions concerning the shipping bill and the Wilson administration's view on the legality of the munitions trade favored the Allies and assured that Britain would have continued access to American goods. The unintended result of Congress's actions and the president's policies would further solidify the economic bond developing between the United States and Britain. The results do not, however, demonstrate that the United States had ended its neutrality. The president mistakenly made his decisions in the hope of presenting his government as an unattached outsider that could be a fair mediator.

Britain and Germany were not interested in ending the war because neither held an upper hand on the battlefield; however, outright rejection of mediation could have a detrimental effect on the vital munitions trade. Grey's strategy was to take a tough line on the sale of contraband to the Central Powers and humor Washington by feigning interest in its pacific overtures. To assure that talks would not actually occur, Britain made stringent demands that it certainly knew Germany would reject. In doing so, Britain's leaders hoped to prevent Washington from ending the sale of munitions and make Germany appear uncooperative because it had refused to come to terms. Despite his best efforts, however, Grey could not deter the president from pursuing peace talks and had to prepare for the arrival of Colonel House.

5

"Twittering of a Sparrow"

February 1915–April 1915

Peace-talk [*sic*], therefore, is yet mere moonshine—House has been to Berlin, from London, thence to Paris, thence back to London again—from Nowhere to Nowhere (Utopia to Utopia concerning the possibility of peace).

—US Ambassador Walter Hines Page[1]

Between February and April 1915 the contradiction between Wilson's goal of mediating an end to the war and his desire to protect the US economy was becoming quite clear. In February 1915 Germany announced a new naval strategy that called for submarine attacks on Allied merchant vessels entering waters around Great Britain and Ireland. Germany's response to the growing United States-British trade relationship created a quandary for the Wilson administration because the destruction of US property and the death of Americans at sea might bring the United States into the war. For Britain, Germany's announcement provided a real opportunity to draw the United States closer. Additionally, Colonel Edward House's European mission would not provide the results that he and the president had hoped for. Neither Britain nor Germany agreed to peace talks and blamed each other for the war's duration. In conjunction with the growing economic ties to London and Germany's declaration of submarine warfare, the progress and the outcome of House's efforts ultimately played an important part in altering the Wilson administration's perception of the war and America's role in it.

House's journey across the Atlantic occurred practically without incident. He left New York on the luxury liner *Lusitania* and spent most of his voyage preparing for his mission. Once the ship reached European waters, however, he learned that British Captain Daniel Dow had decided to fly the American flag to confuse any German submarines in the area. The captain, according to House, was convinced that his ship was destined to meet with a torpedo.[2]

Dow had no idea how right he was to fear U-boat attacks in early February 1915. As the ship steamed toward its home port of Southampton, Secretary of State William Jennings Bryan received the first of many messages from Berlin about a change in German strategy. On February 5, Counselor Robert Lansing learned of an "alleged declaration of the Admiralty at Berlin" that proclaimed its intention to attack Allied merchant and military vessels sailing near the British Isles.[3] According to German Undersecretary of State Arthur Zimmermann, his country had no choice but to defend itself against Britain's effort to "starve Germany out."[4]

In the official declaration on February 7, the German government complained that Britain was interfering with trade between neutrals and Germany. It claimed that London had banned the shipment of certain items that were not contraband. Berlin had deduced correctly that the Allies were trying to harm the German military and the civilian population. The formal statement also asserted that Britain was not the only culprit. In many cases, neutral governments aided Britain by making only "theoretical protests." Even though Germany tried "in vain" to convince neutrals they should oppose Britain's violation of international law, they had accepted the argument that London had to protect its vital interests. In accusing neutrals of compromising their status, Germany cut to the heart of their problem, the economic relationship that had developed between Britain and its most important trading partner, the United States. The Allies' unfettered access to US-made munitions provided them with a military advantage, and German leaders hoped that the U-boat campaign would deter merchant ships from carrying goods to the British. For these reasons, beginning on February 18, Germany declared that all waters around the British Isles were officially a war zone. Germany "will endeavor to destroy every enemy merchant ship that is found in this area of war, without its always being possible to avert the peril that thus threatens persons and cargos." Germany also issued a clear warning to neutrals that they should not enter the war zone: "[I]t is advisable for their ships to avoid entering this area" because of Britain's "misuse of neutral flags . . . [neutrals] becoming victims of torpedoes directed against enemy ships cannot always be averted."[5] In a separate letter, German Ambassador Johann Heinrich von Bernstorff complained further about Britain's use of neutral flags to protect its ships at sea. He tried to increase tension between the United States and Britain by arguing that the practice would endanger neutral shipping, adding, "I venture to leave it to your excellency's kind consideration whether representations to the British Government against the improper use of the American flag by British vessels are in order."[6]

Germany did not begin the war planning to use submarines against merchant shipping. However, on November 3, 1914, Britain declared the North

Sea a war zone in response to German attempts to mine waters along the main trade route between Liverpool and the United States. The announcement convinced the German Admiralty to reconsider. After Admiral Alfred von Tirpitz mentioned the idea to the media in November, public opinion in Germany became increasingly supportive of a major operation to attack British commerce—especially since many Germans thought that Britain only had six to eight weeks of food available. As political and public pressure increased, Wilhelm II gradually accepted the idea and in late January 1915 he approved the use of U-boats to blockade the British Isles.[7]

Germany made the choice to attack commercial vessels in the hope of wearing down the British but failed to fully consider how Wilson might respond. Until Germany announced its submarine blockade of Britain, the problems facing US-German relations were minimal. Wilson did not want Germany to win the war; however, he was also committed to neutrality. In the meantime Germany wanted to prevent America from openly siding with the Allies and did not want to injure its relations with Washington. Yet its policy shift threatened US interests as much as Britain's. With House away, Wilson and Lansing collaborated on a rejoinder. They were gravely concerned about the submarine campaign and understood that how the United States reacted might have a serious effect on the course of the war. Wilson and Lansing concluded that the United States had to respond before Germany acted on its declaration and together they penned a stern but cautious reply.[8]

The president sent US Ambassador James Gerard the official response several days later. In the letter, signed by Bryan, the ambassador was instructed to inform Wilhelm II that his country's decision could cause tension between the United States and Germany. The message made clear that the United States did not regard a submarine cordon as a legitimate form of warfare and that the belligerents were limited to "visit and search unless a blockade is proclaimed and effectively maintained." Keeping public opinion in mind, Wilson defended American policy, claiming that the United States was "open to none of the criticism of unneutral action." Obviously not viewing his capitulation on the Order in Council as a violation of US neutrality, Wilson claimed that other countries might have complied with Great Britain's demands but that the United States had not. The president still thought that by protesting British seizures of American cargoes on a case-by-case basis he was defending his country's rights and insisted that his government was actually putting pressure on Britain to leave its trade alone.[9] Wisely, Wilson and Lansing chose vague language that was open to interpretation, culminating with the ambiguous assertion that Washington would "hold the Imperial German Government to a strict accountability for such acts of their naval authorities and to take any steps it might be necessary to take to safeguard American lives and property and to secure to American citizens the full enjoyment of their acknowledged rights on the high seas." How the United States would hold Germany strictly accountable was not clear, and intentional or not, such a vague statement gave Wilson a substantial degree of flexibility for a future response to German actions.[10]

To British Ambassador Cecil Spring-Rice, the German declaration played right into Britain's hands. He realized that the volatile situation could draw the United States nearer to the Allies. Observing American public opinion, he told British Foreign Secretary Edward Grey that people seemed incensed about the use of submarines: "If a ship or even a United States citizen is blown up a serious situation will ensue." He thought that a submarine attack on US property might force the United States into the war. The best course of action was simply to wait and allow the Germans to hurt themselves: "Time works for us if we do nothing."[11]

Spring-Rice, however, did not expect that all of London's troubles with Washington would disappear. Wilson felt compelled to address the German complaint that Britain was using the American flag to protect its ships at sea. Late on February 8, Bryan received word that the Foreign Office had posted a statement in British newspapers that defended the Allies' right to use neutral flags. Such action was a "well established . . . *ruse de guerre*" and under the Merchant Shipping Act of 1894, Britain recognized the right of other states to use the British flag in an effort to evade enemy vessels.[12] Wilson agreed with London's position and stated his personal opinion at a press conference the following day. He noted that it had become a common practice, and in an off-the-record comment, he added that there was no international law preventing such tactics.[13]

Wilson's official policy, however, was driven more by public opinion than by international law. The use of the American flag irritated many people across the country. Spring-Rice claimed that the population was as angry at Britain as it was at Germany. Editors of German-American newspapers argued that Britain's allowing vessels to fly the US flag justified attacking unarmed ships. In the ambassador's view, the practice damaged Britain's image.[14] Public opinion was so strong that it forced the United States to protest Britain's use of the US flag. Bryan sent an official note to US Ambassador Walter Hines Page declaring that British merchants needed to stop the practice immediately because it endangered neutral ships.[15]

At the next cabinet meeting, Prime Minister Henry Asquith considered Bryan's message and instructed Grey that he should formulate a reply.[16] That afternoon Grey prepared a draft response in which he noted that the *Lusitania* flew the American flag on its inward voyage to deceive the submarines and that when it departed Britain, American passengers, not the crew, insisted that the captain should raise the American flag for their safety. Defending his government, Grey argued that since the German submarine attacks were "regarded by the opinion of the world not as war but as piracy," Britain could not demand that its merchant vessels stop raising foreign flags. He tried to compromise, stating that the British government was prepared to notify British ships that such practices were only acceptable when under attack or trying to escape capture. Nevertheless, he bluntly stated that it was Germany's responsibility to "ascertain definitely for itself the nationality and character of a merchant vessel before capturing it and *á fortiori* before sinking and destroying it." This practice, he added, has been "universally recognised." If Germany shirked this responsibility, it would have to accept blame for any damage.[17]

To the president, the debate over Britain's use of neutral flags was simply a formality to placate public opinion. Wilson did not object to private belligerent merchant vessels using neutral flags. Several days before Grey sent his defense to the White House, Wilson demonstrated his irritation over the issue of neutral flags when he told House that he did not like having to send a note to Britain that protested "unauthorized use of [our] flag." Wilson, however, reasoned that Bryan's letter was necessary because the Germans might accidentally sink a US vessel.[18]

Germany's decision to use submarines challenged Wilson's sense of morality. Attacking unarmed merchant vessels was much worse than Britain's form of economic warfare because it threatened the lives of US citizens. Over the course of the war, the British blockade did cause the starvation of hundreds of thousands of German civilians; however, evidence suggests that in February 1915 Wilson failed to grasp this fact. When Wilson's reaction to the British blockade is assessed alongside his refusal to protest against rumors of German atrocities in Belgium, it is apparent that regardless of the inhumane method that Britain used, the president had no intention to oppose a policy that did not endanger Americans. Additionally, later in the year the Germans claimed they did not need more food and opposed a US proposal to convince Britain to allow foodstuffs into Germany if the imperial government would end its submarine campaign. Therefore, the president did not think the British blockade had caused the death of German citizens.[19]

When House reached London on Saturday, February 6, he did not let the German declaration dampen his enthusiasm for finding a way to bring the belligerents together. Over the next four months, however, he discovered that neither Germany nor Britain would compromise and begin talks. Both continued making inflexible demands, purposely hindering US efforts. Along with the declaration of unrestricted submarine warfare, Zimmermann finally responded that he could not offer any reparations for his country's invasion of Belgium. The undersecretary said he would welcome a chance to talk but insisted that Germany had made major sacrifices to defeat its neighbors and an indemnity would cause domestic unrest.[20]

On Sunday morning, House sat down with Grey and confronted a similarly rigid stance from the Allies. House understood that he was fighting an uphill battle. During the next several weeks, he talked to Grey, William Tyrrell (Grey's personal secretary), and Page but found Britain uncooperative. Grey employed the same tactic he had used before the colonel arrived, stressing that the Allies expected major concessions from Germany before they would sit at the same table. House countered that the sole objective of his mission was to "bring them together," not to press for terms.[21] Grey and Tyrrell claimed that the Allies would not negotiate from a position of weakness and could not "*propose* peace till they have won some more convincing military victory." Their stance did not mean they were unwilling to consider discussions, only that they would not initiate them. In doing so, they successfully placed the ball in Germany's court.[22]

The situation frustrated Page. "Nobody can see past his nose," he wrote the president; all the belligerents wanted to negotiate peace only after they had a significant advantage. He therefore argued that House would not succeed in the near future. Britain could not propose peace because doing so would cause a domestic uproar that "no Government could weather." In the end, Page accepted the Foreign Office view that the only chance for peace was to see what Germany might propose. This, too, he saw as a daunting challenge. Page claimed that House would not get a reasonable offer from the German government. Indeed, he would face an even more difficult problem than he now confronted in London. Germany, the ambassador fretted, had "given up hope of winning American sympathy. They are having poor success getting American copper and food. American hostility is possibly the only American thing they can now utilize." Therefore the war would not end until German forces were exhausted and defeated in the field. Page had no confidence in House's mission and clearly believed that the colonel was naïve to think he could succeed. Later, Page wrote in his diary, "PPeace-talk [*sic*], therefore, is yet mere moonshine—House has been to Berlin, from London, thence to Paris, thence back to London again—from Nowhere to Nowhere (Utopia to Utopia concerning the possibility of peace)."[23]

On February 11, House sent Wilson a letter containing a similar admission: "The difficulty is to get conversations started. Neither trusts the other and neither desires to place themselves at a disadvantage." House, however, still had faith in his mission and its success, as long as Germany was amenable. House stated, "The [outlook] is fairly hopeful provided I can get to Germany by invitation and provided Germany does nothing foolish to create fresh irritation."[24]

Despite his optimism, House's pro-British bias doomed his mission from the start. Within days, Grey and Tyrrell convinced House that Germany was unwilling to talk about peace. House informed the president that he was unsure how to deal with Germany, which he claimed was led by militarists who did not want peace. It was winning on the eastern front, the colonel informed Wilson, and "[a]s long as the military forces of Germany are successful as now, the militarists will not permit any suggestion of peace."[25]

After meeting with Asquith, Grey, and Page on February 16, House informed Wilson that the British did not want him to go to Berlin. They claimed Russia might be in trouble and did not want House negotiating with Berlin while it had an advantage over the Allies. If Russia could defend itself, Asquith and Grey asserted that the colonel "should take that opportunity to go there [Germany]" and inform the German government that if it would withdraw from all foreign territories it presently held and accept a permanent peace, Britain would agree to talk. If Germany disagreed, Britain would continue fighting. House warned Grey not to "close the door too tightly" in case Germany agreed. He suggested that they give Germany hope that peace was possible. Britain should "keep the gate ajar, not too widely, but enough to let hope linger." Asquith "smiled and said, 'If you can do that successfully, you are a clever man.'" Privately Asquith was even more cynical. Seeing House's actions as a waste of time, he noted that the colonel's mission was that of a "twittering of a sparrow in the tumult that shakes the world."[26]

Several days later, House learned of other reasons why the Foreign Office wanted him to delay his trip to Berlin. Grey informed him that Allied forces planned to open a new front in southeastern Europe, at the Dardanelles. In attacking the straits, Britain hoped to take the Ottomans out of the war, give Russia an outlet to the Mediterranean, and convince neutral states in the Balkans to join the Allies.[27] House wrote Wilson, "[Grey] thought that after matters had quieted down upon the Eastern Front and a deadlock had once more been arrived at, and the Dardanelles had been forced it would be well for me to go to Germany."[28]

Britain's effort to deter House worked. He eventually replied to Zimmermann that he planned to come to Berlin in the near future, but that at the moment, he was reconsidering such a move. Because of his earlier conversations with Bernstorff, Wilson concluded that Germany would agree to withdraw from Belgium and compensate its government for damages. Now that House realized this assumption was false, a trip to Berlin did not seem worthwhile. Yet he did not give up. House told Zimmermann that they could table the Belgian issue if doing so would mean the "beginning of conversations." Additionally he tried to convince the undersecretary that if Germany agreed to a parley, the move would offer Berlin a "great moral advantage" over the Allies in the eyes of neutrals.[29]

House's hesitation to make the trip to Berlin irritated the president. Wilson did not want to delay mediation and replied that House should not let the British decide when he planned to go to Berlin. The president recognized that the British government would intentionally delay the trip as long as necessary in the hope that House traveled to Germany only after the Allies had an upper hand in the war. More important, Wilson feared that if House seemed to be under Britain's thumb, the German government might view him as Grey's and Asquith's "spokesman rather than my own."[30] Though he agreed to travel to Berlin within the next several weeks, House tried to convince the president that success was a long way off. He explained that Grey had told him the Dardanelles campaign would not take more than two weeks to complete and that once the Allies broke through, House would have an opportune moment to approach Zimmermann.[31] Still, meeting with the German statesman did not mean he would succeed. The belligerents had demands he had to overcome. "Therefore," House informed Wilson, "not even the beginning of the end is in sight."[32]

From his work in London, House became convinced that Germany was not interested in mediation and that it had provoked the war. He wrote the president that "[s]ince the war has begun and since they [Britain] consider that Germany was the aggressor and is the exponent of militarism, they are determined not to cease fighting until there is no hope of victory, or until Germany is ready to concede what they consider a fair and permanent settlement." Again showing sympathy for Britain, House stated that if the war did "not end militarism, then the future is full of trouble for us." Britain had succeeded in convincing House of its view of Germany, and he was blind to the fact that Britain was equally unwilling to participate in serious peace talks.[33]

By late February, House had already concluded that a trip to Berlin would end in futility, but he let Wilson know that if Zimmermann replied to him, he planned to make the journey.[34] Britain had successfully placed the blame for the failure of peace talks squarely on Germany even before they could begin. By the time House decided to go to Berlin, he was convinced that the kaiser's government would not agree to peace talks and that it was the sole reason that talks would fail.

Casting doubt on German sincerity was not Grey's only objective. Throughout their conversations, Grey suggested the establishment of an organization that could ensure a permanent peace once the war concluded. In one of their early meetings, House noted, "There was one thing that

[Grey] was fairly insistent upon and that was that we should come into some general guaranty for worldwide [peace]."[35] This was not the first time the British foreign secretary proposed the idea of an international peace organization that included the United States. Previously on December 23, 1914, Spring-Rice told House that Grey believed the only way to assure a lasting peace after the war's end was to establish an organization that assured "mutual security and preservation of peace." House recognized the implications of such a proposal. It was not in accord with traditional American isolationist sentiment and House replied that Wilson would refuse to join any alliance that could force the country into participation in European affairs.[36]

When Grey again broached the issue in February 1915, the colonel tried to avoid the subject as much as possible. He declared only that entering an accord with Britain would oblige the United States to help uphold the "guaranty" and could require a military intervention. Nevertheless, Grey was insistent. The following day, Tyrrell mentioned that if Wilson could help broker a lasting peace, Britain would consider "the absolute freedom of merchantmen of all nations to sail the seas in time of war unmolested."[37] This was an astounding suggestion and sparked further conversations on "freedom of the seas." It ran counter to Britain's policy both past and present but was directly in line with American beliefs, which further suggested that the Foreign Office was making such an offer to remain in the good graces of the United States and draw Washington into a quasi alliance. House wrote that he found the conversations very interesting but knew his country could not accept the proposal: "I told him [Grey] it was impossible for us to enter into such a *pact* [House's italics], but that we would be glad to take part in a [separate convention] including all [neutrals] looking to the laying down of [principles of civilized warfare]."[38] House's comment to Grey was most likely congruent with the president's views in February 1915. Wilson's mediation effort was motivated by a desire for world peace; however, at that moment he had not fully formulated his ideas about collective security for the postwar world.[39] Nevertheless, freedom of the seas was destined to become an important issue in the months to come, and House found ways to raise the topic in his negotiations with Zimmermann.

House's conclusion that Germany was the chief barrier to peace negotiations was one of the most important turning points for Anglo-American relations. Grey had swayed Wilson's confidant, and the numerous letters House sent back to Washington had a profound influence on the president's perception of the belligerents. While it was true that Germany was not interested in US mediation, Grey's conversations with House had led the latter to ignore the fact that Britain was equally uninterested in a negotiated peace.

While House tried to build the foundations for mediation, Bryan and Lansing worked hard at the State Department to find a way to end the British and German blockades. Soon after Germany announced that it would sink Allied merchant ships around Britain, the secretary of state received a letter from Bernstorff that proposed an end to the campaign if Whitehall agreed to allow free passage for foodstuffs to the German civilian population. On February 12, Ambassador Gerard told Bryan that after talking with Zimmermann, he liked the suggestion. Gerard wrote, "[I] am convinced from [the] conversation with him [that the] German proclamation will be withdrawn if England will adopt [the] Declaration of London or allow food to enter for the German civil population."[40]

Germany's proposal came on the heels of the British decision to detain another American merchant vessel, the *Wilhelmina*, on February 11. When the *Wilhelmina* sailed in late January, Grey claimed he had not planned to "interfere with the cargo" but revived the assertion that the German government managed the distribution of all foodstuffs in the country and that "all food in effect belongs to the army." Therefore, the secretary added, the British could not allow the food to reach the enemy. Consequently, the Royal Navy would detain the ship and Britain would purchase the cargo to prevent the owners from suffering a financial loss.[41]

Britain's action provoked a controversy over its claimed right to prevent food from reaching the German people and seriously disturbed Bryan because of the humanitarian crisis it could cause. Days after Wilson made his "strict accountability" proclamation, Bernstorff expressed to Bryan that his government needed food to ward off starvation among the civilian population and that Britain's attempt to starve Germany was "murderous" and interfered with neutral trade.[42]

Struck by the ambassador's seeming desperation, Bryan wrote Wilson, "If I am not mistaken the efforts to bring this 'economic pressure'—as they [the British] call it—upon women and children of Germany will offend the moral sense of our country and, of course, still further arouse those who are inclined to sympathize with Germany." Bernstorff's offer to end submarine warfare, contingent on British compromise, convinced Bryan that the United States now had an opportunity to negotiate a deal between Britain and Germany.[43]

Bryan knew, however, that he also had to oppose Britain's interference with American trade, and on February 15 he sent a formal protest. In the memorandum, he asserted that Britain had the right to detain the *Wilhelmina*, but that Washington viewed confiscating the cargo as "not justified" because the food was intended for civilian consumption and because the German government gave assurances that it would not end up in the hands of the military.[44] The following day, Bryan sent Page a second message to pressure Britain into accepting Germany's offer. The secretary told Page that by guaranteeing that foodstuffs reached the civilian population and not the military, Berlin had "remove[d] the reasons given by Great Britain for stopping food intended for non-combatants." Bryan wanted the message relayed to Grey and expressed his concern to Page that if London rejected the proposition, American and world opinion could turn against London: "It will certainly create . . . a strong revulsion of feeling in this country."[45]

Bryan made his argument based on Bernstorff's original proposal, yet he soon learned that the ambassador was incorrect about what Berlin would accept and that reaching an agreement on ending the submarine campaign would be much more difficult than he expected. Gerard informed him that leaders in Germany had met to discuss the plan and could not agree on the initial suggestion. In the new offer, Berlin complicated the discussions by stating that it would withdraw its submarines only after Britain permitted foodstuffs *and* raw materials to enter the continent.[46]

Unaware of Germany's increased demand, Page met with House, Grey, and Asquith on February 16. Over lunch, the four men discussed the possibility of constructing a compromise. Similar to Germany, however, Britain complicated matters further by declaring that it could not accept any arrangement without certain additional stipulations. Page informed Bryan that while it "is not certain and must not be known," Britain might not place food on the absolute contraband list if Germany ended submarine attacks on merchant vessels *and* stopped placing mines in the North Sea.[47] Despite the amendments, Bryan believed Page's news offered a "*ray of hope.*" He and Lansing then let the president know that they wanted to compose a formal proposition that incorporated both British and German demands.[48] Not recognizing that Germany and Britain were making unacceptable demands on each other, Wilson was pleased to see the possibility for a compromise and declared that they should put their ideas "into shape for immediate use in dispatches."[49] Without delay, Bryan went to work drafting two identical letters for Page and Gerard. Before Bryan could send his missives, however, Page told him that he did not think Britain and Germany could come to an agreement because of the latter country's decision to cut off all of Britain's imports. In his opinion, if Britain accepted any compromise it might impair its ability to strangle Germany into submission.[50]

Britain's true intentions were evident in Grey's official reply to the State Department over the *Wilhelmina*. He declared publically that Germany had announced that all grain and flour imported into the country after January 31 would belong to the government. Because of the decree, Grey claimed, Britain had no choice but to detain the vessel. The foreign secretary noted that Germany repealed the order on February 6, but only after the Royal Navy seized the *Wilhelmina*. As in many of his letters, Grey attacked the Germans by accusing them of being warmongers who assaulted civilian populations along the English coast and sank ships carrying women and children. It was on these grounds that he defended Britain's actions. If Germany was not going to abide by fair rules of engagement, he asserted, Britain could not be expected to do so either.[51]

According to Grey, Germany had changed the face of the war, leaving Britain no choice but to respond. If Germany intended to assail British ports and sink merchant ships carrying contraband to the United Kingdom, London had the right to reciprocate: "The German Government cannot have it both ways. If they consider themselves justified in destroying by bombardment the lives and property of peaceful civil inhabitants of English open towns and watering-places, and in seizing and sinking ships and cargoes of conditional contraband on the way thither, on the ground that they were consigned to a fortified place or base . . . His majesty's Government must be at liberty to treat Hamburg, which is protected by fortifications at the mouth of the Elbe, as a fortified town."[52]

The timing of Grey's letter suggests that he was not simply reacting to the *Wilhelmina* or the food proposal. He was setting a precedent by releasing his country from any obligation to follow existing international law:

> Faced with the situation, His Majesty's Government consider it would be altogether unreasonable that Great Britain and her Allies should be expected to remain indefinitely bound, to their grave detriment, by rules and principles of which they recognise the justice if impartially observed as between belligerents, but which are at the present moment openly set at defiance by their enemy . . . If therefore His Majesty's Government should hereafter feel constrained to declare foodstuffs absolute contraband, or to take other measures for interfering with German trade, by way of reprisals, they confidently expect that such action will not be challenged on the part of neutral States by appeals to laws and usages of war whose validity rests on their forming an integral part of that system of international doctrine which as a whole their enemy frankly boasts the liberty and intention to disregard.[53]

Grey's comments did not deter Bryan from his mission to bring about a compromise. The following day he dispatched an official proposal, which incorporated the demands made by both belligerents, to the American ambassadors in London and Berlin. After Page delivered the message to Grey on February 22, the British cabinet took up Bryan's suggestion. Members of the Foreign Office reported that they did not think the scheme would benefit Britain. According to British legal advisor C. J. B. Hurst, only

Germany would profit from the plan because it would allow Germany free access to food "in return for the discontinuance of the illegal methods of warfare which she is now adopting." Great Britain should, he advised, reject the proposition and claim that it was simply following international law. The next day, Assistant Undersecretary of State Eyre Crowe told Grey that he agreed. The compromise, he asserted, would benefit Germany alone.[54]

The British admiralty charged that Bryan's proposal was "strongly unneutral in character" and that the American note required Britain to end a legitimate form of warfare in exchange for what it considered the end of Germany's illegal actions. The British refused to acknowledge similarities between their actions and those of Germany. The admiralty complained that Germany was killing innocent people, a practice condemned "even in the middle ages." In protest, the admiralty stated that Washington stressed the importance of allowing supplies to reach the civilian population of Germany but did not recognize that all of the German population helped with the war effort: "What is the civil population in a war in which the whole nation is taking part?" Even before the war the Royal Navy viewed the German civilian population as its main target. Callously, naval commanders did not consider that the same was true for the British people. They refused to accept that their blockade was in anyway similar to the German U-boat attacks and zeppelin raids. Thus, the admiralty asserted that the American note would fail because it was "far from being in the interest of humanity," or Britain.[55]

Complying with the cabinet's consensus, Grey drafted a response to Bryan's proposal. The British had no intentions of accepting the deal, but they had to find a way to reject the plan without seeming like the villains. He began by playing to American sensibilities. Grey wrote that Britain understood America's compassionate motives and defended his own country's actions as legal and civilized but added that "on the German side it has been very different." Before confessing that Britain would not agree to allow foodstuffs to reach German civilians, Grey listed a number of actions—including the invasion of Belgium, treatment of British prisoners of war, and the bombings of English towns—as evidence that Germany was resorting to criminal acts. Such activities, Grey argued, prevented the Allies from consenting to a compromise. "It is difficult," he concluded, "to see how Germany's enemies can feel any serenity, as long as Germany is not prepared to discuss terms of peace, which will free those nations who are now resisting her from the menace of German aggression and the risk of being injured by bad faith."[56]

Grey's statement was evidence of a tougher policy by which Britain intended to approach the war. On the same day Grey presented his draft to the cabinet, Britain tightened its naval blockade of Germany.[57] London sent word to neutral governments that it intended to stop all German trade regardless of whether it was contraband or not. The Foreign Office defended its actions by claiming that Germany's submarine declaration violated international law. U-boats, Grey argued, could not abide by the established rules of naval warfare: "Law and custom of nations in regard to attacks on commerce have always presumed that the first duty of the captor of a merchant vessel is to bring it before a Prize Court." In Britain's opinion, it was the duty of the attacking vessel to discriminate "between neutral and enemy vessels, and between neutral and enemy cargo . . . [Germany's] methods of warfare are therefore entirely outside the scope of any of the international instruments regulating operations against commerce in time of war." Grey added the assertion that Germany's policy was not just a threat to the Allies but to neutrals as well. Disregarding the fact that Britain was doing the same thing, Grey wrote, "Germany is adopting these methods against peaceful traders and non-combatant crews with the avowed object of preventing commodities of all kinds (including food for the civil population) from reaching or leaving the British Isles."[58]

Using the same argument with which it handled the *Wilhelmina* and foodstuffs cases, the British government claimed that Germany's strategy forced the Allies to respond by keeping "commodities of any kind from reaching or leaving Germany." Considering that Britain was conducting its blockade for the same reason that Germany decided to begin using submarine warfare, the British tried to differentiate their policy from its enemy's by asserting that the Allies did not pose a threat to "neutral ships or to neutral or non-combatant life and [was] in strict observance of the dictates of humanity." But because Germany threatened to prevent all goods from reaching the Allies, Britain and France claimed the right to detain any ship "carrying goods of presumed enemy destination, ownership, or origin."[59]

In painting Germany as a rogue state, Grey hoped to keep Wilson from turning the British blockade into a major issue. Making matters worse for the Germans, at midnight on March 2, Bryan received a telegram from Gerard, who explained that German Foreign Minister Gottlieb von Jagow had presented a counter offer to the US proposal regarding the submarine campaign. Von Jagow stated that Berlin would not end the use of mines but would agree to use anchored rather than free-floating mines.[60] According to Gerard, Zimmermann and German Chancellor Theobald von Bethmann-Hollweg wanted to accept the American proposal, but the decision was not theirs to make. The ambassador asserted that the German military was in control of diplomatic affairs and "Admiral Von Tirpitz did not want England to accept our proposal and therefore added conditions . . . so as to make acceptance impossible."[61]

Although Page asserted that he was not criticizing the administration's policies, he certainly made his opinions clear in a March 10 letter to Wilson. Europe was not embroiled in a "war" but rather a "break-down of civilization." Page claimed that the conflict was devastating the continent and that the United States should stop urging Britain to recognize neutral rights. The State Department, he asserted, had no idea what was really going on across the Atlantic: "Half the requests that I am instructed to make of Sir Edward Grey provoke merely a tolerant smile these days, as you'd smile at a child who ask[ed] you to take your automobile and run back 10 miles to look for a marble he had lost." In Page's opinion, the United States had made a major mistake by trying to convince Britain to accept the Declaration of London and the proposal for ending the submarine blockade in exchange for the free passage of food to Germany. The effort, he thought, would only damage America's standing with the Allies.[62]

Declaring a blockade of the European coast would undoubtedly upset American business interests, and the Foreign Office apparently realized the necessity of offering certain concessions to US merchants in an attempt to stave off diplomatic controversies. Days after Grey's announcement, State Department Foreign Trade Advisor Robert F. Rose, joined L. Wolf, a New York cotton merchant, in warning Spring-Rice that the blockade would harm cotton exports. He told the ambassador that he had advised cotton merchants to "take advantage of the demand for cotton in Germany" because it was on the free list. The change in British policy meant that many shippers might lose money on existing contracts. Spring-Rice in turn sent a message to London asking if it would consider pushing back the deadline for the sale of cotton to Germany. The cabinet responded in a similar manner as with the *Wilhelmina*. On March 8, it announced that the Royal Navy would not confiscate cotton destined for Germany if it had been sold before March 2 and had shipped no later than the end of the month. As soon as they heard the decision, Georgia Senator Hoke Smith, Mr. Rose, and Mr. Beer, Wolf's attorney, met with the ambassador to confirm the public announcement. They learned that Britain would not allow cargoes to reach German ports but would compensate the owners "for any loss at [the] contract price."[63] The decision temporarily ameliorated the problem and prevented an outcry by southerners that could have threatened the Wilson administration's political future and Anglo-American relations by reviving congressional support for legislation that favored munitions embargos.

In addition to providing a concession to the cotton South, Spring-Rice informed Bryan that his government had decided to amend its position on the purchase and transfer of German ships. It still had no intention of allowing unlimited acquisitions, but Britain was willing to make some exceptions. By mid-March, Grey declared that he was "now in a position to indicate the conditions on which His Majesty's Government would be prepared to recognize as valid the transfer of a ship, the beneficial interests in which were American prior to the outbreak of the war."[64]

Before the fighting began in August 1914, Americans held majority interest in a number of vessels registered in Germany. Britain realized this and agreed not to oppose the transfer of these ships to American registry as long as they carried a certificate proving that the "beneficial interests in them were American before hostilities commenced." Together the cotton arrangement and the relaxed approach to the transfer of certain merchant vessels were consistent with Grey's efforts to appease the United States just enough to prevent a split in relations. The compromises that Britain offered did not hurt Allied interests and were obviously approved to make the blockade easier for the US public to swallow.[65]

Compromises alone were not enough to soothe Anglo-American relations, and neither government wanted to jeopardize US neutrality or the American export trade more than was necessary. After reading the British blockade declaration, Lansing informed Bryan that responding would be difficult. The former noted that the proclamation contradicted itself and, in his opinion, did not amount to a legal act. Lansing focused on the Allied statement: "[T]he British and French Governments will therefore hold themselves free to detain and take into port ships carrying goods of presumed enemy destination, ownership or origin. It is not intended to confiscate such vessel[s] or cargoes unless they would otherwise be liable to condemnation." He picked the sentences apart, stating that the first declared a blockade in effect and that the second suggested "no blockade existed." This contradiction, according to Lansing, placed neutrals in a difficult situation because they had "no standard by which to measure their rights or to avoid danger to their ships and cargoes."[66]

Bryan agreed and worked with Lansing to compose a reply. The secretary of state emphasized to the president that they should request that Britain offer a better explanation because the Allied declaration "appears to contemplate a blockade of German coasts but fails to announce the establishment of such blockade or to use the word in the declaration."[67] Wilson replied that the note needed some adjustments before he could send it to Page. To the president, the message seemed "abrupt in expression and also a bit difficult to interpret as it stands." Ultimately Wilson sent Page an edited copy of the missive Lansing gave to the secretary on March 2. Lansing's version, Wilson wrote, was "lucid and conveys the matter in just the right tone of inquiry."[68] Sending off the letter on March 5, it seems evident that the president hoped the reply, like all previous replies, would not threaten House's mission to bring about mediation.

Britain did not immediately respond when it received the message. It was in the process of formulating a new Order in Council and decided the best way to answer would be all at once. On March 15, Asquith's government dispatched two messages to Washington. Bryan received the first letter late that evening. It rejected the secretary's proposal on foodstuffs. Planning to announce a major policy change, Britain did not intend to approve Bryan's proposition. London was also unwilling to admit any fault for the initiative's failure. Grey asserted that the British were not persuaded that Germany would stop conducting submarine warfare and deploying mines at sea. In light of this conclusion, Grey could not see any reason to accept the US proposal but chose to outline the British position nonetheless. He claimed that Britain, unlike Germany, followed international law when prosecuting the war. Germany had, he further charged, violated human rights in Belgium and regularly broke the rules of war by using zeppelins to bomb the civilian population. He also tried to differentiate between British and German policy, claiming that merchant ships should be taken before a prize court to determine their fate—not indiscriminately sunk by submarines. Such German actions, Grey argued, justified the Allies' decision to stop "all passage to and from Germany by sea."[69]

In its second message, the Foreign Office unveiled the new Order in Council titled "Reprisals Restricting German Commerce." Officially dated March 11, the directive announced that in response to the German submarine campaign, Britain had "an unquestionable right of retaliation." Such reciprocity entailed preventing all goods from reaching the enemy. The Royal Navy had orders to stop every ship headed to or from German ports after March 1. As a sop to neutral countries, it was stated that Britain had no intention of confiscating noncontraband cargo without compensation to the owner. To reduce tension with neutral shippers, the British planned to send all detained cargoes to Allied ports and place them "in the custody of the marshal of the Prize Court." Once discharged, the government would requisition noncontraband or return it to the owner. The Order also offered merchants some recourse by allowing appeals to the prize court's decisions. When Britain announced that it intended to retaliate against the German submarine campaign, it was vague about what type of cordon of the continent it planned to establish. The Order in Council was void of the term blockade because British officials did not think the new policy conformed to international law. Therefore they were intentionally unclear, implying that a blockade was in existence without tying their hands with indefensible claims.[70]

Grey followed up by attempting to resolve any confusion over what actually existed and assuage American concerns. Britain intended to "minimize inconvenience to neutral commerce." The government wanted to settle any future problems as quickly as possible by giving the prize court plenty of discretion to "facilitate claims." Grey claimed the Royal Navy and customs agents were under express instructions to respect neutral trade as much as possible. He also addressed Lansing's argument that the blockade was not effective, asserting that Britain had to promulgate a vague policy because the laws governing a blockade were too detrimental to neutral trade. Britain had to prevent Germany from obtaining goods but changed the rules of the blockade and avoided using the term in its Order in Council because it did not want to anger the United States government. Yet Grey knew that changing the wording did not alter the fact that Britain had established a distant blockade. In a message to Spring-Rice, the foreign secretary wrote, "His Majesty's Government have felt most reluctant at the moment of initiating a policy of blockade to exact from neutral ships all the penalties attaching to a breach of blockade. In their desire to alleviate the burden which the existence of a state of war at sea must inevitably impose on neutral sea-borne commerce, they declare their intention to refrain all together from the right to confiscate ships or cargoes which belligerents have always claimed in respect of breaches of blockade." Ultimately Grey's message was an effort to convince the United States that Britain valued neutral trade and respected American rights at sea.[71]

Wilson and his cabinet were divided over how they should respond. On March 19, the president sent Bryan the draft of a letter that he wanted to send to the Foreign Office. Wilson asserted that because the Order in Council covered such a large area of the European coastline, US ships would have to traverse the blockade to reach other neutral ports and that his administration took it for granted that Britain would not interfere with trade among neutrals inside the blockade, unless it was searching ships believed to be carrying contraband destined for Germany.

Wilson noted that his government recognized the "unusual conditions of modern warfare at sea" that Britain used to justify its actions and agreed that submarine attacks were "inconsistent with the best usages of warfare in the dealings of belligerents with neutrals at sea." Wilson also expressed appreciation for Britain's assurance that it would try to limit the interference with neutral trade but asserted that his administration would hold Britain responsible for any violations of international law and neutral rights.[72]

While Wilson wanted to take a moderate stance that acknowledged the blockade's existence yet still held Britain accountable for any breach of law, Page strongly urged outright acceptance of British policy. He informed Bryan that the only real difference between the past and present was that the current blockade was a distant blockade using cruisers to intercept ships before they reached port. The new Order, the ambassador argued, would not injure American commerce. US trade with Britain was still on the rise and, according to Page, even if cargoes could not reach Germany, the upward trend would continue for the duration of the war. Moreover, he warned that the United States wasted its breath with protests. The Allies, he argued, did not take the State Department's complaints seriously, stating that Britons "smile at our love of letter writing as at Fourth of July orations. They quietly laugh at our effort to regulate sea warfare out of textbooks."[73]

Lansing argued that the United States should take a different position. In addition to Wilson's draft, Lansing prepared his own response to the British in which he asserted that its actions were unprecedented and that it had not instituted an official blockade of the European coast. "This Government," he wrote, "should not be led into a trap of admitting that a blockade has been established by the Order in Council."[74] One hindrance to Britain's position was its adherence to the 1856 Declaration of Paris. In signing the treaty, London accepted the doctrine of "free ships, free goods," which declared that neutral ships should be able to trade with anyone. Additionally, the March 11 Order in Council stated that neutral ports within the cordon line were also off limits. Thus, Britain had an extremely long line to monitor and the only way to do so was with a distant blockade that would be porous. Under the Declaration of Paris, for a blockade to exist it must be "effective" or complete. A country could not simply declare a blockade to exist and expect neutral governments to respect it. A navy must have the ability to enforce the proclamation.[75]

During the American Civil War, however, the United States had set a precedent in maritime law that ran counter to the 1856 accord. When trying to shut off the Confederacy's trade, President Abraham Lincoln declared a blockade covering 3,000 miles of coastline of the southern states. The problem was that the US Navy's size prevented it from actually guarding every dock and secluded inlet that the Confederacy might use to off-load goods. This meant that the Union blockade was not "effective." But Lincoln asserted that it was not necessary for the Navy to control every harbor. Just because it was permeable did not make it a paper blockade.[76]

With a similar perception, Bryan informed the president that he felt the biggest difference between Lansing and Wilson originated in Britain's decision not to use the word "blockade" in its newest Order in Council. The secretary contended that whether the word blockade was in the announcement or not was a frivolous detail. In Bryan's opinion, Britain's decision to avoid the term was irrelevant, adding that the United States should not attach "so much importance . . . to a single word." The "word 'blockade' describes a method of procedure" and the British decision to use a different term to explain their actions "cannot be material." Bryan told the president that if Lansing demanded that Britain use the term and thereby comply with strict rules, Wilson's position would be "better sustained." Nevertheless, after reading the Order for himself, Bryan concluded that Wilson was incorrect in assuming that Britain would not stop "non-contraband goods destined for neutral ports." The pronouncement suggested otherwise, leading Bryan to ask, "If the [Wilson's] assumption is clearly inconsistent with the language of the Orders in Council, would it not lead to a contradiction that would embarrass us?"[77]

Ultimately, Wilson agreed with Bryan. Britain, he emphasized, had no right to blockade neutral ports, yet the president claimed the United States had no other option than to accept a de facto blockade. Wilson admitted that Lansing's comment was "convincing; but [it] would lead only to debate" with the British government and "is at present of no practical avail." Wilson suggested that arguing with the British was futile considering that he did not expect Britain to compromise: "We are face to face with *something that they are going to do,* [Wilson's italics] and they are going to do it no matter what representations we make." The only thing that Wilson assumed the United States could do was clarify its neutral rights and assure the British that the US government intended to hold them "strictly responsible for every invasion of our neutral rights." Wilson ended his letter by stating that he hoped Lansing could compose a response that was in line with his thinking and that the three men could meet to "put the thing into a shape that will thoroughly hold water (and exclude it, too, as a maritime paper should)."[78]

Before their meeting, Lansing stressed that the government should consider the effect that any answer would have on US public opinion. If the message did not include a list of American rights under international law, people might conclude the administration either did not care about the threat or was ignorant of neutral rights. He admitted that stating these rights probably would not change the situation but would set a precedent concerning neutrals in future wars.[79]

Together, Wilson and Lansing crafted a response to the March 11 proclamation that addressed the latter's concerns and protested in a way that acknowledged the existence of the blockade while holding London responsible for any violations of neutral rights. Wilson stated that the Order in Council and Grey's explanatory notes had a great impact on neutral states and that they "appear to menace their rights of trade and intercourse not only with belligerents but also with one another." Consequently he was making a "frank comment" in the hope that "misunderstandings could be avoided." He asserted that if the Order was enforced in its existent form, it would offer Britain "unlimited belligerent rights over neutral commerce" and "an almost unqualified denial of the sovereign rights of the nations now at peace." Wilson acknowledged that belligerent countries had the right to search and even capture ships that tried to run the blockade, but he added that these rights were the limit of a belligerent's authority over a "nation not engaged in war."[80] He therefore expected Britain to allow American merchant ships to travel through the blockade to neutral ports.

To demonstrate that precedent supported the US position, Lansing noted that following the Arbitration Commission of 1871, the United States paid compensation for its condemnation of the British flagged merchant vessel *Peterhoff*. In 1863, the *Peterhoff* carried contraband, which was ultimately bound for the Confederacy, to the neutral port of Matamoras, Mexico. On its return voyage, the USS *Vanderbilt* captured the vessel because the *Peterhoff* had conducted a broken voyage. Lansing also pointed out that under the 1856 Declaration of Paris "free ships make free goods" meant that Britain could not interfere with American trade bound for neutral ports. Therefore it was unprecedented to treat ships headed for such destinations the same way as ships headed for belligerent ports. If Britain went beyond "visit and search," its actions would be a "distinct invasion of the sovereign rights of the nation whose ships, trade, or commerce is interfered with."[81]

The US government acknowledged that because of the circumstances of modern warfare, particularly the advent of the submarine, the nature of a blockade changed as well. Submarines made the traditional close blockade of enemy ports impossible and mandated the use of a distant blockade. The administration, however, did not concede that the blockading force had the right to seize neutral merchant ships headed to and from neutral ports inside the blockade's limits. After declaring the American position, Wilson noted that he expected Britain to make restitution or reimbursement for any violations of existing international law. If Britain planned to enforce the Order in Council, the United States would "impose upon His Majesty's Government heavy responsibilities." After the president approved the final version, Bryan sent the message to Page on March 30.[82]

As Wilson and Lansing composed their reply to the Order in Council, House continued searching for a starting place from which he could initiate mediation. On March 1, the colonel met with King George V. He wrote Wilson that he thought the king wanted to discuss plans for negotiations but quickly realized that the monarch was the "most bellicose Englishman that I have so far met." George V had no interest in discussing an early settlement to the war. He emphasized to House that the only way to have lasting peace with Germany was to beat the country into submission. The king's attitude surprised House, who informed Wilson that the king detested his cousin the kaiser and "denounced [him] in good sailorlike [*sic*] terms." Upon reflection, House concluded that George V was the "most pugnacious little monarch that is loose in these parts."[83]

His experience with Zimmermann was not much better. House received a message from the undersecretary on March 2 that expressed disappointment in the colonel's decision to delay his trip to Berlin. Zimmermann stated that he "read with interest what you believe to be a possible beginning to the desired end." Nevertheless, he asserted that House seemed to want to negotiate based on the idea that Germany was almost defeated. This was not the case, he argued, and reemphasized that the German government was not willing to consider an indemnity for Belgium. True to form for all the belligerents, Zimmermann added that Germany did want peace but only after its enemy conceded something that it was certain not to forfeit: "If England would consent to give up her claim to a monopoly on the seas together with her two to one power standard, I think it might be a good beginning." House dutifully forwarded Zimmermann's message to the president and added, "I am not downhearted and trust there may be more light when I am once there [Berlin]."[84]

When he reached Berlin in late March, House met with Zimmermann, who welcomed him "enthusiastically." House wrote Wilson after the meeting that he reasoned that the differences between Germany and Britain were not that great and that the two governments could sit down together. The only major barrier to talks was that the French and German people "have been led to expect much more than is possible to realize." The public's expectations were so high that neither government could accept less stringent demands than they had already proposed without risking a coup. House then declared that he did not know what else he could do in the interim, stating, "[I]t is plain at the moment that some serious reverse will have to be encountered by one or other of the belligerents before any government will dare propose parleys." He did not think the end was near and argued that the United States must wait until events changed for the better: "I can foresee troublous times ahead, and it will be the wonder of the ages if all the governments come out of it intact. The world is upon a strain as never before in its history, and something is sure to crack somewhere before a great while. It looks as if our best move just now is to wait until the fissure appears."[85]

Despite his discouraging tone, House did not concede defeat. He decided he had one last trick in his bag that might spark a conversation between German and British diplomats. House told Wilson that the only way to get Germany to release Belgium was to find a way for the government to save face with its people.[86] He added that Germany might consider a peace accord if Britain agreed to accept the idea of freedom of the seas. Having already talked to Grey, House thought this was a reasonable concession that everyone could support. On March 27, House told Bethmann-Hollweg that it was simply a starting point and emphasized that "some one [*sic*] would have to throw across the chasm the first thread, so that the bridge might have its beginning." House reasoned that if Britain would accept the proposal, Germany could easily go to its own people and explain that "Belgium was no longer needed as a base for German naval activity." Zimmermann and the German chancellor liked the proposal and agreed that it would open the way to a conference. Wilson replied that he found House's suggested compromise "very promising" and hoped it might offer the United States the leverage needed to start peace negotiations.[87]

But before the president could follow up the opening, diplomatic relations with Germany and Britain again reached a pivotal moment. On April 2, Wilson faced a direct challenge to his vague policy of strict accountability. Bryan notified him that a German U-boat had torpedoed a British merchant vessel called the *Falaba* on March 28, killing an American passenger named Leon Thrasher.

The belligerents' new policies toward neutral trade and the difficulties facing House's mediation efforts were significant factors behind Wilson's eventual open support for the Allies. Berlin's response to the unfettered flow of materiel from the United States and other neutrals to the Allies created a serious problem for the US government. Wilson opposed using submarines against unarmed merchantmen. The naval campaign threatened the country's neutrality in that an attack on an American vessel might force the United States into the war. In what the British claimed was a reaction to an illegitimate and inhumane form of combat, the Foreign Office took the opportunity to tighten its blockade on the Central Powers. This action, too, placed the United States in an awkward position since the new British Order in Council prevented US ships from traversing the Royal Navy's distant blockade to reach neutral European ports. Treading carefully, the Wilson administration decided that the best solution was to protest both German and British actions by using ambiguous language.

Historians have argued that by approaching the German and British blockades differently and using rhetoric that implied a harsher and threatening tone toward Germany and a weaker tenor in his letter to Britain, Wilson was no longer neutral.[88] It is true that the words "strict accountability" suggest that the United States would respond quickly to a submarine attack. Yet this is not enough to argue that the administration was outwardly supporting the Allies in early 1915. The "strict accountability" warning to Germany simply reveals the president's concern and frustration over submarine warfare. Wilson viewed it as barbaric. To Wilson, Britain's use of a distant blockade was supported by historical precedent dating back to the American Civil War, but submarine warfare was relatively new and could endanger US citizens. This is why the president and his advisors stated that they would "take any steps it might be necessary to take to safeguard American lives and property."[89] While these words would eventually come back to haunt Wilson later in the year, in March 1915 the president was trying to avert a problem with Germany. Additionally, his inaction spoke louder than his words. When Germany eventually attacked ships carrying American passengers, Wilson did not retaliate with military action or the severance of American-German relations. Instead he continued using diplomatic channels.

As Wilson dealt with the belligerents' blockades, he also hoped to preserve American neutrality and prevent the growing crisis from threatening House's mission in Europe. Britain and Germany were not interested in mediation, however, and did all they could to discourage House without appearing to oppose peace talks. Both belligerents made proposals that they certainly knew their counterpart could not accept and then blamed each other for the impasse. The failure of House's trip to Europe is significant because, when examined together with the changes in German and British naval policies, Grey's ability to influence House's view on mediation started a definitive shift in Anglo-American diplomacy that would aid in moving the United States closer to open support for London by the end of the year.

6

"The Palliations of Piracy"

April 1915–June 1915

They seem to think that all this Government has to do is stiffen its back and peremptorily demand respect for the rights of its citizens, and that the belligerent governments, though they may fume and bluster, will submit rather than have an open breach with the United States.

—State Department Counselor Robert Lansing, May 3, 1915[1]

Prudence is an impertinent intruder *this week*, and Wisdom intolerable!

—Wilson to Edith Galt, May 8, 1915[2]

By mid-1915, the paradox created by Wilson's pragmatic and idealistic goals was clearly evident. The president was becoming more focused on his country's economic bonds with Great Britain, which complicated his effort to be a fair mediator. Anglo-American trade relations made Britain very important to US economic health and helped to provoke the submarine crisis with Germany. When U-boat attacks resulted in the death of American citizens, they challenged Wilson's sense of morality and further shaped his negative perception of Germany. The submarine cordon created a diplomatic quandary. Wilson wanted to remain neutral yet demonstrate that "strict accountability" was not just mere rhetoric. Disagreements over the correct approach to the crisis caused a major shake-up in Wilson's administration culminating with Secretary of State William Jennings Bryan's decision to resign from his post. Additionally Colonel Edward House's mission to Europe was not having the effect that the president hoped. The belligerents' aversion to peace talks would play a critical role in solidifying Wilson's and House's conviction that Germany was the major barrier to peace talks. Collectively, the intertwining of his ideological outlook and economic interests affected the president's approach to the war and became the catalyst for Wilson's eventual decision to abandon US neutrality.

Tension over the use of submarine warfare intensified when the U-28 sank the British steamship RMS *Falaba*. Germany had killed an American civilian and many people in the United States wanted a strong response from Wilson. British Embassy Counselor Colville Barclay and British Ambassador Cecil Spring-Rice sent newspaper clippings to the British cabinet pointing out the US public's outrage. The ambassador quoted the *New York Times* as stating, "[I]t has not even the palliations of piracy, for the pirate, like the highwayman, kills for gain, not because he delights in slaughter . . . It is a crime directly chargeable against Germany for which she will be held responsible in the judgment of civilization."[3]

The challenge for the Wilson administration was to hold Germany accountable for the death of Americans without provoking permanent domestic or international political problems. Bryan argued that the United States could not protest the attack unless it was willing to denounce the "methods employed" by the Germans as "improper in warfare." Additionally Bryan maintained that when Leon Thrasher decided to board the *Falaba* he took his life into his own hands. Thrasher, he pointed out, was aware of the risk of traveling on a British-flagged vessel, and thus his death, while regrettable, did not call for US government protest.[4]

In a letter to Bryan, Counselor Robert Lansing observed that a number of options lay open to the department but warned that it had to choose prudently because the response would "determine our policy in this case and in the event other Americans meet death in the same way." The United States had to discover whether the ship tried to escape and if the U-boat complied with international law by surfacing and allowing the ship's passengers and crew to disembark. Only then could Wilson and his staff decide about the attack's legitimacy and respond to Thrasher's death. An American, Lansing asserted, should be able to depend on Germany to comply with the "established rules of visit and search and of protection of non-combatants." According to The Hague Convention of 1907, prior to sinking a belligerent vessel the attacker must provide for the "safety of persons on board." If the United States accepted this principle, Lansing concluded, the government would have to protest the attack and demand that Germany pay reparations.[5]

The day after Wilson learned of the *Falaba*'s sinking, he admitted to Bryan that the case was "full of disturbing possibilities." He maintained that the U-boat violated international law by firing on the ship and that the administration probably needed to stress to Germany that American lives "shall not be put in danger." Nevertheless, he knew that his office had to handle the matter with caution.[6] In Lansing's opinion, the United States needed to stand firm and "state the remedy which we expect." If it did not display "firm determination," Germany would "show contempt for its weakness." If the United States responded hesitantly, it would "amount to an admission of Germany's right to perform lawless acts in that area." Lansing argued that the German commander of the U-28 violated international law and that he should have given the ship fair warning before the attack. Additionally, he asserted that Germany must condemn the incident, punish the U-boat commander, and pay compensation for Thrasher's death.[7]

Bryan and US Commercial Attaché Chandler Anderson were more cautious. The secretary of state did not want to act before the United States knew all the facts. Recognizing that the attack could pull the United States closer to war, Bryan argued that it should not risk the security of the entire country because of one man's actions. "[R]ights and obligations of citizenship," he claimed, "[were not] so one-sided that the Government which represents all the people must bring the whole population into difficulty because a citizen, instead of regarding his country's interests, thinks only of himself and his interests."[8] Anderson added that Germany may have misunderstood the American note on "strict accountability" to apply only to US vessels and that it probably did not know the *Falaba* carried an American citizen. Therefore, he argued that the sinking of the *Falaba* was not a "question of national affront, but merely a question of whether a German submarine was acting lawfully or unlawfully."[9]

Bryan also feared that the wrong response could inflame public opinion. He argued the administration needed to be cautious in its reply because German-Americans might doubt the White House's impartiality if it aggressively condemned Germany's actions. The secretary also thought that if the government sent a harsh response to Berlin, it might stir pro-Allied Americans' demand for a declaration of war.[10]

On the afternoon of April 7, the US consul-general in London, Robert Skinner, contacted Bryan and gave him several eyewitness accounts of the *Falaba* attack. These reports suggested that the ship tried to escape until the submarine threatened to fire, at which point passengers began to disembark. Bryan read that the submarine launched a torpedo only ten minutes after the *Falaba* had surrendered. The survivors claimed that many people were still visible on board when the U-boat attacked. They "[s]aw people swimming near [the] submarine crying to it for help," but the crew did not attempt to aid any of the survivors. Other accounts claimed that the submarine was able to get close to the *Falaba* by flying a British flag and switching to a German flag before the attack.[11] When Lansing learned from Skinner that of the 147 passengers on board, 89 were rescued, he concluded that the U-boat captain must not have thought the vessel was armed. If he had, he would have attacked immediately and without warning. The real problem, as Lansing saw it, was that while the captain gave "some time" for passengers and crew to get off the ship, he obviously did not offer enough.

To the counselor, the issue was not simply a matter of legality but one of humanity as well.[12]

The US government's frustration over the matter mounted when days later US Ambassador James Gerard sent Bryan a dispatch containing Germany's version of the attack. It claimed that the U-boat chased the ship for fifteen minutes as the *Falaba* fired signal rockets for help. When the ship finally stopped, the German commander waited 23 minutes before launching a torpedo.[13] Frustrated after hearing the German account, Wilson wrote Bryan. "What are we to believe? . . . This version is absolutely in contradiction of that given by both passengers and petty officers of the FALABA!"[14]

Bryan demonstrated his concern by resurrecting his proposal to end the blockade as a means of ending the impasse. The only way to ensure America's neutrality was to impose a compromise on the belligerents: "Our identical note was well intended & Germany indicated a willingness to negotiate—would it not be wise to make another effort to pressure Gt B. [Great Britain] to join in some agreement which will, by permitting food into Germany, do away with the torpedoing of merchant vessels?"[15]

The matter weighed heavily on Wilson's mind. Without responding immediately to the secretary's proposal, he stated that he had outlined a series of points that he wanted Bryan to include in the State Department's answer to the German government. The president insisted that despite the exigencies in modern warfare, Germany must follow accepted rules of engagement set out in international law. Therefore, he expected Germany to "acknowledge her responsibility in the present instance." Taking Lansing's view, Wilson challenged the use of submarines against merchant vessels because they could not ensure the safety of the crews and passengers of the ships they attacked. He told Bryan to issue "a very moderately worded but none the less solemn and emphatic protest," one not based solely on legal grounds but also on "humanity, fair play, and a necessary respect for the rights of neutrals."[16]

Despite his reservations, Bryan instructed Lansing to prepare the response. The secretary, however, told Wilson that the message would heighten the "hostile feeling against us in Germany" mainly "because of its contrast with our attitude toward the allies." The United States, asserted Bryan, was claiming that submarine attacks on noncombatant vessels were "inhuman" but simultaneously looking the other way while London kept "food from reaching non-combatant enemies." He correctly asserted that if one was a form of uncivilized warfare, so was the other. To view it otherwise, he argued, was "partiality." In such an atmosphere where Germany already suspected that the Americans favored its enemies, Bryan stressed that Wilson's suggestions for the "Thrasher note" would further complicate

US-German relations. He insisted that the alternative was to pressure the belligerents to discuss peace openly and claimed that the United States could not wait for one side to have the upper hand, especially since it claimed to be neutral. Additionally, he worried that if the war continued, America could wind up a participant: "Is it not better to try to bring peace for the benefit of the whole world than to risk the provoking of war on account of one man?"[17]

Even Lansing assumed that protesting Germany's actions would make American neutrality more difficult to sustain. He told Bryan that no matter how much he softened the language, Germany would view the note as "further evidence of our partiality for the Allies." Nevertheless, he thought that the United States had to react because the American public would not tolerate "silence" on the matter. "The tension in our relations with Germany is becoming greater; the situation more and more difficult; almost anything we say or do will be distorted into unfriendliness. I can but be apprehensive of sending an instruction like the one enclosed, and yet it seems impossible to avoid doing so in the circumstances."[18]

On April 28, Wilson told Bryan that he was "not at all confident that we are on the right track" concerning the note. The president acknowledged that composing an official statement on the *Falaba* might not even be necessary. Wilson was also frustrated about the secretary's suggestion that the administration should make a public request for the belligerents to lay down their arms. "I wish I could see it as you do," Wilson told Bryan, but House's messages from Europe convinced the president that he could not. He told the secretary that the Europeans knew that the United States wanted to help and that they could depend on the administration to act as an intermediary between the belligerents. But Wilson had rightly concluded that Germany and Britain were not ready for peace and forcing the issue would "be futile and would probably be offensive. I am afraid, Mr. Secretary, that there is much in this that will seem to you disputable; but I can only state my conviction in the matter, and God knows I have searched my mind and conscience both to get the best, the nearest approach to wisdom, there is in them."[19]

Before the administration could dispatch a note to Germany about the *Falaba*, it found itself in what was probably the most tumultuous week it had yet faced. On May 1, Lansing wrote Bryan that two new issues had severely complicated the whole situation. On April 29, a German aircraft had bombed the *Cushing*, a US merchant vessel sailing in the North Sea. One of the bombs struck the ship's deck, although it did not result in serious physical damage or kill any of the crew.[20] Two days later, the German embassy placed a warning in US newspapers declaring that all ships flying a British flag or those of its allies "are liable to destruction in those waters [around the British Isles] and that travelers sailing in the war zone on ships of Great Britain or her allies do so at their own risk."[21]

Lansing regarded the bombing as a "flagrant violation of neutral rights" and complained that Germany should not have used the American press to publish its warning. Public statements were "highly improper" and the German embassy should have given the warning to the State Department. Bryan disagreed with Lansing. The United States should not consider the warning "a matter of offense," he informed the president. Bryan argued that Germany's decision to publish the warning proved that it wanted to avoid problems with America not exacerbate them.[22]

As Lansing and Bryan explained their views to the president, Germany struck again, this time torpedoing the *Gulflight*, an American tanker. Two seamen drowned after jumping overboard and the captain died of heart failure.[23] The three events produced a delicate situation. Lansing's eye for detail convinced him that the White House had to consider not only the tone of its protest but also the timing of its submission to Germany. He told Bryan that they should first address the Thrasher case because doing so would allow them to raise the moral issue of submarine warfare; focusing on the destruction of US property would only allow for a defense based on the February 10 note announcing "strict accountability."[24]

In the midst of the *Gulflight* crisis, the administration learned of the most infamous U-boat attack of the war. At 3:06 p.m., Bryan received a telegram from American Ambassador Walter Hines Page that read, "The *Lusitania* was torpedoed off the Irish coast and sunk in half an hour. No news yet of the passengers."[25] The message sent a shockwave through the administration. No one knew exactly what to do. After dinner, Wilson received a bulletin declaring that the submarine attack had taken many lives. In a distraught state, he walked out of the White House into the rainy streets of Washington, returning later to discover that as many as 1,000 passengers had died.[26]

The *Lusitania* sank in less than 18 minutes, taking 1,257 passengers with it to the bottom of the Irish Sea. Among the dead were 128 Americans. Immediately, voices from across the country clamored for a vigorous response. Editorials printed in the *New York Times* called the sinking "murder . . . plain and unqualified piracy . . . This cold-blooded, premeditated outrage on [a] colossal scale will cause such a blinding white light of indignation . . . that there can not [*sic*] conceivably, be in Washington any thought of turning back from the note to Germany, sent Feb. 10 . . . No voice will be made, to force, the hand to hasten the action of the President of the United States. But neither he nor any other official in our Government can mistake the temper in which their fellow-citizens wait . . . The nation which remembered the sailors of the Maine will not forget the civilians of the Lusitania!"[27] Spring-Rice reported to Grey that many major American newspapers berated Germany. He added a quotation from the *New York Herald*, which declared, "The 'Lusitania' was torpedoed without an instants warning. Even the rattlesnake gives warning before striking."[28] In a separate note, the ambassador stated that "[t]he White House was flooded with telegrams and letters saying that the time of yielding was past," and that "public opinion demanded energetic words."[29]

Wilson was under great pressure to respond. House cabled him on May 9 that the United States would probably have to enter the war if Germany did not change its policies. "America has come to the parting of the ways," he asserted, "when she must determine whether she stands for civilized or uncivilized warfare." For House, the war had come to the US doorstep. "We can no longer remain neutral spectators." Days later he added that the president needed to respond quickly or risk diminishing America's stature and that if Wilson declared war, "I hope you will give the world an exhibition of American efficiency that will be a lesson for a century or more." The British public also expressed its desire to see the United States join the fight against Germany. Many Britons could not see how the United States could stand by while Germans killed American civilians. If the United States did not declare war, some newspaper editors hoped that Wilson would at least send Germany a serious message by severing diplomatic relations. If it did not, "[t]here [would] not be enough of American dignity and honor left to cover the coffin in which American rights [were] enclosed."[30]

Despite the country's immediate distress and anger over the *Lusitania*, the president did not act impetuously. When Wilson's private secretary Joseph Tumulty tried to convince him to take action, the president told him that they should not be concerned with the details of the sinking. Wilson told him, "If I pondered over those tragic items that daily appear in the newspapers about the *Lusitania*, I should see red in everything, and I am afraid that when I am called upon to act with reference to this situation I could not be just to anyone. I dare not act unjustly and cannot indulge my own passionate feelings."[31]

Wilson also knew that the American public's emotional fervor would wane and that if he reacted too soon people might question why he did not have more patience. Expressing his position and frustration, the president confided to his new love, Edith Bolling Galt, that he found himself torn between pursuing aggressive and cautious action: "Prudence is an impertinent intruder *this week*, and Wisdom intolerable!"[32] The public wanted Washington to defend it, but this did not mean going to war. Even many pro-British sympathizers viewed the conflict as a European affair and accepted that while tragic, the passengers' deaths were not enough to drag the country into the fight. They praised the president for stating that he was not ready for war.

On the evening of May 10, Wilson stood before a crowd of 15,000 people, including 4,000 recently naturalized citizens, at Convention Hall in Philadelphia and emphasized that the country must stay together and that it could avoid entering the conflict without appearing weak: "My urgent advice to you would be, not only always to think first of America, but also, to think of humanity. You do not love humanity if you seek to divide humanity into jealous camps . . . It was but an historical accident, no doubt, that this great country was called the 'United States'; and yet I am very thankful that it has that word 'united' in its title and the man who seeks to divide man from man, group from group, interest from interest in the United States is striking at its very heart."[33] Wilson regarded America as the leading civilized state of the world and maintained that it should guide other countries into a new era of global harmony: "The example of America must be the example, not merely of peace because it will not fight, but peace because peace is the healing and elevating influence of the world, and strife is not. There is such a thing as a man being too proud to fight. There is such a thing as a nation being so right that it does not need to convince others by force that it is right."[34] Wilson's idealism and distress over the war came through clearly in his speech, and his desire to stay out of the conflict seems to have matched the temperament of the American people. Even Spring-Rice observed that Wilson "certainly attained a greater degree of popularity than has been given anybody since Roosevelt."[35] Wilson's "too proud to fight" speech also revealed the weakness of his "strict accountability" warning to Germany. The president's decision not to fight over the *Lusitania* demonstrated that "strict accountability" held no more weight than the US protest over the British blockade.

In his memoirs, Lansing wrote that the path Wilson chose would have been much different if the *Lusitania* had been an American-owned vessel. "There would," he asserted, "have been no hesitation by the President in severing diplomatic relations and in appealing to Congress to declare a state of war with Germany." While this is uncertain, Lansing did point out that most Americans agreed with Bryan that the passengers took their lives into their own hands when they elected to travel on the British ocean liner, and they supported the president's eventual decision to make a formal protest rather than a rash declaration of war.[36] The result was that in Washington, American statesmen sought a way to make clear their anger and expectations without backing the United States, or Germany for that matter, into a corner.

Bryan's pacifism drove him to great lengths to prevent American intervention. In the aftermath of the sinking, Bryan read an editorial in the

Washington Post that detailed the munitions cargo stored below deck on the *Lusitania.* On board were 4,200 boxes of rifle ammunition and 1,250 cases of shrapnel artillery shells. The newspaper editor suggested that the government should declare that ships carrying contraband could not transport passengers as well. His opinion sat well with the secretary of state. Bryan told Wilson that Germany had the right to "prevent contraband [from] going to the allies" and argued that ships carrying contraband should not carry civilians as a means of discouraging U-boat attacks. The passengers' presence acted as a human shield for the cargo, which placed their lives in danger. "It would be like putting women and children in front of an army," Bryan argued.[37]

Lansing maintained that the United States had to take a stand against Germany. He did not oppose war personally but realized that option was not open to Wilson. Lansing informed Bryan that in his opinion the German warning that Americans should not traverse the war zone did not absolve Berlin of the consequences of violating the "principles of law and humanity." He added that several courses of action were available to the administration. It could demand that Germany accept responsibility for breaking international law and pledge that the next time a U-boat confronted a merchant vessel, it must "ensure the lives of American citizens on the high seas, unless they are traveling on a vessel of belligerent nationality, which is armed or being convoyed by belligerent war craft." If Germany did not comply, the United States might sever diplomatic relations. Such a message, he asserted, would demonstrate that the Wilson administration was not willing to compromise on its policy of strict accountability. As far as he was concerned, it was not a "hostile act" and did not mean that a state of war existed between the countries. His second option was to persuade all neutral powers to send Germany and Great Britain messages complaining that they had both breached international law. While Lansing argued that the letters from neutrals would not replace a protest about the *Lusitania*, they would offer the United States the time necessary to write a protest that had a judicious character.[38]

The German government sent the State Department an official letter of sympathy for the deaths of Americans on the *Lusitania* but defended its actions by claiming that the responsibility for the attack lay with Britain. Arguing just as Lansing had expected, von Jagow claimed that Britain's ships were usually armed and on numerous occasions tried to ram surfaced U-boats. Germany had surmised from the British press reports that the *Lusitania* was armed and regularly carried munitions across the Atlantic. He claimed that the ship contained "5,400 cases of ammunition" and that considering the risks involved, the British "lightheartedly assumed responsibility for human lives on board." Though von Jagow did not state as much in his letter, Germany viewed the *Lusitania* as a naval reserve vessel. The *Lusitania* and its sister ship *Mauretania* were listed in the 1914 edition of *Jane's Fighting Ships* as auxiliary cruisers and their distinctive profile made them easy to recognize. Von Jagow added that despite its sympathy for the loss of life, Germany "can not [*sic*] but regret that Americans felt more inclined to trust English promises rather than pay attention to warnings from the German side."[39]

In consideration of the German letter and the suggestions put forth by Lansing and Bryan, Wilson formulated a draft reply. The president decided that his response to Germany should address the Thrasher case, the *Gulflight*, and the *Lusitania*. According to the president, using submarines to attack unarmed merchant ships went against all "rules of fairness, reason, justice, and humanity." Because U-boats could not give quarter or capture vessels as prizes, they had to abandon crews and passengers to the sea. Therefore, the president declared, he could not condone their use.[40]

Following Lansing's advice, Wilson noted that the United States would not accept the German ambassador's warning to Americans as an "excuse" to carry out submarine attacks and that the United States would still hold Germany accountable for all injuries to US citizens and ships. He then offered Germany an opportunity to disavow the attacks, claiming that his administration "cannot believe that the commanders of the vessels which committed these acts of lawlessness did so under orders from the Imperial German naval authorities or with their approval." He then declared that US citizens had every right to take their ships "wherever their legitimate business calls them upon the high seas" and to do so secure that they were not endangering their lives. When examined together, the two statements suggest that Wilson hoped to give Germany a way to escape a confrontation over the current crisis, yet demonstrate that he would not tolerate any additional injuries to American lives or property—in effect condemning the entire submarine campaign.[41]

In the midst of the crisis, Americans got their first glance at a report by former British ambassador to the United States, Lord James Bryce. The report included a 60-page section enumerating the atrocities Germany had allegedly committed against the Belgian people and a 300-page appendix full of depositions from people who claimed to have witnessed the brutal treatment of civilians. In these 1,200 depositions, Belgian refugees and British soldiers asserted that the German troops had mutilated bodies and bayoneted small children for their amusement. The report also included accounts from diaries taken from dead German soldiers that were purported to describe the execution of civilians accused of shooting at soldiers. Like other forms of propaganda, Wellington House used the Bryce Report to describe, with dramatic flair, the destruction of towns and the deaths of civilians and left it to the public to conclude that German soldiers committed wanton and intentional acts of violence against innocent people. The report had a strong impact on the British people and Allied supporters in the United States; nevertheless, it did not appear to influence American policy toward Germany.[42]

That same day, Wilson and the cabinet met for three hours to discuss their response to Germany. They concluded that the American people were not interested in going to war over the *Lusitania* but that they wanted the administration to let Germany know that it disapproved of its actions. Yet how to place pressure on Germany divided the president and his advisors. All wanted an end to the attacks on merchant vessels, but there was no consensus on policy regarding Americans who entered the war zone. Bryan asserted that because the Germans were angry about Britain's "starving-out policy," it would be futile for the administration to pressure Germany to stop using submarines in retaliation.[43]

The following day, Bryan sent the president a personal letter concerning the draft note stating that he "joined in this document with a heavy heart" because its tenor would destroy America's credibility as a "fair peace maker." The secretary asserted that Wilson's note could divide the American people and might drag the United States into the war. While the administration openly objected to Germany's submarine warfare, it did not charge Britain with any violations over its total blockade, using the American flag on its ships, or loading munitions on vessels full of noncombatants. Bryan apparently feared that the lack of even-handedness would lead Germany to conclude that the United States favored its enemies. He urged the president to "prevent irreparable injury [by] issue[ing] simultaneously a protest against the objectionable conduct of the allies."[44]

Once Lansing edited the draft note for Germany, Bryan returned it to the president. Bryan stressed that Lansing's revision was too harsh and that it included phrases that the Germans might find offensive. Challenging the use of submarines, Lansing had asserted that they could not comply with the "rules of fairness, reason, justice, and humanity, which the civilized world regards as imperative." To Bryan, the change suggested that Germany was uncivilized, and he argued that "[t]here is no use calling names—there is sufficient force in the plain statement."[45]

In a separate communication, Bryan warned that the note to Germany would stir up the American "jingoes" because they might think the message "means war." He feared that such a reaction could affect Germany's response. Therefore, he requested that Wilson send an additional statement to Germany that might soften the blow of the official note. Wilson soon replied that he agreed and that he wanted Bryan's separate note to take the form of a "tip" to the German government.[46] Per Wilson's instructions,

Bryan composed a statement to send to Germany. The second communication was to take the form of a newspaper article and not an official statement from the president. In the message, Bryan declared that the United States expected Germany to respond to Washington's official note "in a spirit of accommodation" that suggested "a desire to reach an agreement."[47]

Bryan showed the note to Lansing, who told the secretary that he was pleased. Unbeknownst to Bryan, however, Lansing was furious. The latter immediately told Secretary of War Lindley Garrison and Tumulty about Bryan's and Wilson's plan. All three men feared that the "tip" would undermine the official *Lusitania* memorandum and signal that the US government had no resolve. That afternoon, Tumulty, accompanied by Post Master General Albert Burleson, met the president in hope of changing his mind. Wilson defended his decision, but Tumulty's and Burleson's arguments that the "tip" would anger the American people and suggest that the United States was weak persuaded him to do so.[48] He sent word to Bryan that the message could not go out at the same time as the official response. Lying to the secretary of state, Wilson said that he had "heard something indirectly" from the American embassy in Berlin that convinced him that he would "lose all chance of bringing Germany to reason" if it regarded the official US note as intended merely to open debate on the issue. Wilson therefore ordered Bryan not to send the "tip" and asserted that they should only send a second note after the official statement "has had its first effect."[49]

Reaffirming his decision to remain steadfast, Wilson also opposed Bryan's subsequent suggestion to bar American passengers from entering the war zone. Bryan learned that a British passenger liner, the *Transylvania*, was carrying Americans and munitions into the war zone. He received a telegram from the heads of several German-American and Irish-American societies suggesting that the US government should ask the British to order the *Transylvania* to put all of the American passengers ashore in the Azores, outside the area patrolled by U-boats. Bryan told the president that the administration should consider this course of action.[50] Wilson disagreed. He asserted the action would suggest that Washington did not think Germany would meet US demands.[51] In a final act of desperation before the official response to the *Lusitania* was sent, Bryan told the president that the last paragraph of the memorandum did not emphasize the government's "friendship" toward Germany. He claimed that Lansing did not think it should stress American amity, and he sought the president's opinion on the matter.[52] Despite Bryan's pleadings, Wilson agreed with Lansing, adding that it already "contains a sufficient tone of sincere friendship."[53]

Wilson rejected Bryan's advice about making a public protest against Britain's blockade at the same time the *Lusitania* note went to Germany, but he was not averse to voicing his concerns to Britain. The difference lay in his approach. The president preferred to handle the situation privately, not through official channels. In allowing House to discuss the blockade with Grey personally, Wilson hoped to keep the subject from weakening his message to Berlin.

The United States had good reason to challenge Britain's policy. As Wilson and his advisors pondered how or even if to respond to German actions, Britain continued stopping American cargoes headed into the war zone and the State Department became inundated with letters complaining about the British Order in Council.[54] Making things worse, Skinner told Bryan that the American embassy was having trouble securing the release of US vessels because the British were "acting almost entirely on suspicions and are very slightly concerned respecting legal rights, or for that matter, their own rules." The British, Skinner claimed, were even detaining cotton shipments with "certificates from British consuls" attesting that the goods were sold before the March 2 deadline.[55] According to Page, by May 20, 134 ships or cargoes had been detained. He told Bryan that cotton made up 33 cases and that, of those, eight reached the prize courts. The main shipments ending up in prize courts were copper, foodstuffs, and machinery, all with suspicious destinations.[56] When Wilson contacted House in early May, he stated that public opinion at home was changing because of "England's delays and many willful interferences in dealing with neutral cargoes." Americans were "listening with more and more acquiescence" to the notion that the United States should stop selling munitions to the Allies if Britain's policy did not change, and Wilson did not think he could reverse this line of thinking.[57]

Grey was well aware of the tension brewing in the United States. On April 16, Spring-Rice wrote Grey that they needed to take more precautions to avoid harming American economic growth. He told the foreign secretary that Bethlehem Steel's stock price had risen in recent weeks. The increase, the ambassador asserted, occurred because of Allied munitions orders, but he argued that it might be a short-lived improvement if British companies wrested control of the orders away from US firms. This "would be a very bad thing for us" because as long as Americans were profiting from the war, Britain would have more influence in the "American commercial and political world."[58]

In a subsequent dispatch, he emphasized the importance of the British market to American companies. He noted that the value of US trade with Germany had dropped from $262,000,000 to $28,000,000 over a one-year period. British imports from the United States, however, had increased by $55,000,000 in the same period. Thus, the US gross domestic product jumped by 8 percent between 1914 and 1915. The reason behind the country's economic growth was simple: The war forced Britain to buy more goods from across the Atlantic. According to a US Department of Commerce report, "British territory is the market for one-half the entire exports from this country."[59]

The British government understood the implications of such data and could see their reliance on America increasing almost daily. In a meeting after the sinking of the *Lusitania*, Prime Minister Henry Asquith noted that he and his ministers agreed, "one thing to fear and avoid is that they [Washington] should be provoked to prohibit the export of munitions of war to us, which would be almost fatal."[60] He did not exaggerate.

By late spring, Britain's want of munitions had reached crisis proportions. In a report sent to Chancellor of the Exchequer David Lloyd George, the War Office Armaments Output Committee noted that one of the reasons Britain could not supply sufficient quantities of munitions to the army was the prewar failure to appreciate how many guns would be needed. The board asserted that the style of warfare also played a role: "Owing to the conditions of siege war, more shells per gun are required than was ever contemplated, or has ever been heard before."[61]

Battlefront demand, however, was not the only reason behind Britain's problems. In addition to labor shortages caused by the enormous number of enlistments in the army at the beginning of the war, munitions manufacture was hindered by trade union agreements that protected workers from overwork. As soon as the war began, many companies asked unions for temporary concessions. These accords, however, were not enough to enable productivity to keep up with demand. Seeing a need for intervention, the government sponsored two conferences to find compromises between labor and management. At these meetings in February and March 1915, the government got unions to consent to the use of some female and unskilled labor as long as it was released once the war ended. The labor and production shortages convinced Lloyd George to call a meeting at which union leaders agreed that workers in war-related industries would not strike, all labor disputes would go to arbitration, and certain policies concerning work conditions would be suspended until the war's end. Such domestic efforts, however, did not alleviate Britain's materiel shortages.[62]

Since the war's outbreak, the British War Office had placed huge orders in the United States for a wide variety of military goods, including hundreds of thousands of bayonets, millions of artillery shells, over 400,000 rifles, and more than 5,000,000 cotton sandbags.[63] Yet the war office was apparently unable to ensure that the supplies reached the army quickly and in large enough quantities to satisfy battlefield demands. Lloyd George later recalled that at the Battle of Aisne in January 1915, the army had only 24 6-inch howitzers, "one-sixteenth the number that were being used against us by the Germans."[64] For June 1915, the military had 1,225 18-pound guns available, requiring 195,000 rounds that month alone. However, the army had a deficit of 75,000 rounds. Of the 24 divisions available for June, only 14 could be fully outfitted.[65]

Statistics for rifles were no better. Every division needed approximately 1.5 million rounds per month, but the expeditionary force as a whole had a "deficiency of 6 ½ million rounds." Lloyd George stated that the two reasons behind the deficiencies were the disorganization of the War Office and the British munitions firms' acceptance of contracts for more than they could produce, especially since some companies were also selling weapons to Russia. He complained that "[w]hen they accepted these Russian contracts they must have known that they had not the faintest chance of executing them in time if they were to deal fairly with British orders."[66] Even Washington was aware of the munitions situation faced by the Allies. House told Wilson that the French needed over ten times as many shells per day than they estimated before the war and that they were firing as many as 150,000 a day during intense battles.[67]

In early May, Sir John French complained that during the Second Battle of Ypres his troops found themselves enveloped in the first German gas attack of the war but could not respond because they lacked enough high explosive shells. Frustrated at the government's failure to rectify the situation, the field marshal leaked similar information to the London *Times*, which published the story on May 14, with the headline "NEED FOR SHELLS: BRITISH ATTACKS CHECKED: LIMITED SUPPLY THE CAUSE." The story sparked a public outcry about the shell shortage that could not be ignored.[68]

Adding to the difficulties faced by His Majesty's government, the Allies could not find a way to break the stalemate. Along with complications on the western front, Russia faced major problems in the east. Tsar Nicholas II's generals tried to take the offensive in March but quickly found themselves in retreat and, like the British and French, without adequate supplies to hold the line. Making matters worse, British, Australian, New Zealand, and French troops were bogged down against stubborn resistance from Turkish forces on the Gallipoli peninsula. The campaign, championed by First Lord of the Admiralty Winston Churchill, was supposed to have been a simple naval operation that would open up a path to Russia and drive the Ottoman Empire from the war. Soon after the campaign began on February 19, however, it became obvious that breaching the defenses was more difficult than first thought. Underwater mines and heavily fortified artillery made the strait impregnable, and after the combined French and British fleet failed to run the Narrows on March 18, the naval command withdrew to a safe distance. Finally, it concluded that ground troops were necessary to take out the enemy's guns. This operation too came to a standstill. By the first week in May, five Allied divisions and the Turkish forces that faced them had entrenched for a drawn-out battle that would last until January 1916 and ultimately end in an Allied failure.[69]

At home many Britons were irritated that the war was not going well, and after the *Lusitania* incident, they argued for taking a harder line against Germany. In the days following the sinking, fear of German gas attacks, zeppelin raids, and the submarine campaign inflamed tempers to the point that rioting broke out around London. Editorials in the London *Morning Post* declared "[t]he sinking of the Lusitania marks the end of the first phase of the war . . . it coincides with . . . a new conviction . . . that the German must be broken in pieces before there can ever again be peace and safety, Germany has lost the right to make peace on terms."[70]

Collectively, the shell shortage, the stalemate in Europe, the debacle at the Dardanelles, and the *Lusitania* sinking shook public confidence in the Asquith government and ultimately provoked a shake-up in the cabinet. Members of the conservative Unionist Party were frustrated with Asquith but could not openly express their opposition without seeming unpatriotic. By May, however, the prime minister's government had not produced the results it had promised in August 1914. Matters became worse on May 15 when Admiral Lord John Fisher, one of the most revered officers in the Royal Navy's history, resigned in disgust at the administration's handling of the Dardanelles operation.[71]

The culmination of events gave the Unionists the opportunity to weaken the Liberal Party's decade-long control of parliament and compelled Asquith to call for the resignations of all cabinet ministers except those in the Foreign Office.[72] In August 1914, members of the major parties had agreed to a political truce to focus on the war effort. A respite, however, was not possible because the conduct of the war challenged the Liberal Party's laissez-faire approach to industrial mobilization and "business as usual" attitude toward civil society. To appease the opposition, Unionist leader Andrew Boner Law was offered the position of Lord Chancellor when Richard Haldane resigned under accusations that he held pro-German sentiment, and Arthur Balfour replaced Churchill when he was forced to stepped down as First Lord of the Admiralty because of the failure of the Dardanelles campaign. Asquith also tapped Lloyd George to head the newly created Ministry of Munitions.[73]

While the decision to establish the first coalition government did not cause any immediate changes in Britain's policy toward neutrals or Germany, Grey was certainly in a fastidious situation. He needed the United States more than ever to supply the munitions, but domestic turmoil made him more cautious about granting concessions to America.

Even before the crisis came to a head, evidence suggests that Grey found it more difficult to compromise and at least on one occasion had to reverse his position. When House returned to London from Berlin, he was optimistic about the possibility of a breakthrough with Germany on the freedom of the seas issue. He wrote Grey on April 12 that German Undersecretary of State Arthur Zimmermann was interested in the idea. House stated that he raised the subject because Britain had suggested it in February: "It was on that subject alone that I awoke sufficient enthusiasm to warrant the hope that in it lies the way to peace." House then told Wilson that "[i]f he [Grey] agrees to this I will write to him, even though I am in London, and have him reply." By creating a paper trail House could send copies of the letters to Germany. He hoped this would provoke a response "and we may have them talking to one another before they realize it."[74]

Unfortunately House did not receive the response he expected. Grey stalled on the issue for almost two weeks before replying. When he responded to House, Grey claimed that he faced opposition in the cabinet and had to reject the offer. Defending the government's position, he informed House that "[i]f Germany means that her commerce is to go free upon the sea in time of war, while she remains free to make war upon other nations at will, it is not a fair proposition." To avoid placing Britain in a poor light, Grey countered with a proposal for a "League of Nations" that might ensure peace after the war: "If on the other hand, Germany would enter after this war some League of Nations where she would give and accept the same security that other nations gave and accepted against war breaking out between them, their expenditures on armament might be reduced and new rules to secure 'freedom of the seas' made. The sea is free in times of peace anyhow."[75]

In enunciating this policy, Grey reversed his posture on freedom of the seas and again found a way to circumvent peace talks. Instead of supporting House's proposal, Grey was able to drag out negotiations once more and take the moral high ground by advocating the formation of a permanent peace organization that could prevent future wars.

One month later, House tried a different course in hope of finding a new route to mediation. The colonel dined with Grey on May 14 and discussed the *Lusitania*. To cajole House, Grey stated that Wilson could not have written a more conciliatory note to Germany and that he recognized that the president had to stand up for American rights or risk the possibility of losing credibility among the "great nations." Grey compared Wilson's predicament to Britain's declaration of war to uphold Belgian neutrality. House and Grey then turned to the blockade. House tried to rekindle interest in Bryan's food-for-submarines deal. After listening to the colonel's pitch, Grey countered that if Germany would also stop using chemical warfare Britain might reconsider allowing food through the blockade.[76] Grey's suggestion interested Wilson. Writing to House, the president wrote that he wanted to know if Grey would face any opposition at home to such a decision and noted that he and House needed to act fast because he thought "things are likely to move rapidly now."[77]

In the meantime, Bryan sought to avoid additional confrontations with Germany. On May 14, he again proposed warning Americans not travel on ships owned by Britain or France.[78] Wilson responded that such a caveat seemed "weak and futile." If the government told Americans not to go into the war zone, Germany might view the action as evidence that the administration was willing to abandon American rights at sea: "To show this sort of weak yielding to threat and danger would only make matters worse." Additionally Wilson reasoned that Americans already knew the risks, and those who planned to travel to Europe would not be dissuaded by a warning.[79]

Undeterred, Bryan again discussed the possibility of sending a letter of protest to Britain concerning its interference with neutral trade. Lansing opposed the idea, arguing that doing so would not change the international situation. In a personal memorandum written on May 3, Lansing asserted that neutral states were unable to depend on precedent from previous wars because the belligerents were not following any precedents and were making up rules as they went along. He wrote, "It is obvious that with the belligerent powers desperate and lawless a neutral government seeking to preserve the commercial rights of its citizens has a well nigh hopeless task." The only practical course the United States could take was to exercise "patience and treat the warring nations as if irresponsible for their acts." He sympathized with them as well adding,

> The trouble is that the stakes in this conflict are so great or are believed by the belligerents to be so great, that everything is subordinated to the one object of destroying their enemies. When a government and people believe that their existence as a nation depends upon their being victorious in a war, can you expect them to weigh carefully the legal rights of neutrals which seem to be obstacles to success? Put yourself in their place. What would you do? . . . We must look at the situation from the standpoint of the participants in the war and not from that of a bystander. The warring nations see red . . . They are desperate.[80]

He surmised that much of the American public felt differently. Lansing concluded that they expected Washington to go on the offensive to protect its interests abroad. He admitted that it was not a complete surprise that merchants who were losing money because of the conflict "should resent bitterly the conduct of the belligerents and should feel that the Government was willfully deaf to their appeals." Yet, he continued, protecting American rights was a difficult task: "They seem to think that all this Government has to do is stiffen its back and peremptorily demand respect for the rights of its citizens, and that the belligerent governments, though they may fume and bluster, will submit rather than have an open breach with the United States." A strong stance would simply exacerbate the situation: "You might as well try to drive with an ox-whip a bull, which has been maddened by the banderilleros and stands in the bullring dripping with blood."[81]

Lansing's private writings emphasize his anxiety over the war's progress and suggest that he thought the Wilson administration was doing everything it could to preserve US neutrality. The counselor wanted to protect American prestige and economic interests and intended to use his interpretation of international law to do so. He discerned, however, that similar to his experience with the Declaration of London, he had limited options available. The best course, he reasoned, was for the United States to work with the belligerents to try to reach a workable arrangement. But he knew that moderation was not a popular position. Lansing lamented, "[I]t is not pleasing to an unthinking public who applaud vigor of language as in accord with national greatness." The country needed to follow an unpopular policy of patience and compromise, a strategy that "under normal conditions would be humiliating and contrary to the dignity of the United States . . . To curb this indignation, to ignore the causes, to remain self-possessed and cool under great provocation—that is the difficult task which a neutral government has to perform, however severe the criticism and from whatever source it may come."[82]

His frustration certainly influenced the draft he composed for Bryan on May 15. It read that on March 15, Britain announced in its Order in Council that the Royal Navy was not to "impose restrictions upon neutral trade more burdensome than those which have been regarded as inevitable when the ports of a belligerent are actually blockaded by the ships of its enemy." Yet in the two months since the declaration, Lansing complained, Britain had interfered in neutral trade beyond what was reasonable. He added that its actions "have become intolerable and can no longer be endured without complaint; and that a continuance of these practices so subversive of neutral rights and so destructive of their enjoyment will invite measures by the Government of the United States, which will restore to American citizens the freedom of the high seas and protect them in the exercise of their just rights." Lansing told Bryan that they needed to issue the statement as soon as possible to demonstrate that the United States did not favor the Allies over Germany: "We have complaints against both. We have already been too complacent with Great Britain in the enforcement of the Order in Council."[83]

Two days later on May 18, Wilson informed House that the United States needed to send Britain a letter of protest over its interference with neutral trade to demonstrate Washington's impartiality and neutrality. Seeing a silver lining, he stated that if Britain stopped interfering with bona fide trade on its own, it would put "Germany alone in the wrong and leave her without any excuse that the opinion of the world could accept."[84] Although the message was evidence of the president's favor toward the Allies, its timing suggests that his main hope was that the note might result in Germany's cessation of its submarine operations.

House told the president that he spoke with Grey the following morning. Apparently gulling House again, the foreign secretary claimed that he would "use all his influence" to promote the shipment of food to neutrals on the continent if Germany agreed to end its submarine attacks on merchant vessels and stop using chemical warfare. House immediately instructed Gerard to tell Germany that its response to Wilson's note should express Germany's willingness to accept such an arrangement. Buying the ruse, House told the president that Grey had agreed to this suggestion only to "conform to our wishes."[85]

Wilson wanted House to keep all proposals made to Germany separate from discussions with Britain: "It seems very important indeed that we should not even seem to be setting off one government against the other or trying by any means resembling a bargain to obtain from either of them a concession of our undoubted rights on the high seas."[86] As far as the president was concerned, relations with Germany and relations with Britain were not connected. Taking this approach, Wilson instructed Bryan not to send the protests to Britain until after Germany responded to the American protest because he did not want Germany to use US negotiations with Britain as leverage in its own discussions with the United States over the *Lusitania*. Berlin, he asserted, should consider the American protest "without regard to anything we mean to say or do in the case of England."[87] While this was an illogical assumption, he apparently thought that keeping them separate would prevent one belligerent from influencing America's negotiations with the other and help to preserve US neutrality.

Wilson's desire to keep discussions with Germany and Britain separate was also evident in the State Department's stance toward continuing negotiations between the British government and American trade advisors as they searched for a compromise over the detention of cotton cargoes. Days after deceiving the president by hinting at a new deal on foodstuffs, Grey sent word to Bryan asserting that Britain was taking steps to alleviate the distress of American cotton merchants who had their cargoes detained.

Grey pointed out that his government had purchased a large amount of the confiscated cotton and was in the process of paying its owners the full price of the shipment. On May 22, Spring-Rice claimed that the Wilson administration appreciated the secretary's note but asserted that it did not want to leave the impression that it was accepting the British restrictions on American trade at the same time it was challenging Germany on the submarine crisis.[88]

Grey took advantage of the situation by cabling Spring-Rice to tell him he should emphasize in the press that the US government was not involved in any talks over the cotton issue. He was to make clear that it was "in no sense a party to this agreement and took no part in the negotiations." Britain did not want to place Wilson in an awkward situation with the American people—or Germany for that matter. Shielding US neutrality further, Grey acknowledged that any arrangement made between British and US representatives would not change the American policy toward the Order in Council.[89] This was an effort to keep from angering the US government in the midst of its biggest crisis so far in the war. By emphasizing to the American public that Britain understood its government's position, Grey was trying to forestall any animosity arising against the Allies and therefore keep the public focused on Germany.

The importance that Britain placed on US public opinion was visible in late May when the Foreign Office deliberated sending the United States a response to its March 30 protest against the Order in Council. On May 26, the American vessel SS *Nebraskan* suffered an unexplained explosion off the coast of Lands End, UK, en route to the United States from Liverpool. The ship did not sink and no one was injured, but the first supposition was that the *Nebraskan* had come under submarine attack.[90] Sir Eyre A. Crowe contended that the department should delay its response to the US protest over the Order in Council until it learned how Wilson's government would respond to the incident.[91] Grey echoed Crowe's suggestion when he gave Spring-Rice a summary of the arguments that the Foreign Office planned to use in its reply to the US note. The foreign secretary claimed that he had "held back his answer in the belief that it would be preferable not to revive controversies between us and the United States about principles at the moment when feeling in America is pre-occupied with the idea of a possible conflict with Germany." He added that if a "fresh wave of anti-German feeling" swept the country, he did not want a British reply to provide a "diversion" for those in America who opposed the Allies.[92] Spring-Rice agreed, asserting that London must avoid any statement that "might be turned against us," and that the Foreign Office reply only after Wilson sent his protest over the *Nebraskan* to Germany.[93] Though the affair came to naught because the cause of the attack was never determined, the last thing Grey wanted to do was reduce the attention focused on Germany or increase that on Britain.

While Britain continued making small gestures to pacify the United States and taking measures to avoid further confrontation, Germany did not. Berlin stubbornly defended the use of submarines. The country's leaders still believed that their blockade could strangle the Allies. Gerard contacted Bryan on May 15 and told him that when he spoke with von Jagow, the latter was not receptive to any deals that might require that it alter its naval policy. Gerard reported that von Jagow laughed and commented, "Right of free travel on the seas, why not free travel on land in war territory?" The German foreign secretary then noted that his government would have to formulate a response, but did not intimate that Berlin would stop using submarine warfare.[94]

Ten days later, House sent word to Wilson that Germany refused the foodstuffs proposal because, according to von Jagow, it did not need any more food. This rebuff annoyed House and convinced him that Germany had lied with its February declaration. If Germany did not need food, he concluded, the rejection of his proposition undercut its justification for using U-boats.[95] Von Jagow's comment that Germany did not need food is significant because it helps to explain why the Wilson administration did not view the British blockade with the same disgust as it did the German submarine campaign. Regardless of whether or not the Royal Navy's cordon was actually starving the German people, Wilson apparently did not conclude it was creating a humanitarian crisis in 1915.

To avoid an outright refusal of the foodstuffs proposal, Germany countered by increasing its demands on Britain. Gerard informed the State Department that Germany claimed it would end the submarine campaign if Britain allowed all raw materials that did not "directly enter the manufacture of munitions" to cross the blockade line. Irritated, Wilson told Bryan that he thought the demands were "manifestly impossible to acceptance by England . . . [I]t looks like we are again in a blind alley."[96]

On May 28, Germany sent its official reply to the American note of May 13 concerning the submarine attacks on merchant and neutral vessels. Germany pledged that it would examine the cases of the *Cushing* and *Gulflight* closer and accept responsibility if evidence proved that its navy had made mistakes. As for the British-owned *Falaba* and *Lusitania*, Berlin claimed that evidence suggested that its submarine captains had acted appropriately. Focusing on the *Lusitania*, von Jagow argued that Germany still suspected that the ship was armed and carried munitions. Therefore his countrymen believed that the U-boat was justified in its attack.[97]

Observing the situation from Washington, Spring-Rice told Grey he presumed the Wilson administration feared that Germany might not realize there were "limits to its patience and that it can be provoked too far." Wilson, he stated, continued to weigh public opinion heavily and was "naturally anxious not to be either in front or behind when the public opinion is on the move." Interpreting popular sentiment, Spring-Rice added that despite the German answer on May 28, the tension over the *Lusitania* was declining because Americans preferred to focus on their own economic prosperity and "profit as far as possible by the peace which still prevails on this continent."[98] Additionally he sensed fear within the administration that going to war might tear the country apart. Spring-Rice claimed that many Americans did not trust people of German descent and wondered how German-Americans would react if the government severed relations or went to war. German propaganda and continued loss of American property and lives had, he wrote, "created a situation which is in the highest degree embarrassing."[99] Spring-Rice deduced that the United States would not retaliate over the *Lusitania*. Describing the mood of the population, he stated that "what the country most ardently desires is peace; only gradually could change take place, and the best judges doubt if on the present case, unless new incidents occur, the country would be willing to take any action likely to lead to war."[100]

In this charged atmosphere the US government formulated their responses. On June 2, Wilson asked Bryan for his and Lansing's opinions on the German letter of May 28. He specifically wanted to clarify that the *Falaba*'s attempt to escape did not justify the German U-boat commander's decision to attack without consideration for the safety of the ship's passengers, and he wanted to know if there was a precedent in international law for announcing the existence of a "danger zone" that "neutral vessels enter it at their own risk."[101]

Privately Lansing considered the submarine crisis an affront to his country's national honor and that declaring war was a viable response. He seemed exacerbated that the American public appeared to concede the issue to Germany. Americans, he thought, were becoming too materialistic and were placing economic gain before national honor and patriotism: "Has the blood of patriotism ceased to throb in American veins? Have our eyes grown dim to the glory which has illuminated the past history of the Republic?"[102] When asked for his opinions, however, Lansing kept his views to himself. Instead he told Bryan that Germany was attempting to foment a debate over the "facts and [was] avoiding the questions of the principles involved." When responding to Germany, the government should refuse to discuss specific details until Berlin acknowledged American rights at sea: The "question of liability depends primarily on the principles applicable to the cases which have arisen." Lansing also noted that the German note lacked any "friendly sentiment for the United States" and that Berlin demonstrated that it had no interest in changing its policy. Therefore, he argued, any response from the administration should avoid any "friendly expressions."[103]

Bryan warned Wilson against issuing a hasty reply. To pacify the situation he claimed that the German letter was cordial and that there was no "desire on either side for war." And unlike Lansing, he argued that the US answer should address the facts of the specific case and not larger issues of neutral rights.[104] Wilson responded that the United States needed to reply promptly to drive home to Germany that the crisis was at a critical point. He had no faith that the German government would cease its submarine attacks; they "show[ed] not the least inclination or purpose to change their methods even pending this interchange of views."[105] Yet it seems that he understood how important taking a strong stand was to the American public and the country's prestige.

Bryan tried again the next day to diffuse the issue. In a lengthy letter to the president he concluded that the United States should accept Germany's May 28 response and, when possible, the government should settle its claims through arbitration. He pointed out that America and Germany were parties to treaties that "committed us to the doctrine of investigation in *all cases* [Bryan's italics] . . . [W]e could not consistently refuse to apply this document to all questions that may arise between us." The treaties, he argued, offered the administration an "excuse" to arbitrate and avoid the risk of further damaging its relations with Germany. He also reiterated his conviction that the government should warn Americans not to travel on ships that carried munitions to Europe. Bryan compared such an action to a city notifying its citizens to stay indoors during a riot. The city, he argued, had the responsibility to not only end the violence but also "restrain citizens from the exercise of their rights in order to prevent injuries that might otherwise be inflicted unintentionally." He reminded Wilson that the administration had already advised Americans to leave Mexico after the Tampico affair in 1914 and offered to pay for their trip to the United States if they could not afford the passage.[106]

The split between Wilson and Bryan widened as the crisis continued and neither could find common ground. According to his wife, Mary Bryan, the secretary dreaded cabinet meetings because he came away anxious and dejected. "Mary, what does the President mean! *Why* can't he see that by keeping open the way to mediation and arbitration, he has an opportunity to do the greatest work man can do! I cannot understand his attitude."[107]

Despite continued resistance from Wilson, Bryan did not stop proposing ideas "necessary to insure us against war with Germany." When he read the second draft of the American response to Germany's May 28 letter he told Wilson that it could provoke a showdown between the two governments and pressed the president to reconsider arbitration as a means of ending the quandary. The government, Bryan said, should also send a letter of protest to Britain before replying to Germany. Additionally Bryan pleaded with the president to reconsider arbitration of American claims against Germany and to "prevent passenger ships from carrying ammunition." The secretary then warned that if the administration did not consider these suggestions, "the note as you outlined it at the cabinet meeting would be likely to cause a rupture of diplomatic relations and this might rush us into war in spite of anything we could do."[108]

Wilson, however, had made up his mind. Weeks earlier, he received a message from House that may have reinforced his decision to focus American pressure on Germany. The colonel cautioned Wilson that protesting against Britain might damage US relations with the Allies: "We are bound up more or less in their success, and I do not think we should do anything that can possibly be avoided to alienate the good feeling that they now have for us." Stressing America's future role in world affairs, he added, "If we lost their good will we will not be able to figure at all in peace negotiations, and we will be sacrificing too much in order to maintain all our commercial rights."[109] House's advice dovetailed with Wilson's views of the affair and his private sympathy toward the Allies. In accepting House's guidance, Wilson deliberately started down a road that would draw him firmly into the British camp.

Upon reading Bryan's last plea, Wilson immediately penned a message that would sever both the working and personal relationships between the president and his secretary of state. Trying to soften his rejection of Bryan's proposals, Wilson stated, "I hope that you realize how hard it goes with me to differ with you in judgment about such grave matters as we are now handling. You always have such weight of reason, as well as such high motives, behind what you urge that it is with deep misgiving that I turn away from what you press on me." He told Bryan that he would try to find a "legal" way to prevent Americans from traveling on ships carrying weapons but asserted that sending Britain an official complaint before Germany received the US protest would undermine the administration's position. The president then said that he made some changes to the note that he hoped would satisfy Bryan, but the changes were in no manner what the great commoner had desired.[110]

Bryan concluded that the time had come to resign. The secretary had held on as long as he could, fighting to keep the country from stumbling into the European conflict, but the president's approach to the second *Lusitania* note was more than he could endure. On the afternoon of June 5, Bryan told Secretary of the Treasury William McAdoo he regarded it as his duty to resign—not for the president's sake but for the American people and his own conscience. He admitted that the decision might ruin his political career but that he had to uphold his convictions: "[I]t is after all, merely the sacrifice that one must not hesitate to make to serve his God and his country." McAdoo could not convince him to change his mind.[111]

After his conversation with Bryan, McAdoo went to see the president. His news did not come as a surprise to Wilson. The president simply replied that he hoped Bryan would stay on, not because of any regard for his advice but because he did not want Germany to conclude that the government was divided over policy. Nevertheless Bryan's resignation concerned him enough to confide to Galt, who wrote Wilson that night that she was happy and added that it would be a "blessing to get rid of him."[112]

The following Monday, after sitting quietly through one final cabinet meeting, Bryan pulled the president aside and told him of his intention to resign. Wilson made an insincere request that Bryan reconsider, but after a continued and increasingly heated debate in which neither would back down, Bryan accurately declared, "Colonel House has been Secretary of State, not I, and I have never held your full confidence."[113]

The final version of the US note to Germany went out on June 9 to Gerard. In it the administration expressed it was pleased that Germany acknowledged its responsibility to "meet its liability" for attacking neutral vessels. Wilson and Lansing took a harsher tone concerning the *Lusitania*. They argued that Germany's defense based on the ship's cargo of munitions was "irrelevant to the question of the legality of the methods used by the German naval authorities in sinking the vessel." The "principles of humanity . . . throw into the background any special circumstances of detail that may be thought to affect the cases." The US focused on the loss of civilian life in the attack, arguing that the *Lusitania* carried "more than a thousand souls who had no part or lot in the conduct of the war . . . were sent to their death in circumstances unparalleled in modern warfare." The note condemned Germany's actions and argued that the United States was "contending for nothing less high and sacred than the rights of humanity, which every government honors itself in respecting and which no Government is justified in resigning on behalf of those under its care and authority."[114]

They concluded the message by stating that America expected Germany to satisfy all the US claims concerning the loss of life and violation of neutrality. Additionally Wilson and Lansing stressed that Americans had the right to travel on neutral and belligerent merchant ships and that it was Germany's responsibility to ensure the safety of noncombatants on "unresisting merchantmen." They then demanded that U-boats had to "take sufficient precaution to ascertain whether a suspected merchantman is in fact of belligerent nationality or is in fact carrying contraband of war under a neutral flag." In the final sentence, Wilson and his new Acting Secretary of State Lansing stressed that "[t]he Government of the United States therefore deems it reasonable to expect that the Imperial German Government will adopt measures necessary to put these principles into practice in respect of the safeguarding of American lives and American ships, and asks for assurances that this will be done."[115]

The Wilson administration viewed the sinking of the *Lusitania* and the death of American citizens as crimes against humanity, yet they were not enough to go to war. Instead Wilson addressed the submarine crisis by formally protesting Germany's actions. Doing so demonstrates the limits of "strict accountability" and that it held no more weight than US protests over Allied interference with trade. Nevertheless he did want Germany to end its submarine campaign and decided to complain about the matter prior to addressing the British blockade in the hope of maintaining pressure on Berlin. Sending protests at different times was not a violation of neutrality, and he apparently did not think his approach constituted open support for the Allies.

Despite the protests, Wilson's outlook on the war and America's role in it was changing. Across the Atlantic, House's mission had foundered. Revisionist historian Charles Tansill asserted that House had "badly bungled an excellent opportunity for world peace."[116] When examining House's conversations with German and British leaders, it is clear that there really was no chance for success. Nevertheless House's mission did fail because he accepted Grey's assessment of the war. The main outcome of his European trip was the further deterioration of Germany's reputation in the minds of House and Wilson. The combined effects of the rapidly growing economic ties to Britain, the German U-boat attacks, and the outcome of House's mission would ultimately convince the president that he needed to take an active and partisan role in the conflict; and in the months that followed the second *Lusitania* note, he and his advisors began a deliberate drift away from neutrality.

7

"The Shadow of War"

June 1915–August 1915

Shall we ever get out of the labyrinth made for us all by this German 'frightfulness'?

—Wilson to Edith Galt, September 6, 1915[1]

In the first 11 months of the war, Wilson repeatedly placed US neutrality in question. Yet during that period his actions did not violate the letter of the law. By the summer of 1915, the Wilson administration began an important and intentional shift in its approach to the belligerents. After Secretary of State William Jennings Bryan's resignation, hawkish policy makers dominated the administration, and Wilson permitted his pro-British leanings to influence his policies. He concluded that American economic and political development depended on a healthy Anglo-American friendship. Britain also understood the significant contribution the United States would make to an Allied victory. By late 1915, Britain had almost depleted its cash reserves and could not raise further capital from domestic sources. The quandary forced Britain to seek loans in the United States in order to continue purchasing vital war materiel. At the same time, the ongoing submarine crisis convinced the president and his advisors that Germany was unwilling to negotiate a resolution. In this volatile environment, the British and US governments came together in the hope of protecting their financial and ideological interests.

Bryan's resignation brought about a wide mix of reactions. British Ambassador Cecil Spring-Rice asserted that Bryan's decision was good for the British war effort. With Bryan out of the way, the United States might get in line behind the Allies. Spring-Rice did, however, fear that his resignation might temporarily have a negative effect since Bryan would "give a visible head to the 'long-haired men and short-haired women' who are agitating this country for peace, prohibition, woman suffrage and the prohibition of the export of arms." In the ambassador's opinion, the former secretary was going to become an outspoken leader for the peace movement and the

German-Americans who "accepted him as a Heaven-born leader."[2] Spring-Rice later wrote that Bryan's resignation would aid the peace party's propaganda against the war. His "motives were perfectly honest, but the result of what he has done had been to give the effect of international treason to the President."[3] Even Wilson privately denounced Bryan's resignation as a "desertion."[4] Colonel Edward House, on the other hand, saw the great commoner's exit as a boon for the United States and Allies alike. In a letter to British Foreign Secretary Edward Grey, House said that US involvement in the war was "inevitable unless Germany changes her policy in regard to submarine warfare" and that with Bryan gone, America was much closer to entering the fray.[5]

War was still in the distant future for the United States, but the colonel predicted correctly that the government would begin to actively support the Allies. With Bryan gone, there was no one to offer Wilson a cautious perspective that might counterbalance the viewpoints taken by House. The president and House discussed several individuals to appoint as secretary of state. They wanted someone who would not challenge Wilson's policies, and on June 16, House advised the president that he should consider State Department Counselor Robert Lansing. Wilson's first impression of Lansing was that he was not a "big enough man" for the job and that he lacked the necessary initiative. For House, this was a positive attribute of Lansing because he was "a man with not too many ideas of his own and one that will be guided entirely by you."[6]

The president eventually agreed with House that Lansing was a good choice. According to House, Wilson was his own secretary and "Lansing would not be troublesome by obtruding or injecting his own views." Assuring the president that Bryan's departure was for the good, the colonel added that Bryan "had never done any serious work in his life; that he was essentially a talker." Finally he asked Wilson if he should brief Lansing on his recent European mission, to which the president responded "No." Lansing should only know "enough to get him to work in harmony with us."[7] Wilson was looking for a sycophant who could take care of public diplomacy. In Lansing, he thought he had found his man.

Even before Wilson officially selected him to be the new secretary of state, Lansing was hard at work tightening the relationship between the United States and Great Britain. In June, the Foreign Office was still debating over when to reply to the American April 2 note. On the evening of June 10, Grey notified Spring-Rice that Britain's reply was almost ready; however, he sought advice on the matter before he sent it to Washington.[8] The ambassador replied that the dispatch should be postponed until a later date, arguing that at the moment it might generate a "dangerous discussion and crisis" in the United States.[9]

On June 12, Lansing learned from American Ambassador Walter Hines Page that Britain had formulated an answer but planned to send the official reply after tension between the United States and Germany subsided. After reading Page's summation of the proposed British answer, Lansing told the president that "from the confidential information obtained here" the note defended London's retaliatory blockade. If his information was correct, he feared that the British response would complicate the situation with Germany. Thus he too wanted the British to delay publication of their reply. Consequently, he sent a telegram to Page instructing him to tell Grey not to send the message unless it supported the US position.[10]

In a meeting with Lansing on June 11, Spring-Rice stated that Britain had to respond but stressed that he did not want to trigger a problem between the governments.[11] After hearing back from Spring-Rice, Grey decided to send a draft of the British reply unofficially and have the ambassador talk to Lansing in private. By doing so, Grey hoped to eliminate the need for an immediate public notice. Private talks would also allow both parties involved to agree on the appropriate time to send an official note to the United States.[12]

Replacing Bryan with Lansing was not the only reason that the Wilson administration dropped any pretense of neutrality. Arguably one of the most important influences was House's assessment of his unsuccessful trip to Europe. When House returned from his mission, he blamed all of his failures on German stubbornness and militarism. On the same day he recommended Lansing's appointment, the colonel told the president that the stalemate on the battlefield had decreased Germany's interest in making peace. He maintained that the sinking of the *Lusitania* and Germany's use of chemical warfare made any discussion on freedom of the seas or the "formation of a peace covenant" difficult. As a result, he blamed Berlin for ruining the chance for mediation. House inferred that Germany had internal problems as well. Tension between the German Foreign Office and the navy prevented any real progress. Admiral Alfred von Tirpitz, House surmised, was determined to continue submarine warfare and leave the diplomats to justify the "'unfortunate incidents' as best they may." House then told the president that German actions would eventually force the United States into the war and speculated that American participation would bring the conflict to a quick end. He argued that joining the Allies would allow the administration to play a vital role in "aid[ing] the other great democracies in turning the world into the right paths."[13]

House's accusation that Germany was the barrier to peace had a serious effect on the president's thinking and Wilson began taking actions that were clearly unneutral. In the summer of 1915, the administration was dealing with three major international issues: the continuing cotton crisis, the ongoing disputes with Germany over the use of submarines, and Britain's need for loans. Wilson's and his advisors' response to each demonstrated that they had moved away from neutrality. Moreover, Wilson's letters and the actions he took in the late summer of 1915 prove that he understood that his decisions had ended the country's role as a spectator.

During the *Lusitania* crisis, Wilson assumed that the American people still did not want to go to war, and he made an effort to continue US-German relations. In his second *Lusitania* note, he dropped the demand for the cessation of submarine warfare. When Germany responded on July 8, the president again pondered how to reply as delicately as possible. Foreign Minister Gottlieb von Jagow had once more justified the attack, claiming that had the U-boat surfaced, the liner would certainly have rammed it. He also offered a compromise by asserting that Berlin would instruct submarine commanders "to permit the free and safe passage of such passenger steamers when made recognizable by special markings and [when Germany was] notified a reasonable time in advance."[14] Numerous American newspapers quickly denounced the note, claiming that it did not satisfy Washington's demands. Despite von Jagow's defense of the attack, however, the country was apparently not ready to end discussions with Berlin. Many people still preferred a peaceful solution to the crisis. In an editorial to the *Chicago Tribune*, a concerned writer declared that the government should act carefully and avoid allowing the affair to spin out of control: "All we have to do is accept [the] present conditions, keep whatever opinion we wish to hold regarding the violations of law and humanity, and preserve not all our rights but a practical working application of them."[15] When Wilson sat down to begin drafting a new note to Germany, he certainly kept public opinion in mind.

The president also weighed how his response would influence the US reputation among the belligerents and the trustworthiness of Berlin's word. Weeks before, on June 6, Grey sent House a note warning that "the desire of the people of the United States to keep out of the war with Germany may lead to burying the Lusitania issue inconclusively." The foreign secretary warned that such an occurrence could be detrimental to Washington's reputation. Germany and the Allies, he claimed, would "disregard . . . American influence in the future and the tendency will be to discount it."[16] Wilson took this specious argument to heart, writing House days later that Grey's comments carried weight.[17] House was also beguiled by Grey's note and told the president that any "inalienable rights" conceded to Germany might be perceived as a sign of weakness. Reminding the president of von Jagow's comment that Germany had plenty of food available, House claimed Germany acted fraudulently when it claimed the British blockade was starving the German people. The colonel also argued that Germany had declined America's suggestion that Britain should allow the safe passage of foodstuffs to Germany in exchange for an end to the submarine campaign. In turning down the offer, he concluded, Germany had either lied or demonstrated its intransigence. Either way, the colonel regarded the Imperial Government as untrustworthy.[18]

After examining Germany's July 8 reply Wilson asserted that the United States could not acquiesce to von Jagow's suggestion regarding the transit of passenger liners into the war zone. He also expressed frustration with the American people, whose seemingly conflicting demands for both peace and a forceful reply to Germany made an answer very difficult. The "[two] things," he declared, "are plain to me, in themselves inconsistent." Nevertheless, Wilson reasoned that his administration's response should meet the public's desire for an end to the crisis without making an "unfriendly issue inevitable." In other words, he sought to construct a letter that included a definitive solution yet avoided a war with Germany.[19]

Before offering his views on the issue, Lansing read a report from US Ambassador James Gerard that offered him a perspective on German thinking. The ambassador noted that Germany was under the control of the military and that a "sort of junta" including von Jagow, von Tirpitz, Admiral Georg von Muller, Vice Admiral Paul Behncke, Chief of the Imperial German General Staff Erich von Falkenhayn, and Emperor Wilhelm II made all the important decisions. Gerard also said that the German people still envisioned a victory: "As to Germany's war methods, they have the full approval of the people; the sinking of the *Lusitania* was universally approved, and even men like [Arthur] Von Gwinner, head of the German Bank, say they will treat the *Mauretania* in the same way if she comes out." The ambassador speculated that most people in Germany wanted to keep Belgium: "They say the sacrifices of the war demand compensation . . . People in Government circles say that to give up Belgium would be to invite revolution and the expulsion of the Hohenzollerns. The whole German people is dangerously mad."[20]

Gerard's message must have influenced Lansing's impression of the July 8 German note. The United States, he informed Wilson, should not take offense to its language because it was written for "home consumption." Nevertheless Lansing agreed with the president that replying would be difficult because "[w]e are to an extent bound to respond to a similar chord in this country." He shared the president's perception that most Americans did not want war but wanted the government to stand strong against Germany and force it to "submit to our demands." Fulfilling such demands would be "nigh impossible"; however, he asserted that the government had to consider public opinion when drafting the next note to Germany.[21]

Lansing told Wilson the administration should not compromise until the "principles" involved were addressed, including a reasonable resolution of the *Lusitania* affair. Lansing emphasized that the State Department needed to show the American people and Germany the government's resolve to defend US interests. He also explained that while he wanted to seem steadfast in protecting American interests, he realized that the United States would have to bend to avoid war. The secretary acknowledged that "the demands we make will be the most difficult part of the note." Expressing his unease, he pondered the question, "Is it possible to be firm and at the same time to compromise?"[22]

Lansing sent Wilson his first draft of the answer to Germany on the evening of July 16. He proposed stating that the United States found Germany's July 8 note "unsatisfactory" because it did not contain an acceptable resolution to the *Lusitania* affair or offer to cease submarine warfare. Lansing mentioned that Berlin must "offer reparation for the wrong done to citizens of the United States." Only then could the United States consider any agreement between the two countries.[23]

Finding it too bellicose, Wilson required a second draft. In the new version Lansing eliminated specific demands (such as requiring reparations before any compromise could take place) but stressed that Germany must recognize the principles of freedom of the seas for neutrals. One major addition to the second draft was his acknowledgement that German submarine officers had restrained themselves in the months following the sinking of the *Lusitania*. He asserted that this was evidence that Berlin found a way to use submarine warfare without endangering neutrals.[24] Lansing concluded that if Germany continued infringing on American neutrality, it would be responsible "for the inevitable consequences," and that the United States would take whatever "steps necessary" to protect its rights. Wilson told Lansing that he liked most of the new note but regarded the last paragraph as too harsh. The president argued that it seemed like an "ultimatum" and added, "I do not think that we need [to] add a *sting*." When they completed the final draft, Lansing immediately telegraphed a copy to Gerard for the German government.[25]

Using a more appeasing tone and trying to avoid an additional confrontation with Berlin indicates that Wilson sought to avoid going to war with Germany; yet by mid-1915, the idea of maintaining a balanced approach to the belligerents had lost its grip on the president. Up to that point, he had hoped for an Allied victory but apparently believed that he should not do anything that might tip the balance at the expense of what he considered America's neutral position. By August, confrontations with Germany and closer economic and political ties to Britain convinced Wilson to reverse a number of his previous policies.[26]

On July 14, the day after Wilson received the German note, House again approached the president about strengthening the US armed forces. The colonel claimed Germany respected martial power and viewed anything else as weakness. He wrote Wilson, arguing, "I wonder whether the time has not come for us to put our country in a position of security . . . If war comes with Germany, it will be because of our unpreparedness and her belief that we are more or less impotent to do her harm."[27] This time, the president was more receptive. Wilson informed Secretary of War Lindley Garrison and Secretary of the Navy Josephus Daniels that he wanted to increase the size of the military. He instructed them to provide information he could use in a speech to Congress about buttressing US security. As he stated to Daniels, "[I]t should be a programme planned for a consistent and progressive development of this great defensive arm of the nation, and should be of such a kind as to command itself to every patriotic and practical man."[28]

After the sinking of the *Lusitania*, the preparedness movement gained strength and the president assumed that a majority of Americans supported a stronger military force. His reaction to international events—including the failure of House's mission and the *Lusitania*—suggests he thought the only way to convince the German government to respect US rights was from a position of power.[29]

At the same time that Germany's standing with Wilson sank, Britain became less willing to make major concessions to American demands and focused on tightening the blockade. On June 11, Grey's private secretary, Eric Drummond, told the British secretary of state for India Lord Robert Crewe that Spring-Rice thought the United States might try a new proposal to lift the prohibition on food. Drummond urged the cabinet to give the United States a definitive answer. The cabinet should decide whether to "relax the restrictions" against Germany in return for an end to submarine attacks on merchant vessels, placing mines at sea, and using gas warfare. Grey had already mentioned to House that the cabinet would entertain the proposition, but as Crewe put it, the secretary learned that Germany had "turned down" the offer, stating it did not need food. Drummond told Crewe that he wanted the American people to know that Britain was willing to discuss the accord. This, Drummond added, might increase American support: "It seems worth consideration whether some such formal offer ought not be made to the United States, in order to put ourselves right with public opinion there."[30]

In a letter to Crewe, Grey stated that under the circumstances, such a proposal would increase tension between Washington and Berlin. "We shall retain and probably improve the good will and the advantageous position which we hold in the United States." The alternative was to maintain an "inflexible attitude" and "face the consequence of possible trouble with the United States." The cabinet disagreed, concluding that harming Germany outweighed the risk of problems with America.[31]

In his memoirs, Winston Churchill claimed that the submarines were only a minor nuisance to British shipping in 1915. He asserted that the admiralty actually thought Germany's February pronouncement would aid Britain and its enforcement of the blockade: "We were sure that the German declaration and the inevitable accidents to neutrals arising out of it would offend and perhaps embroil the United States . . . We looked forward to a sensible abatement of the pressure which the American Government was putting upon us to relax our system of blockade."[32]

To justify the cabinet's opposition to the US proposal, Grey suggested that Britain should argue the March 11 Order in Council had originated as a "measure of reprisal against the illegal warfare on merchant shipping" and that the impact of the cordon was slow in coming. Grey then exaggerated further, arguing that the submarine attacks had had an immediate impact on Allied shipping. He concluded that "it is accordingly unreasonable to expect His Majesty's Government to acquiesce in this destruction of British life and wealth . . . almost before the enemy has commenced to feel its effects."[33]

In addition to rejecting the foreign secretary's foodstuffs proposal, the cabinet wanted to tighten its economic warfare against Germany by eliminating certain loopholes left open for neutral trade. The challenge for Grey was to do so without arousing American ire.[34]

In late June, he sent Page a letter and asked to have it printed in US newspapers. It defended the Royal Navy's detention of American vessels. London claimed that it had taken numerous steps to minimize interference with neutral shipping; nevertheless, it received many complaints from Page "as to the particular hardships alleged to have been wrongly inflicted on American trade and shipping." Grey asserted that Britain had fairly handled American cotton and noted that his country continued to purchase bales in order to prevent financial injury to merchants. He claimed that the Board of Trade had already bought £450,000 worth of cotton since the beginning of the war and that it intended to pay for more as quickly as ownership of the cargoes could be confirmed. Of the 27 ships still detained by the British, only eight had cotton on board, all of which the government had agreed to purchase. Grey also emphasized that three months had passed since the issuance of the March 11 Order in Council, and he deemed this a sufficient amount of time for business contracted before March 1 with Germany to have been transacted. Yet his office still received requests from Page asking that American companies be allowed to continue shipping goods to Germany after June 15 as long as they were purchased before

March. Again Grey stressed that London had deferred to the United States by allowing such transactions to take place at all and that Britain would still "give special concessions to cases presented to them and involving particular hardships."[35]

If Grey hoped the public notice would forestall American protests, he quickly found otherwise. On June 22, Lansing received word from the US consul-general in London, Robert Skinner, that despite British claims that it would limit interference with American trade, the Royal Navy had seized a number of cargoes shipped under the "so-called cotton agreement." Making matters worse, Skinner accused Britain of purchasing the American goods and then selling them to the "same destinations from which our own trading ships are excluded."[36] Skinner informed the secretary that Britain exported nearly 500,000 more bales of cotton in 1915 than in 1914, including 376,263 bales shipped to Holland and Sweden, an increase of over 340,000 compared to the previous year.[37] Weeks later, Lansing received a complaint from Morris Stern, the president of the Galveston Commercial Association, which stressed that Britain's seizure of US cotton harmed US merchants. He wrote that there was a "large surplus" of cotton in the United States and that shippers needed access to as many international markets as possible. If companies could not sell cotton overseas, the price of the commodity would "probably again be depressed below the cost of production as [it was] last year when the largest part of the crop was out of the hands of the farmer before the cotton market even partially recovered."[38] Such protests prompted Lansing to instruct Page to tell the British "unofficially" that the United States opposed their decision to detain cotton that it thought was destined for Germany. Lansing asserted that public discontent over British policy was on the rise and stressed that it might reach a point where finding a solution to the cotton issue could become impossible.[39] When the ambassador met Grey days later, the latter complained: "It was difficult to see how we could satisfy the United States, unless we threw up the sponge altogether, and gave up any attempt to prohibit any quantities of goods of all kinds reaching Germany through neutral countries."[40] Grey told Page that Britain would not end its blockade of the European coast and that the government refused to permit "unrestricted American trade" with neutral countries. In his opinion, Britain might as well abandon the cordon all together.[41]

In the meantime, after reading an article in the London *Times*, Assisstant Undersecretary of State Eyre Crowe asserted that Britain needed to send its reply to the April 2 US note quickly. He argued that "[the] Americans are exploiting the position in which they are placed by their ability to pretend that they do not know our views." Crowe argued that if Britain published its position, Washington would have a harder time making its case against London: "Our answer would largely take the wind out of their sails."[42]

At the request of the cabinet, Grey formulated two different ways that Britain could approach the United States concerning the blockade. In the first, Grey suggested that the government continue following the March 11 Order in Council; however, he noted that the result "will lead to a deadlock; protests from the United States about particular cases, such as the 'Neches,' will accumulate; and the attitude of the United States towards us will become increasingly disagreeable." The alternative was to "abandon our Order in Council . . . rather than argue with the United States and have a difference of opinion with them." Grey claimed that if Britain adopted this approach, it could use existing laws related to "contraband and continuous voyage," rules accepted by the United States during the American Civil War. The drawback of such a policy was that Britain would "abandon at a stroke all restriction upon the export trade of Germany to neutral ports." In the end, the cabinet decided that it had to maintain economic pressure on Germany even if doing so risked a confrontation with the United States.[43]

When Grey penned his July 23 message to Washington he simply defended Britain's position. He argued that in light of German atrocities, including the use of poison gas and the sinking of the *Lusitania*, Britain was justified in using any method at its disposal to survive. He also supported the naval blockade by arguing that during the American Civil War, Washington had found itself in a similar position. The US Navy had cordoned off the southern coastline and had intercepted shipments to Mexico, destined ultimately to the southern states. In response to the White House's comments about the *Peterhoff* (see Chapter 5), Grey stated that the Allies now acted in the same manner as had the United States: "Your Excellency will no doubt remember how, in order to meet this new difficulty, the old principles relating to contraband and blockade were developed and the doctrine of continuous voyage was applied and enforced under which goods destined for enemy territory were intercepted before they reached the neutral ports from which they were reexported." Grey argued that the neutral states next to Germany constituted an analogous situation. Because of the network of rail lines connecting neutrals like the Netherlands to Germany, shipping goods to such ports was practically the same as sending them directly to Britain's enemy.[44]

Regardless of the letter's assertiveness, Spring-Rice told Grey in early August that it was well received by the American public: using precedents from the American Civil War improved Britain's standing in the United States. The public, he noted, was "most quick to resent anything which recalls to them the argument advanced in a recent German note, that changed conditions of warfare require a new application of the principles of international law." The note, he claimed, persuaded many Americans that Britain was following the rules and Germany was not.[45]

Grey hoped the communications would demonstrate that within reason, Britain was doing everything it could to protect American property. Nonetheless he knew that at the same time his government needed to do the opposite. Germany used American cotton in its arms manufacturing process, and the British government was compelled to stop the trade. When the March 11 Order in Council was published, many Britons were not satisfied because it did not make cotton absolute contraband. A number of chemists in England stressed in a letter to Lord John Fletcher Moulton, head of the Explosives Supply Department in the War Office, that Germany needed cotton for its munitions industry. As long as Germany had access to US cotton, they asserted, it could continue the war.[46]

By late summer, the cabinet reconsidered its decision to leave the southern commodity on the free list. The Foreign Office claimed that the government had successfully dealt with the issue of cotton shipments reaching Germany by using the blockade and buying most of the cotton sold by American merchants. The problem, however, was that such measures had not stopped the US government or cotton dealers from protesting London's policies and placing Britain in an awkward situation. Thus in order to undercut US protests and prevent future disputes, it was decided to add cotton to the absolute contraband list.[47]

Such a decision required a coordinated and timely effort on the part of the Allies. The Foreign Office asserted that if the cabinet declared cotton absolute contraband, it should "consult secretly with the French, Italian, and Russian Governments so as to get them to act simultaneously." Doing so would demonstrate a show of unity and make it more difficult for the United States to object. And it urged that if the government adopted this policy, it should act immediately—before the United States had the chance to renew its protests. Otherwise, Americans might view such a declaration as "deference to the American demand" to abandon existing blockade policy because it would suggest that the policy had failed. As a result, it would appear that Britain was using the cotton issue as a way to "hide our withdrawal" from the existing policy.[48]

One question remained: how would the United States react? Grey recirculated a note to the cabinet that had been sent to Washington the previous October. In it, the government declared that it would not place cotton on the absolute contraband list. He reminded his colleagues that at the time, the government did not want to anger cotton interests in the United States. Additionally, keeping cotton on the free list was a concession to counterbalance placing copper, rubber, "and all the articles which we considered really important to Germany for supplying her army" on the absolute contraband list.[49]

Grey was concerned that if Britain made any change in policy it would have to offer an unassailable rationale. Spring-Rice agreed on July 6 that something had to be done; however, he feared that if cotton was declared absolute contraband without some waiver for the 1915 crop, it might generate a "bad political situation."[50] For one thing, the ambassador was still concerned about the continuing congressional debate over the sale of munitions. Even though he believed the president would oppose it, Congress might compel him to sanction an embargo. If Wilson vetoed such legislation, Spring-Rice concluded that Congress might override it.[51] With that outcome in mind, the ambassador urged the British government to "steady the price" of cotton.[52] But the following day, he told Grey that making cotton absolute contraband could also have a positive effect. It would strengthen Britain's position since the United States did not recognize the blockade's legality. Yet taking cotton off of the free list was a delicate matter because doing so would aggravate the American South, "which is dangerously strong, and would bring most southern senators and representatives into line against export of arms and ammunition."[53]

Following up his suggestion that the British government intervene in the cotton market, Spring-Rice informed Grey on July 15 that American brokers sold 2,700,000 bales annually to Germany and Austria. The "visible balance of [the] 1914 crop will be about 2,000,000 bales." To keep the surplus off the market, the ambassador recommended that the British government needed to create a syndicate of banks to buy the entire amount normally exported to Germany and Austria-Hungry and store it until after the war. At that point, Whitehall would extract a guarantee from its allies that they will buy up the cotton. He asserted that if this was done Britain could add cotton to the absolute contraband list.[54]

By late July, Spring-Rice was more confident that the United States would not ban the sale of arms to the Allies. Nevertheless he still stressed that London must continue trying to appease "the various interests that are arraying against us," especially in the cotton South. The president, he added, had to heed the will of the populace regardless of his personal convictions. The peace party had gained a unifying figure when Bryan resigned and Spring-Rice claimed this situation could revive efforts to end munitions sales.

On the other hand, he speculated there were limits to American patience and that Germany could push the United States into war by taking a hard-line stance. If Germany decided to back away from submarine warfare and made "appeals to the American pocket," it might be able to turn "important interests against us . . . The dollar against honour;—and, after all, the passengers on the Lusitania are dead and the cotton people are much alive. Dead people have no votes and no pockets. We have not threatened either the honour or the lives of Americans but we have threatened and are threatening their pockets."[55]

By July 22, Britain decided to add cotton to the absolute contraband list but also buttress the market by guaranteeing the price of cotton at ten cents a pound. Page informed Lansing that Grey had instructed the British commercial attaché in Washington, Richard Crawford, to meet with cotton dealers and establish an agreement to purchase "large quantities at a good price."[56] In a rough draft of the declaration circulated to the cabinet, Grey explained that because cotton was so important to producing munitions, Britain had to place it on the absolute contraband list but stressed it was aware of its significance to the southern United States. Britain, he asserted, was "most anxious not to take any step that would cause disaster to the material interests in those States, and [it was] therefore prepared to enter into negotiations with those interested in cotton-growing," to the extent of purchasing the entire amount that would otherwise go to Germany and or Austria-Hungary.[57]

Initially Britain's decision concerned Wilson. He told House that such a move might alter American views toward the Allies and provoke Congress to bar the sale of munitions to all belligerents.[58] He immediately contacted Lansing to clarify Britain's existing policy. The president thought Britain had pledged months earlier that cotton would not become contraband. Lansing confirmed that Wilson was correct. The secretary then asserted that Britain's policy change would aggravate many Americans and that domestic pressure to retaliate "will embarrass us seriously." In a conversation with Spring-Rice, Lansing warned that the US public would resent the British decision because of the "feeling that Great Britain had broken her promise."[59] Americans, he argued, would oppose any ban on the cotton trade unless Whitehall made an "arrangement for preventing [the] fall in price." As Grey had suspected, Lansing concluded by warning that declaring cotton contraband implied that the blockade of Germany was ineffective.[60]

The difficulty facing the White House lay in deciding how to handle the affair without creating any additional problems with Great Britain or Germany. The British decision to make cotton contraband was still unknown to many Americans, and complaints continued to roll in. In a letter to Dr. G. S. Barkdale of Fernbank, Alabama, Senator John H. Bankhead from Alabama wrote that he had spoken with Wilson about the cotton crisis and concluded that the president was doing everything he could under the circumstances. Bankhead seemed to understand how cautiously the president had to move: "If we should become involved in a serious quarrel with

Germany it would not help the cotton market, and a misunderstanding with England of a serious nature would completely destroy it. It seems our finger is in the trap, and it is the part of wisdom to work at the spring rather than jerk it out of the trap, but I am persuaded there is relief not a great ways in front of us."[61]

The following day, on July 31, Spring-Rice reported that US Commercial Attaché Chandler Anderson and Lansing reconsidered the situation and privately admitted that making cotton contraband was not a bad idea as long as Britain ensured that the cotton industry did not lose money. They also agreed that declaring cotton contraband would prevent problems over search and seizure on the high seas. US businessmen could not complain if they illegally shipped goods abroad. The key was that Britain needed to make the declaration concurrent with a statement that it planned to "take measures to prevent as far as possible disastrous results to cotton growers in the United States."[62]

Making the decision easier to stomach was the discovery that the cotton crop might be smaller than predicted. According to William P. G. Harding, the chair of the Cotton Committee of the Federal Reserve Board, the United States would produce only 12,000,000 bales, and he estimated an increase in home consumption because US textile companies would produce more to fill the void created by the drop in textile imports caused by the war. Harding also noted that American munitions companies would require more cotton to manufacture ammunition.[63] Spring-Rice later wrote that Harding had predicted that despite the closing of German and Austrian markets, international and domestic consumption would "absorb every bale that is likely to be cultivated." With such information in hand, Grey concluded the time was right to inform Washington in confidence that his government was definitely going to declare cotton contraband.[64]

As the White House deliberated on how to respond, Lansing received a message from Skinner informing him that between March 11 and May 19, Britain had detained 204,633 bales of cotton and 28 ships. Only 8,891 bales had been released to consignees. But he added that even though Britain had detained many American cotton shipments, its own purchases had jumped significantly over the previous year and it was "compensating for the damage wrought." Consequently he reasoned that while London was interfering with US trade, it was taking important steps to prevent American merchants from losing much money caused by the closing of the "German market." He speculated the European conflict actually had a positive effect on the US cotton trade.[65] Increased manufacture of munitions had boosted Britain's purchases of American cotton, prompting him to claim, "[I]t cannot be said, therefore that the war had been disadvantageous to American cotton interests since it has caused an enormously increased consumption of cotton for the manufacture of explosives, whereas up to the beginning of the war, the cotton manufacturing business had been dull and the general demand, at least as far as Great Britain was concerned, far below normal."[66] Furthermore Britain had brokered a deal with American cotton interests to purchase the latter's surplus. On August 13, Spring-Rice told House that London agreed to buy enough cotton to keep the price from falling below ten cents per pound and that Britain would guarantee that neutral nations received their "normal amount of cotton."[67]

The next day, Spring-Rice told Lansing that Britain would declare cotton absolute contraband in the near future. In the conversation, the secretary of state took a new position. Statistics on the industry seem to have convinced him that the American public would not view such a move adversely. He asserted that US citizens would understand the need for such a measure but added that he hoped to receive the statement from London soon because he wanted it before he responded to Britain's note of July 23.[68] In coordination with the State Department, the Foreign Office wisely waited until after the market closed on Saturday, August 21 to make a public announcement. In the hope of preventing a sharp decline of cotton values when the markets reopened, London agents began purchasing all available cotton at the previous Saturday's closing price.[69]

Unknown to the Wilson administration, many southerners accepted Britain's August 21 declaration because they realized that the decision was not going to hurt their pocket books. On August 23, the New Orleans *Times-Picayune*'s editor asserted that the southern economy would survive because "[w]ith a moderate crop and the Allies supporting the market, there is no reason why the south, aided by the Federal reserve system, should not obtain prices that will make those of the last autumn look unreal."[70] This argument clearly echoes the Wilson administration's perspective on the cotton issue. Equally important, the president and his advisors in turn did not interfere when Britain again violated US rights at sea. These related decisions were more than simple acquiescence to British policy. Advising the British on how to violate American rights at sea by adding a vital US commodity to the absolute contraband list was a clear departure from neutrality. By accepting Britain's cotton policy without protest, the Wilson administration willingly helped to tighten the blockade of Germany and thus become an accomplice to the Allies.

In addition to cutting off German access to US cotton, Britain found itself dealing with an economic crisis. During the latter months of 1915, the Allies, especially Britain, were feeling the crushing fiscal weight of the war. Prewar Britain imported more than it exported but covered the deficit through interest received from foreign investments and on profits from the merchant marine, leaving a trade surplus of £150,000,000 a year.[71] By

December 1914, that surplus had evaporated. Britons could not make new foreign investments, and the government exhausted all its available funds to finance war spending and loans to its allies—especially Russia. As of March 1915, Britain had spent $6,000,000,000 and increased income taxes to cover its expenses and by June the government was unable to cover its military expenditures with domestic financing.[72]

Making matters worse, over the first 11 months of the war, the British suffered a drop in the value of the pound because foreign investors started doubting the country's ability to continue a long war. And as the dollar gained in value against the pound, Britain found it difficult to buy dollars to pay for American goods. The exchange rate was turning against the United Kingdom and it had to act fast to locate new sources of funding.[73] A cabinet report of June 1915 stated that Britain could cover the costs of imports through the "restoration of our export trade to something approaching the prewar magnitude, or the realization of a sufficient part of our overseas investments to furnish the requested sum." Unfortunately, these were long-term adjustments and London needed funds immediately.[74] The only feasible solution was to start borrowing money from US financial firms.

This situation prompted the Bank of England to ask J. P. Morgan and Company to call for a $50 million private loan backed by gold and American securities held in the United Kingdom. Technically this was still a private transaction because Morgan received collateral from the Bank of England and in turn made a private loan so the company could continue purchasing for the British government. As historian Kathleen Burk points out, the advance made by Morgan merely "provided money for the down payments" on Britain's current expenditures. By mid-August, the money was almost gone and the value of the pound had again dropped, this time to $4.725. Estimates for the year 1915 suggested that the British debt to US firms would soon reach more than $2,500,000,000 and that the difficulty of paying off Allied debts was reaching critical proportions.[75]

Across the Atlantic, Spring-Rice was well aware of the dilemma and feared that addressing the issue may be difficult: "We have, I fear, to pay blackmail if we want to retain freedom of trade in munitions of war, and if we wish to float a loan . . . The time for the latter, according to New York opinion, is drawing near, and longer delay may entail very bad terms." He warned Grey to bear in mind that Britain purchased most of its goods on the US market, and he did not want to injure his country's public standing. "I think that the whole matter should be considered in the light of the necessity of using this country as a base for supplies, and for money."[76]

Like Spring-Rice, Chancellor of the Exchequer David Lloyd George was quite concerned about the predicament. In June 1915, the British Expeditionary Force required 261,000 rounds of artillery ammunition per week, yet British factories were only able to deliver 153,000 rounds. Because of this deficiency, Lloyd George reported to the cabinet that "less than 60% of [the] requirements was being delivered on the whole . . . and High Explosives insufficient in almost all natures, the 60-pounder being the only gun which was getting approximately its requirements."[77] During a war policy meeting on Wednesday, August 16, 1915, Lloyd George added that he was uncertain whether the government could supply the army with the needed munitions.[78] As a consequence he concluded "it is now agreed that we shall not be ready for a new offensive," until additional supplies were obtained in the United States.[79]

In addition to supplying existing divisions, Lloyd George wanted the government to be able to outfit as many as 100 divisions. Despite Kitchener's opposition to stockpiling enormous quantities of weapons and ammunition, Lloyd George wanted to avoid another "shell crisis." The Ministry of Munitions therefore contacted Bethlehem Steel and Midvale Steel with orders for hundreds of artillery pieces, which the Pennsylvania-based companies were happy to accept.[80]

While problems continued to mount in Britain, the situation in America was quite the opposite. US businesses reaped the profits accruing from the massive trade imbalance. In a speech given on May 3, Chief of the Bureau of Foreign and Domestic Commerce Edward Pratt noted that at the beginning of the war, the United States owed nearly $7,000,000,000 to European creditors, including $4,000,000,000 to Great Britain alone. Things were now different: "At the end of the first nine months of the fiscal year 1915, instead of owing Europe considerable sums, Europe actually owed us $452,500,000."[81]

Pratt noted that the rise in the dollar's value against the pound meant that America's financial position was rapidly improving. "The real meaning of this low rate of sterling exchange in New York is simply that . . . London owes New York." He added that the United States sold more than $100,000,000 worth of goods "in excess of the amount she needed to sell in order to pay for her imports and to meet foreign obligations." As long as Britain continued purchasing goods in the United States, the country would enjoy robust growth. As Pratt concluded, "With the issue of foreign securities in London prohibited and with the French and German markets all practically closed to the issue of international securities, New York has the whole field of international finance at her feet."[82]

This economic expansion did not go unobserved in Britain. Crowe wrote Spring-Rice in late June expressing his wish that the United States would enter the fighting on their side. The United States, he exclaimed, was "the only country . . . really unassailable by Germany." More important, US intervention would mean that the "financial and economic position of the Allies would be rendered very much stronger, if not impregnable," and German trade "would practically come to an end."[83]

By late summer, the Allies faced a difficult situation because they had exhausted their existing sources of capital. Reginald McKenna, who replaced Lloyd George as chancellor of the exchequer, explained to the cabinet that Britain was practically supporting all of its Allies financially. As of August, Britain had a total of £335,000,000 outstanding and McKenna estimated that the war was costing an average of £1,000,000 each day.[84] Britain had to continue making purchases in the United States, but buying American goods was hampered by the lack of credit: "A loan," McKenna concluded, "is the only remedy on a large scale that [we] can use." More bluntly McKenna warned Churchill that if Britain continued to supply the Allies into 1916, "the liabilities we have entered into during this year and next are already in excess of our power unless we can borrow in America, sell securities, or greatly reduce domestic consumption."[85]

Many American banks were eager to loan money to the British government but were unwilling to do so without the White House's approval. McAdoo sided with the banks and urged Wilson to furnish it. He argued that since selling munitions was legal so was loaning money to purchase them.[86] The secretary claimed that Britain needed a minimum of $500,000,000 in credit and admitted that legal considerations were trumped by economic ones: "We have tied our hands, so that we cannot help ourselves or help our best customers."[87]

Expanding Anglo-American trade caused further deterioration of US-German relations. Spring-Rice reported that many Americans "believe that Germany means to force on a war." In addition to the continuing *Lusitania* crisis, rumors of German-American sabotage and agitation had reached the Wilson administration.[88] As early as July, Lansing privately expressed his irritation at German efforts to sway US public opinion. He was also aware that German agents were trying to stir up anti-American feeling in Mexico and across Latin America. Berlin, he claimed, was trying to keep Washington focused on the Western Hemisphere in hope of preventing America from entering the war. This situation prompted him to advocate a robust policy that included strengthening the military and launching "secret investigations of German activities in Latin America."[89]

Then on August 19, Britain received a gift from the Germans when a U-boat sank the SS *Arabic* sixty miles off the coast of Queenstown, UK, killing two American passengers.[90] The incident infuriated Wilson, who was losing all faith in Berlin's word. That night he confided to Edith Galt, now his fiancée, that the United States' third *Lusitania* letter may have tied the government's hands. The president stressed that he told Berlin another attack would be "'a deliberately unfriendly act' . . . You may easily imagine, therefore, my precious One, my sweet Counsellor, what sober forebodings are in my mind tonight." He added, "Certainly the Germans are blood-mad." Twice he stressed that since the *Arabic* was "bound *out* from Liverpool," it could not be transporting weapons, and the attack was a blatant "disregard of international law and of brutal defiance of the opinion and power of the United States."[91]

Wilson wrote Galt the following day and stated he was "very blue." The *Arabic* sinking might cause the "final parting of the ways" between the two countries. To express his grief, Wilson told her "it was as if I had taken my hand from yours for a moment, to turn a page—a page with the shadow of war upon it—and that when I sought it again and looked to get the reassurance in your eyes you were not there!" He still did not want the affair to lead to open hostilities and did not regard war as inevitable. He had options to pursue first. Washington could recall Gerard and send German Ambassador Johann Heinrich von Bernstorff home. But he also worried that such acts might provoke Germany to declare war "and the guidance of our policy be taken out of our hands."[92]

Lansing informed Wilson that newspapers reported that the *Arabic* was part of a convoy and that the passengers were watching an attack under way on the *Dunsley* when the torpedo struck. If correct, the government needed to consider whether the U-boat had to offer a warning because "it is not required to visit a ship under convoy." He also wondered if the submarine commander thought that the *Arabic* intended to ram his vessel or chase it away. Either way, he did not want to give any official statements until he knew all the facts. According to Lansing, the best way to address the situation was to call publicly for a cabinet meeting to consider the attack. This action, he felt, would demonstrate to the American people that the administration took the issue seriously and at the same time "would not have a bad effect on the German Government."[93] Despite his growing frustration, Wilson agreed that the government needed all the facts but worried that holding a cabinet meeting so soon might send the "wrong impression." He thought that acting too fast might suggest that the White House was preparing for drastic measures and he wanted things to calm down first.[94]

Wilson then contacted House and stressed his assumption that Americans expected him to keep them out of the war. He also reasoned that he could still bring about a negotiated peace: "It would be a calamity to the world at large if we should be drawn actively into the conflict and so deprived of all disinterested influence over the settlement."[95] Wilson obviously did not consider that the volume of US trade with Britain and his consequent approval of the cotton arrangement had compromised American neutrality. Germany indubitably would not regard the United States as an honest broker. Neither would Britain. Britain was certainly less likely to sit down at the bargaining table because American support provided them an advantage over the Central Powers.

House agreed with Wilson that Americans wanted to avoid the war, but he was not interested in being an intermediary. The colonel asserted that the time had come to take aggressive action, asserting that notes of protest were no longer effective. He wanted to send Bernstorff home and recall the American ambassador to Berlin. These moves, he asserted, would act as a warning to Germany about the seriousness of the crisis because the next logical step was a declaration of war. House was ready to join the Allies. In his diary, he wrote that he would "begin preparations for defense and for war, just as vigorously as if war had been declared."[96]

Exacerbating Wilson's irritation, on August 22, House forwarded a letter from Bernstorff stating that before Germany would consider mediation, the US government had to provide assurances that "Wilson wishes to give us a square deal." In what was a fair accusation, Bernstorff complained that munitions sales to the Allies and the lack of protests over Britain's policy toward American cotton frustrated the German people and that no one assumed the United States was impartial in its dealings with the belligerents. As he did on numerous occasions, Wilson sent the official letter to his fiancé. Despite Bernstorff's reasonable argument, Wilson expressed his anger, stating, "What an impertinent Prussian Bernstorff is!"[97]

In a separate message to Wilson, Galt sent several newspaper articles that warned Americans to be cautious when traveling on English-owned ships. Aggravated, Wilson made the irrational assertion that Americans had the right to travel on any ship they pleased, belligerent or not. "[Y]ou came near being corrupted there, young lady by *Bryanism*!" He wrote, "It was your friend W. J. B. who took the ground that we must let Americans understand that they took passage on British ships . . . at their own risk and peril. Beware of heresies!" Once again adding a bias assertion, Wilson claimed that Bryan's argument was probably the "more reasonable and practical one . . . but it is not the doctrine of international law, and we must base our claims of right on the undoubted practice of nations,—for which Germany is showing such crass and brutal contempt."[98]

On August 24, the Wilson administration received two messages from Germany concerning the *Arabic*. Bernstorff informed Lansing that Germany did not have any "official information about the sinking of the *Arabic*," and he hoped the United States would not make any decisions based on incomplete information and without allowing Germany to prepare an informed response.[99] Additionally Bernstorff assured Wilson that his government did not want to hurt Americans and that if any had died on the ship, Berlin "would deeply regret this fact." The same day, von Jagow told

Gerard that if the submarine captain attacked without warning, he had disobeyed orders.[100]

Wilson recognized a ray of hope in these letters but suspected that the ambassador's request that the United States move slowly was an attempt to buy time. The president stated that he was unsure how long they should wait before responding. On the other hand, Wilson expressed concern that if the United States severed relations with Germany, German-Americans might begin a sabotage campaign in major cities and he did not know how the government could prepare for such an event.[101]

Regardless of this apparent break through, Wilson's ardent support for the Allies remained intact. On August 29, Lansing learned of a deceitful British attack on a German U-boat that was following international law as it approached a merchant vessel. Page sent the secretary two eyewitness accounts of the surprise assault on the German submarine by the *Baralong*, a reserve auxiliary vessel of the Royal Navy that was disguised as a merchant vessel. This "Q-ship," as such vessels were called, signaled that it wanted to aid the damaged *Nicosian*. Flying the Stars and Stripes, the *Baralong* moved behind the *Nicosian*, lowered the US flag, and fired on the submarine when it came back into view. Both witnesses claimed that the German crew jumped into the water to escape and as the men swam for the *Nicosian* the British crewmen shot at them in the water. Some reached the *Nicosian* and tried to hide, only to be discovered and killed. After murdering the U-boat crewmen, British sailors tossed the bodies overboard.[102]

Wilson told Galt, "Isn't this one of the most unspeakable performances . . . It's horrible!" Lansing stated that the deed shocked him but hoped news of the account would not become public.[103] Wilson agreed and decided not to act, choosing instead to look the other way as long as he could. Wilson's pro-Allied stance had become egregious. Wilson had condoned Britain's use of the American flag to disguise a combat vessel whose crew killed unarmed Germans at sea.

Even as Wilson sought to ignore the Q-ship attacks, on September 1 Bernstorff informed the US government that Germany planned to restrict the use of submarines. He told Lansing that prior to the attack on the *Arabic*, his government had instructed him to state that Germany would not torpedo any more liners "without warning and without safety of the lives of noncombatants" as long as the ships did not try to run from or ram the U-boats. The president was elated over the *Arabic* Pledge, and regardless of his limited influence over Germany's decision, he received enormous praise and numerous letters of congratulations for his success in the matter.[104]

In time the excitement surrounding Bernstorff's announcement dissipated. Within weeks, an explosion damaged the British liner SS *Hesperian* on its voyage from Liverpool to Montreal, killing eight passengers, none of them Americans. The cause of the explosion was unknown, but Wilson immediately suspected German perfidy. When Wilson penned his letter to Galt on Monday morning, he told her that the "triumph" of the so-called *Arabic* Pledge did not last long. He claimed that the explosion on the *Hesperian* demonstrated that "nothing can last long which depends on Germany's good faith." The lack of evidence was irrelevant to him. Wilson had made up his mind that Germany could not be trusted. The facts might "put a different face" on the incident, he admitted, but added that this was a "very slim possibility." Writing to House the following day, Wilson pondered, "Shall we ever get out of the labyrinth made for us all by this German 'frightfulness'?"[105] Wilson's comments further illustrate the flagrant bias against Germany and his willingness to support the Allies. The president had eyewitness accounts of the HMS *Baralong*'s deceitful assault on German sailors, yet he condemned Germany without any evidence at all.

Concurrent with the *Arabic* and *Hesperian* affairs, Washington continued tightening its relationship with Great Britain by finally allowing the London government to seek loans in the United States. In response to a query from Lansing enclosing letters from US bankers, Wilson stated that the White House would not stand in the way and that Lansing might inform bankers that the government "would take no action either for or against such a transaction." Although he added that this policy was not to be put in writing.[106]

Later that day, Lansing told McAdoo in a confidential letter that he agreed with the secretary about offering loans to the Allies and that the president quietly approved.[107] The discretion demonstrates that Wilson understood the diplomatic implications of his actions. Making loans to Britain would assure that it could continue the war and not worry about a constant flow of materiel from across the Atlantic. It also illustrates that he knew the importance of an Allied victory to American prosperity. Just as important, US-German relations hinged on the president's decision remaining secret. In giving his approval of American loans to the Allies and not offering the same to the Central Powers, Wilson certainly recognized that he was disregarding US neutrality, which could provoke a rupture with Germany.

The decision to look the other way, however, was not enough. US banks would remain wary if they did not receive the manifest support of the White House. Lansing informed Wilson that since December 1914, American exports "have exceeded our imports by nearly a billion dollars" and noted that estimates for 1915 showed the United States would have an excess nearing $2,500,000,000. The secretary wrote that even though European banks had about $3,500,000,000 in gold, using a large portion of these funds to purchase American goods would "disastrously affect the credit of the European nations." Plus if Europeans stopped importing from the United States, American production would be limited, causing "industrial depression, idle capital, and idle labor."[108]

Lansing argued that the US government had to change its official policy regarding loans. He reminded Wilson that Bryan had announced on August 15, 1914, that making loans to belligerents ran counter to the spirit of neutrality. Lansing stated that maintaining that loans were "'inconsistent with strict neutrality' is now a source of embarrassment." American public opinion was already divided, and Lansing doubted that approving loans to the Allies would make things worse. Demonstrating that he recognized the importance of Anglo-American trade he asked, "Can we afford to let a declaration as to our conception of 'the true spirit of neutrality' made in the first days of the war stand in the way of our national interests which seem to be seriously threatened?"[109]

Wilson replied on September 8. Still averse to putting his views on the subject in writing he told Lansing that their "oral discussion of this matter yesterday suffices." Nevertheless his approval was clear.[110] Wilson's support for the loan did far more than just tighten the economic bond between the United States and the Allies.[111] The president's decision to keep his approval private clearly indicates that he understood the implications of his actions and suggests that he wanted to both protect the US economy and provide support for the Allies.

After 13 months, American relations with the belligerents reached a critical juncture. US and British financial interests were tightly bound together, and each relied on the other for its well-being. At the same time, US-German relations deteriorated because Wilson perceived Berlin as the sole barrier to peace talks and the submarine crisis still clouded the diplomatic horizon. The combination of events convinced the president to actively support Britain's decision to place cotton on the absolute contraband list, turn a blind eye to the *Baralong* incident, and choose to keep his policy reversal on loans quiet. Consequently during July and August 1915, the Wilson administration changed course and regardless of its official policy the United States could no longer claim to be neutral.

8

"He Has Thus Crossed the Rubicon"

September 1915–December 1915

> I propose therefore to keep in hand all concessions that we can make, in order that when we do reply to this American Note the effect of them all together may be as favourable as possible.
>
> —British Foreign Secretary Edward Grey to Ambassador Cecil Spring-Rice, November 6, 1915[1]

Washington's public protests over the treatment of neutral trade continued throughout the period of American neutrality, even though US and British officials did not take them as seriously. Neither government wanted to disrupt the business relationship that had developed. At the same time, Germany's attempts to relieve the growing tension over the submarine crisis and the *Arabic* Pledge did not end the problems between Berlin and Washington. From September to December 1915, evidence surfaced that German agents in the United States were trying to disrupt the country's commerce. Additionally the Imperial Government tried to defend the submarine captain who attacked the *Arabic*. These factors contributed to worsening American-German relations and Wilson's decision to support mediation under circumstances seriously disadvantageous to Germany.

On August 31, American Ambassador Walter Hines Page informed Secretary of State Robert Lansing that the British had arrested American journalist James Archibald for transporting official documents for the Central Powers. British agents knew he was using his US citizenship to protect himself as he traveled between Germany and America, but they could not detain him in New York without provoking an international incident. Archibald was one of a number of people suspected to be German spies. In late August, the British discovered that Archibald planned to carry several letters for the Austro-Hungarian ambassador to the United States, Konstantin Dumba. When he reached Falmouth, England, he was stopped and searched.[2] After confiscating a number of messages from the German and Austrian embassies in the United States, authorities allowed him to continue onward to Holland. In the seized letters, Dumba wrote to Baron István von Burian, the Austro-Hungarian minister for foreign affairs, that he and German military attaché Captain Franz von Papen agreed that inciting a strike among Hungarian-American workers in the United States would "disorganize the manufacture of munitions of war at Bethlehem and in the Middle West and hold it up for months."[3]

British Foreign Secretary Edward Grey told Ambassador Cecil Spring-Rice he was having difficulty "guaging [*sic*] what its effect would be on American public opinion" if the letters were published and added that it was up to the ambassador to decide how to convey the information to the State Department. Spring-Rice exhibited no qualms about making the most of the situation. Within days, the reports showed up in national newspapers, including the *New York Times*.[4]

Spring-Rice's act was based on his beliefs that the United States was gradually being drawn closer to overt involvement in the war and his fear of a German "fifth column" in America.[5] Lansing was not consumed with such apparent paranoia but did understand the implications that the Archibald case could have on US–Austro-Hungarian relations. He summoned Dumba on Tuesday, September 7, to offer an explanation of his actions. In his memoir, Lansing stated that he asked Dumba, "Do you think it proper for a diplomatic representative of a belligerent government in the United States to employ an American citizen traveling under the protection of an American passport as a messenger to carry official dispatches through the lines of the enemy?" Fearing his answer would incriminate him, Dumba replied that he must "think it over" and suggested that his government might give him a leave of absence to prevent further embarrassment. Soon after the interview, Lansing officially requested Dumba's recall.[6]

On September 8, German Ambassador Johann Heinrich von Bernstorff addressed the submarine crisis, informing Lansing that for several months U-boat commanders had been under orders not to attack passenger ships "without warning and safety for non-combatants." He assured the secretary of state that "[t]hese instructions are and will remain in force which as we hope will in the end lead to a complete understanding on all questions of maritime warfare."[7] This announcement did not mean, however, that Germany intended to offer an indemnity in the case of the *Arabic*. On September 9, Lansing received the German account on the sinking of the vessel, which claimed that when the submarine stopped the *Dunsley*, its captain noticed the *Arabic* approaching in the distance. The *Arabic*'s course led the captain to conclude that vessel intended to ram his boat.

In presumed self-defense, Commander Rudolf Schneider submerged and attacked the *Arabic*. The German government expressed its grief over the death of American citizens; however, because it deemed that the U-24 acted properly, it denied responsibility for an indemnity. But German Foreign Minister Gottlieb von Jagow added that if the United States was dissatisfied with Germany's decision, it could be submitted to the international tribunal at The Hague.[8]

Lansing did not view the response as conciliatory. Soon after Berlin sent the note, US Ambassador James Gerard expressed to Lansing that Germany reversed its position after Bernstorff presented the *Arabic* Pledge because the government was following the Imperial Navy's, not the Foreign Office's lead. Gerard claimed that the Imperial Navy convinced the German government that Bernstorff's pledge had undermined the entire submarine strategy and "would mean the total failure of that method of warfare." Adding fuel to the fire, Lansing learned from Gerard on September 10 that when he asked von Jagow about the *Hesperian*, the foreign minister responded that "he did not see what business it was of the United States unless American citizens had lost their lives." Consequently he refused to give Lansing the German report on the incident.[9]

Clearly irritated, Lansing replied on September 11 that it was Washington's business. Even if Americans were only "endangered," the government would take an interest in the case.[10] Apparently under American pressure, von Jagow responded days later that after reviewing the *Hesperian* case, the government concluded that a submarine had not attacked the ship. He asserted that there were no U-boats in the vicinity of the vessel and that it must have hit a mine.[11]

On the same day that Lansing wrote to von Jagow, he reviewed the German note on the *Arabic* attack and informed Wilson that on the basis of information he had from London and survivors of the sinking, he found Germany's response was "unsatisfactory." The *Arabic* was apparently over two miles away from the *Dunsley* and was traveling in a zigzag pattern, a "method of avoidance" with which the submarine captain should have been familiar. The German captain, he claimed, must have known that the *Arabic* was not trying to attack. Thus the "whole tenor of the note is a cold and uncompromising declaration that the commanders of submarines have practically a free hand though bound, technically, by some general form of instructions, and that if they make mistakes, however unwarranted, the Government will support them." According to Lansing, the note was unacceptable and the German government should disavow the assault. If Germany did not agree to the American demands, the secretary argued that the United States would have to consider the act as unfriendly and "sever diplomatic relations with Germany."[12]

Lansing subsequently spoke to Bernstorff and pressed him to include more than passenger ships in Germany's declaration, especially since some merchant ships might have American crewmen onboard.[13] On September 14, Lansing sent Gerard a message containing affidavits from sailors and passengers on the *Dunsley* and *Arabic*. He noted that witnesses claimed the submarine had attacked without warning. The secretary asserted that they did not see the U-boat and only spotted the torpedo once it was within several hundred yards of their vessel. Days later, the State Department's legal counselor Frank L. Polk told Gerard that the United States could not accept the "*Arabic* note" in its current form. He argued that because Germany supported the captain, Bernstorff's promise to respect American rights at sea was "valueless." Polk added that until Berlin disavowed the U-boat commander's actions, the United States would not capitulate to international arbitration.[14]

The impasse further affected Wilson's view on the war. On the afternoon of September 22, House met with the president. They discussed the German account of the *Arabic* incident and agreed that unless Berlin renounced the attack, the administration was going to have trouble satisfying US public opinion. More significantly, Wilson was now questioning his decision to remain officially neutral. House was surprised when Wilson stated "he had never been sure that we ought not take part in the conflict and if it seemed evident that Germany and her militaristic ideas were to win, the obligation upon us was greater than ever."[15]

Over the next ten days, Austria-Hungary and Germany acquiesced to American demands on two major counts. On September 22, Polk informed US Ambassador to Austria-Hungary Fredric Penfield that Vienna had officially granted Dumba a "leave of absence" and called him home.[16] Then on October 2, Bernstorff gave Lansing a short message concerning the *Arabic*. It contained a promise that similar attacks would not happen in the future. Despite defending the U-boat's actions, Germany acknowledged that the officers and crew of the merchant ship had a different perspective on the matter and that the U-boat captain might have made a mistake: "[T]he attack of the submarine, therefore, was undertaken against the instructions issued to the commander." Finally he stated that while Germany was not obligated to pay repatriations, "in the spirit of conciliation and friendship," it would offer an indemnity.[17]

After reading the note, Lansing recognized a new opportunity to put pressure on Bernstorff for more concessions. He told the ambassador that Germany contradicted itself by accepting the submarine captain's assertion that the *Arabic* intended to ram him but claiming that he did not follow orders. Bernstorff agreed to change the letter to meet American demands. Lansing edited the letter to state that Germany not only regretted the attack but also "disavow[ed] the act" and that Germany would pay reparations "in the circumstances . . . for the American lives."[18] Bernstorff, fearing the severance of diplomatic relations if Germany did not comply with US demands, took it upon himself to tell Lansing that his government approved the changes and declared that Germany would "pay an indemnity for American lives" with no reservations.[19] He also emphasized in a personal letter to Lansing that "[t]he orders issued by His Majesty the Emperor to the commanders of the German submarines—of which I notified you on a previous occasion—have been made so stringent that the recurrence of incidents similar to the Arabic case is considered out of the question."[20]

This was not the first instance the United States and a belligerent cooperated on the wording of an official document, yet this was significantly different than previous ones between the Wilson administration and Britain. Unlike negotiations with the Allies, Lansing dictated the terms to Bernstorff, and Germany's acceptance of his terms seemed to solve the crisis. Wilson was so pleased that he wrote Edith Galt that he could now focus on their engagement plans: "[M]y heart is light . . . And now we are free to be gay and happy!"[21]

At the same time that the Wilson administration pressured Germany over the *Arabic*, the economic and political bonds between Britain and the United States tightened even further. In the last quarter of the year, Washington renewed its public protests against the British blockade, but the seriousness of the protests, as far as Wilson and his advisors were concerned, declined because they understood the importance of US commercial ties with the Allies. London too made additional concessions to the American business community because of its growing financial and materiel demands. The states' dependency on each other cemented their interests together. During the early summer of 1915, US Consul-General Robert Skinner suggested to the State Department that he should privately organize a meeting of US shipping interests to discuss their grievances concerning the March 11 Order in Council. Eventually Skinner changed his opinion. He wrote Lansing on September 16, that he no longer thought such a meeting was necessary: "[A] considerable amelioration is noticeable in the situation." American merchants were able to trade with the Netherlands by transferring their cargoes to the Netherlands Overseas Trust (NOT), and US goods, including "tobacco and southern fruit," were now reaching their markets "as in normal times." Moreover the Merchants Guild of Copenhagen worked similar to the NOT and allowed Americans to trade with Denmark without much difficulty. As for cotton, Skinner noted that Britain found ways to avert problems by making agreements with both Sweden and Norway that enabled US businessmen to sell their goods in those countries. Finally the number of ships detained since the

Order in Council went into effect declined from a high of 114 in April to 37 in August. According to the consul-general, the majority of the recent detentions resulted from the "ignorance of shippers, practically all of whom are entirely familiar with prevailing conditions."[22]

It was with such information in hand that the State Department evaluated complaints made by US meat-packers against the detention of their goods by the Royal Navy. In mid-September, the "High Court of Justice of Great Britain" confiscated a number of meat shipments bound for Norway because the British government claimed they were ultimately destined for Germany. The cargo owners complained to Lansing, challenging the decision. Simply because the consignment was "in excess of normal consumption," the British assumed that any surplus was bound for Germany.[23]

On that same day, Spring-Rice forwarded a message to Lansing from London defending the court's ruling. The Foreign Office asserted that the food shipments were destined for the enemy, making the meat "liable to confiscation." It also pointed out that if the court had ruled in favor of the packers, Britain would have released the meat and allowed the sale to continue at the agreed upon price of 1.3 million pounds. If the court decided to confiscate the shipments, the office declared, the shippers should not incur any serious financial loss because Britain intended to compensate the packers by paying "a round sum of 2,250,000 pounds."[24]

The State Department received a second letter from Spring-Rice on October 12. The ambassador claimed that some American meat-packers worked covertly with German agents in Europe, who purchased shipments for use by the military. The agents, he argued, told the shippers what ports to enter in an effort to evade the Allied blockade. In some cases, German agents wrote American last names on orders to deceive British censors.[25]

With the *Arabic* crisis behind it, the White House sent the long-postponed protest to London.[26] The dispatch outlined a number of broad grievances about the disruption of trade since the beginning of the war. Washington protested against Britain's practice of detaining American ships without proof that they were acting illegally and asserted that the Royal Navy did not have the right to deny access to neutral ports within the blockade's limits. Lansing noted that despite Britain's pledge not to interfere with legitimate trade with neutral countries on the European continent, it continued to disrupt American shipping and was "unsuccessful in her efforts to distinguish between enemy and neutral trade." He also attacked the legitimacy of the blockade. He pointed out that, among other issues, the belligerents had agreed in the Declaration of Paris that for a blockade to exist, they themselves could not trade with ports within the perimeter. Therefore since Britain routinely exported US goods to the neutral states in Europe, London was breaking long-established practices.[27]

Historian Author Link asserts that with this letter "the construction of the edifice of American neutrality was finally completed."[28] By this point, however, the protest was simply a veneer on the bygone US neutrality. On October 31, House handed the president a dispatch that Spring-Rice planned to send to the Foreign Office. The ambassador, most likely after speaking with House or Lansing, wrote that the United States government would have to keep sending protests with harsh language until the public was "convinced of the necessity of taking sides . . . [A] Policy of pin pricks against one or the other party will only give the impression of prejudice and one sidedness." Spring-Rice suggested that his government should address the "non-essential" issues in the US protest and leave the "essential" ones to arbitration. In effect, he urged Britain to concede on small points, which might appease US opinion, and discuss larger ones later. House told Wilson that he was pleased: "I am told that Sir Cecil is now more pro-American than the worst of us." He also sent Spring-Rice a complimentary letter: "I am glad you are advising Sir Edward so wisely. There can be no serious controversy between us, and what has been done and is to be done, will in the end be of more advantage to you than to us."[29]

After reading the note, Grey told Spring-Rice there was room for "compromise." The foreign secretary asserted that he could work with certain meat-packers who were shipping goods to Europe and only demand the "extreme penalty . . . against those meat packers of whom we have proof . . . that their goods were definitely destined for Germany." He also wanted to allow American tobacco free passage to German ports. Grey agreed with Spring-Rice's recommendation but noted that the timing was an important factor to consider. "It would be easier" he added, "for us to concede these points, not necessarily in the actual reply to the American Note . . . but simultaneously with our reply to it." If Britain offered to compromise before it sent its official rebuttal, "the good effect will have evaporated before we reply to the American Note, on which public opinion will subsequently concentrate . . . I propose therefore to keep in hand all concessions that we can make, in order that when we do reply to this American Note the effect of them all together may be as favourable as possible."[30] This move was intended to assure Americans that Britain was willing to work with them to protect their trade as much as possible. If Britain gave in on certain points, it would be easier to prevent serious outcry in the press.

Despite his explicit support for the Allies, Wilson still had not abandoned his desire to mediate an end to the conflict. This time, he would not attempt to play the role of an honest and disinterested broker. All previous efforts to start peace talks failed because none of the belligerents would agree to initiate a discussion. Consequently by the end of 1915, Wilson reasoned that he would have to manipulate the situation in favor of the Allies.

In early September, House sent two letters to Grey asking if the time was right for Washington to propose a peace conference. He assured Grey that Wilson "would never be a party to any terms not including the liberation of Belgium and France and the end of Militarism" and that he wanted to "return as nearly as possible to the 'status quo'" antebellum.[31]

On October 8, House told the president the extent of his plan, which included cooperation with the Allies and possible American intervention. The colonel insisted that severing ties with Germany over the *Lusitania* was no longer a viable option and that he feared it might win the war and turn its aggression toward the United States: "Therefore, we should do something decisive now—something that would end the war in a way to abolish militarism or that would bring us in with the Allies to help them do it." Outlining his scheme to the president, House proposed something he had already done. "My suggestion," he declared, "is to ask the Allies, unofficially, to let me know whether or not it would be agreeable to them to have us demand that hostilities cease." House then added that the way to justify the proposition was to "put it upon the high ground that the neutral world was suffering along with the belligerents . . . and that peace parleys should begin upon the broad basis of both military and naval disarmament." If the Allies secretly agreed, he would then send out a public note that condemned both navalism and militarism.[32]

Although House wanted the official announcement to have a neutral tone, in reality he hoped it would deceive Germany into making the first call for peace: "If the Allies understood our purpose, we could be as severe in our language concerning them as we were with the Central Powers, the Allies, after some hesitation, could accept our offer or demand." If Germany agreed, House wrote, "We would then have accomplished a master-stroke of diplomacy." If it refused, the United States should then end diplomatic relations and enter the war. "The President," House claimed, "was surprised by this plan [yet] . . . [h]e seemed to acquiesce by silence."[33]

Over the next week, House discussed his ideas with Polk and Lansing. He told the former that the United States needed to step in before "the Allies reached a point where they could not be of assistance in the event we had war with the Central Powers." House also took an ideological tack, asserting that the United States had a responsibility to prevent Germany from becoming the "dominant military factor in the world."[34] Lansing apparently agreed, admitting that if the Allies lost, "we would follow in natural sequence."[35]

On October 15, House finally received Grey's response. The latter did not think the time right to make peace proposals and refused to commit Britain without consulting the rest of the Allies. He stated that Germany would have to surrender Alsace Lorraine and Russia would have to have access to the Mediterranean Sea before peace talks could occur. More important, Grey argued that there needed to be an assurance of a lasting peace. He asserted that the best way "of securing the elimination of militarism and navalism is to get security for the future against aggressive war." He asked House "how much are the United States prepared to do in this direction?" His solution was the establishment of a "League of Nations" that included the United States.[36]

House regarded the proposal of a League of Nations as the perfect opportunity to put forward his plan to force Germany to the peace table. House described his plan to Grey in detail: "In my opinion it would be a world-wide calamity if the war should continue to a point where the Allies could not, with the aid of the United States, bring about a peace along lines you and I have so often discussed." House assured Grey that the Wilson administration was ready to press Germany "whenever you consider the time is propitious for this intervention" and that when Grey thought the moment right, he would come to London to coordinate their efforts. He would then travel to Berlin and inform the German government that Wilson planned to intervene on the "side that accepted our proposal." He would not tell the Germans that he had made any agreements with Whitehall and wanted them to think the Allies would ultimately "reject his proposal." House theorized that if the Germans thought the United States might enter the war on their side, they would accept the proposal. Germany would then act first, breaking the stalemate on opening peace talks. If Germany did not accept his suggestion, "it would nevertheless be the [United States'] purpose to intervene." In other words, if the offer was rejected, Germany's public standing would suffer and the United States could justify entering the war on the Allied side.[37]

Wilson made several small editorial changes to House's draft that he thought would make little diplomatic impact. House had stated, "If the Central Powers were still obdurate, it would be necessary for us to join the Allies and force the issue." Wilson looked at the wording and changed the sentence to say, "It would, 'probably' be necessary for us to join the Allies and force the issue." The president claimed that his changes were "two unimportant verbal changes . . . but they do not alter the sense of it." Wilson wisely wanted to keep the United States from finding itself cornered if circumstances changed. "I do not want to make it inevitable *quite yet* that we should take part to force terms on Germany, because the exact circumstances of such a crisis are impossible to determine."[38]

The president's decision to edit the letter and offer Washington more room to work demonstrates that he was still not ready to draw his country into the European conflict. He opposed sending soldiers across the Atlantic and he was convinced that the American people would not support military involvement. Nevertheless, by approving House's initiative Wilson was willing to sacrifice America's traditional isolationist position if doing so might lead to mediation.[39] More important, his decision to endorse and send the secret letter to Grey provides more evidence that Wilson had concluded that active and partial diplomacy—in support of the Allies—was necessary.

While House was concocting his scheme, problems between the United States and Germany continued to mount. Throughout the early weeks of November, the White House pressed Germany for a resolution on the sinking of the *Lusitania*. The administration soon concluded that Germany intended to drag out negotiations as long as possible. During a series of conversations with Bernstorff, Lansing decided that Germany did not intend to reach a solution with the United States.[40] The secretary had received word that Germany regarded its attack as justified since the submarine campaign occurred in response to Britain's "unlawful starvation campaign." Nevertheless Bernstorff argued that his government did not intentionally kill "noncombatants" and that it was prepared to submit the issue to The Hague.[41] Lansing wanted immediate restitution and found the ambassador's argument unsatisfactory. Lansing told the president that the two countries were "coming to an *impasse* [Lansing's italics] in the matter of the LUSITANIA." He reported that Bernstorff did not think his government would accept responsibility for the death of Americans who chose to travel on British ships. The secretary added that he had learned from several sources that Germany planned to stall until the United States "let it drop." If Germany did not accept the American viewpoint, Lansing warned, the United States would have to sever relations or submit the issue to Congress, "the branch of Government charged with [the] power to declare war."[42] Wilson replied that the United States needed to stand firm on the *Lusitania* case and told Lansing to inform Bernstorff that he expected Germany to settle the issue in a manner similar to that of the *Arabic* case. Anything less, he argued, might "lead back to the very crisis that was then so happily avoided." Wilson was gambling. He hoped that Bernstorff would once again concede to American demands.[43]

Along with the ongoing debate over the *Lusitania*, on November 7 the United States became embroiled in another controversy with Austria-Hungary. Two submarines under Austrian colors attacked an Italian passenger liner, the *Ancona*, off the coast of Sicily.[44] Many in the United States and Europe assumed that the attack was the work of the Germans and not the Austrians.[45] While waiting for reliable information on the attack, Wilson told House that the attack meant that the United States would now have to deal with Austria-Hungary as well as Germany.[46] Austria-Hungary's Chargé d'Affaires Baron Zwiedinek informed Lansing that his country accepted responsibility for the attack, but the Wilson administration presumed that the submarine was actually German and displayed the Austrian flag to avoid problems with Washington. In his memoirs, Lansing asserted that the U-boat captain's decision to fire into the side of the *Ancona* and launch a torpedo as the passengers tried to escape had "exhibited so little regard for moral obligation and was so wanting in human instincts . . . [that the] act was that of a Prussian and not of an Austrian."[47]

House saw the affair as an opportunity and asked Wilson if they could "immediately let some of the obnoxious underlings of the offending Embassies go?" He also urged the president to break off relations with Austria-Hungary, arguing that the *Arabic* Pledge "should have bound [Germany's] allies as much as it bound her."[48]

On Sunday, November 28 House met Lansing to discuss US relations with Germany and Britain. The former stated that the United States should inform the Allies that "their cause [was] our cause" and that it was "impossible to maintain cordial relations with Germany . . . It was evident that the Government there was looking for some excuse for failure and the easiest and best in their opinion, seemed to be the United States' 'unneutral attitude in regard to the shipments of munitions of war, and the lending of money to her enemies.'"[49]

Considering his secret mediation efforts, House was trying to decide how to strengthen relations with Britain and hold a tough line with Germany while posing as an unbiased neutral. Together he and Lansing concluded that the best solution was to request a new ambassador from London, "provided [that] the President consented." House then advised Lansing to "find some excuse to send as many of the Germans and Austrians [diplomats] home as he reasonably could" and again urged severing relations with Austria. Doing so would serve as a warning to Germany, which he accused of pulling the strings in Vienna anyway. The State Department should not send Bernstorff home, he stated, because the United States could not break relations with Germany, but expelling Austrian officials might warn Germany not to push the United States too far. House reiterated his opinion to Wilson. The president agreed that the Allies should know "how our mind is running," but that asking Britain to replace Spring-Rice was not the answer.[50]

Over the same period, British allegations of German propaganda and sabotage in the United States were bearing fruit. While the German saboteurs were few in number and accomplished little, British articles in US newspapers gave the impression that German spies were everywhere. This British propaganda generated witch-hunts for subversives. Americans, Lansing recalled, became "spy mad." The State Department received numerous letters from the British government complaining about German activities, and Lansing seems to have believed that the accusations were true and assured Spring-Rice that the United States was taking steps to capture anyone caught in the act of damaging British property.[51]

According to Lansing, between March and September 1915, 13 explosions had occurred on outbound ships and ten in munitions plants across the nation. None, however, were proven attacks. "All of these explosions," declared Lansing in his memoir, "were believed to be caused by bombs placed by German plotters and fired by clockwork, a fact of which there was little doubt but which was difficult to prove."[52] Nevertheless Lansing's comments to Spring-Rice demonstrate that such rumors caused frustration in the White House.

At the same time that rumors of German sabotage spread within the Wilson administration, the pro-German organization Friends of Peace made numerous verbal attacks on the president. On November 18, John Brisben Walker, national chairman of the Friends of Peace, decried Wilson as "unneutral" and condemned his decision to approve the British loan. Attacking the administration's defense of munitions sales, he added, "Upon Mr. Wilson rests the responsibility of this crime—the greatest the world has ever known."[53] When he finished his speech, the *New York Herald* reported that shouts of "Shoot the President!" were heard, "to which no member of the audience objected."[54]

When Joseph Tumulty, Wilson's personal secretary, read the articles about the Friends of Peace, he forwarded them to Wilson along with editorials that criticized the "unchecked secret warfare which the Teutonic allies have waged here." Tumulty claimed that Americans were tired of pro-German agitation in the United States: "The country everyday reads of the efforts of these hyphenated Americans to destroy manufacturing plants, to poison and control public opinion in every way, and is astounded at the seeming indifference of the Administration toward these efforts to undermine us and to injure our people." In his opinion, Washington had to respond. The administration lacked "*aggressive* assertiveness" and "the time has come for *action,* and ACTION and MORE ACTION all along the line."[55]

Wilson in fact was ready for action. In addition to evidence that the German embassy had forged passports for German reservists who wanted to fight in Europe and rumors of sabotage, several major events stirred Washington and the American public. Previously on July 24, German Commercial Advisor Dr. Heinrich Albert left a briefcase containing secret documents on an elevated commuter train in New York City. Before he could retrieve the portfolio—which contained files implicating various German officers in plots to conduct espionage and sabotage along the American east coast—a US secret service agent who was following him grabbed the satchel.[56]

On August 15, the documents found their way into the pages of the New York newspaper *The World*.[57] Albert's letters deepened the administration's distrust of Germany and furnished proof that Germany was trying to disrupt US industry. Lansing decided that publishing some of the letters would also quiet the anti-administration propaganda of German-American newspapers, especially *The Fatherland*. One of the publicized documents suggested that the Imperial Government was funding the paper. Lansing's strategy evidently worked. He later noted that from that point on, the public viewed *The Fatherland* as a publication of the German government.[58]

The rumors and activities generated much anti-German literature. Books such as *The German-American Plot* reached a wide readership. Wilson echoed the sentiment of many Americans who were frustrated with what they considered "hyphenism." In a patriotic address to the Daughters of the American Revolution on October 11, 1915, the president argued that he was ready to have a "line-up and let the men who are thinking first of other countries stand on one side—Biblically, it should be the left, and all those that are for America first, last and all the time on the other side." He enjoined his listeners to maintain a spirit of neutrality but let his own sentiment shine through when he added, "[T]rue Americans must haze irresponsible persons who sought to use American influence for other than American aims."[59]

Days after Wilson's speech, many American newspapers denounced Germany's decision to execute Edith Cavell, a British nurse working in Belgium who was helping soldiers sneak across the front lines.[60] Like Allied papers, US newsmen described her as an innocent, young, and beautiful nurse murdered by the evil Hun. The *New York Evening Post* claimed the slaying of "a pure and good woman adds to the blackness of Germany's record, which is already one of the blackest in history." Additionally editors received numerous letters condemning the Germans and in some cases demanding a declaration of war.[61]

In November the contents of Albert's portfolio gained a new lease of life. While Wilson and his advisors could not send home Berlin's ambassador, they decided to use the papers as an excuse to expel a number of lower-level German diplomats. Lansing informed Wilson that the administration had to deal with the German spies and saboteurs working out of the embassy.[62]

Lansing promptly met with Bernstorff and Zwiedinek to inform them that the State Department planned to publicly "request the withdrawal" of three low-level diplomats. In separate meetings he told them that these men were "unacceptable to this Government, and we desired them to withdraw from this country."[63] When Zwiedinek sought to delay the expulsion of one, Wilson intervened to urge speed and suggested that Albert be expelled as well.[64]

The president had had enough. By early December 1915, he no longer feared the German-American vote and was ready to respond to those who were constantly berating the administration for its increasingly obvious pro-British stance. In his annual State of the Union address before Congress on December 7, Wilson made public his new agenda for the country and criticized the unpatriotic sentiments that he surmised existed within the German-American community. He asserted that the United States would remain neutral and that he did not see any immediate threats to the "amicable relations" existing with both Germany and Britain. Nevertheless, he stated that the country needed to increase the size of the military. In late 1914, he assumed that the belligerents might view an expansion of the US Army and Navy as a threat or, at the very least, a nonneutral act that would hamper his mediation efforts. Moreover he did not want to cause a domestic crisis. The events of 1915 changed his mind. He now argued that military preparedness was necessary to the defense of his country and to the implementation of his policies. "[I]f our citizens are ever to fight effectively upon a sudden summons," he proclaimed, "they must know how modern fighting is done, and what to do when the summons comes to render themselves immediately available and immediately effective."

Wilson called for expanding the army to 400,000 men. He also proposed a building program that would make the US Navy a formidable force on the seas. In addition he stated that the country could not depend on other nations' vessels to carry its goods around the globe. In a time of war America might find itself unable to conduct overseas trade: "If other nations go to war or seek to hamper each other's commerce, our merchants, it seems, are at their mercy, to do with as they please . . . [W]e can develop no true or effective American policy without ships of our own,—not ships of war, but ships of peace."[65]

As for the state of the Union itself, he pointedly criticized those who although "welcomed under our generous naturalization laws to the full freedom and opportunity of America . . . [had] poured the poison of disloyalty into the very arteries of our national life." Never in American history, he exaggeratedly claimed, had the nation experienced such activities by its very own citizens, and he called on Congress to pass laws to punish disloyalty.[66]

Wilson also called for economic and industrial mobilization since the country's safety depended on a strong economy. "We cannot adequately make ready for any trial of our strength unless we wisely and promptly direct the force of our laws into these all-important fields of domestic action." He pledged to coordinate efforts between military and industrial leaders to assure a smooth transition to a war footing. The overarching aim of his proposals, Wilson concluded was, "national efficiency and security."[67]

Commenting on Wilson's address to Congress, Spring-Rice told Grey that when the president condemned "the disloyal action of the hyphenated citizen [he] was greeted with great applause." The ambassador asserted that Wilson considered withdrawing the statement, but in the end he had decided to include the denunciation. To Spring-Rice, this was an important turning point. It confirmed to the ambassador that Wilson was no longer going to kowtow to the German-American vote. "He had thus crossed the Rubicon," exulted Spring-Rice. "He had openly attacked the German Americans who have as openly attacked him." He also assumed that the president's speech showed the sentiment of the American people. The ambassador expressed that Wilson felt he could not act unless he had the will of the people behind him and that the president "has continually waited for an indication of what is the popular will . . . When the popular will has been expressed he has done what the popular will seemed to demand." Spring-Rice told Grey that the president's "policy from the first was to maintain absolute neutrality and he certainly did his best to keep the straight line. If the people desire action in regard to foreign affairs inconsistent with neutrality and the desire is clearly expressed he will no doubt take it but not until the expression is clear and definite." Americans, Spring-Rice deduced, were gradually realizing their interests in the European struggle and that their security was at stake: "The visible sign of the struggle which is plain to all is the odious policy of treachery, disloyalty, outrage, and crime which is being pursued before the American people and on American soil by the agents of a foreign government, and which is more and more working its effect upon public sentiment."[68]

Spring-Rice felt that Germany was injuring itself with such tactics and that the wisest thing the Allies could do was "not allow the situation to be complicated by any action on our part which may appear to have an unfriendly character to-ward this people and its interests . . . The main thing before us however is that a great issue is making itself more and more clear before the minds of this people and that they are beginning to see things as they never saw them before." The ambassador knew that the direction of American sentiment was not something London could control. The growing agitation within the United States, he asserted, might not last and American public opinion could change in the future. However, he added with a sense of satisfaction, "we can tell that there is a change which is operating at the present moment and that this change is in favour of the allies."[69]

While Spring-Rice's observations about the sentiment of the American people may be exaggerated, he hit the mark in that president had become extremely frustrated with Germany in the latter months of 1915. The submarine crisis, rumors of German sabotage, growing trade with Britain, and the failing mediation efforts had exacerbated the president's perception of the belligerents. In promoting preparedness, he was sending a signal that German submarine attacks were becoming intolerable. Building up the navy would help the nation protect its merchant shipping against German attacks. Additionally expansion of the US Army was an effort to deal with national security—specifically a theorized German invasion of North America. Berating the German-American population and promoting the expansion of the military and merchant marine were not unneutral acts; however, as the ambassador indicates to Grey, the State of the Union address is a clear indicator of Wilson's new stance on the war.

On the morning of December 15, House went to the White House to meet with the president. The colonel was surprised to find Wilson "not quite as belligerent as he was the last time we were together." He noted that the president did not think that at present the US military could have an immediate impact on the war. This was a reasonable assumption considering that the expansion of the naval and ground forces would take time, but his comment to House did not mean that he was reconsidering his approach to neutrality. He still wanted House to go to Europe to discuss his secret proposal with Grey. Wilson and House decided that the latter should travel under the pretense of conferring with the American ambassadors in Britain, France, and Germany. Doing so, they hoped, would keep his true intentions hidden.[70]

Conclusion

July 1914 to December 1915 was the critical period in the Anglo-American quest for diplomatic rapport. During these months, London and Washington cultivated economic and political bonds that convinced Wilson to violate US neutrality. The transition was neither simple nor smooth. When the war began, the president tried to uphold neutrality in spite of his private desire for an Allied victory. In the months that followed, British and US diplomats navigated a maze of domestic and international issues, communicating through official and backdoor channels and compromising when necessary in pursuance of their separate political and economic objectives. By the end of the period, however, relations between the two countries reached a point where US interests and UK interests became Anglo-American interests and Wilson could no longer claim to be a neutral spectator of the war.

When the conflict began in 1914, British and US interests were at odds. The Royal Navy's prewar plan to keep Germany off the seas and strangle it into submission had the unavoidable consequence of interference in neutral commerce. The British strategy challenged the age-old US philosophy that neutral merchants were free to trade without interference. In addition to defending its commercial rights, the United States had its own wartime goals. The president thought that his administration could bring the belligerents together and mediate an end to the European conflict. He also wanted US firms to reap financial rewards through increased exports to the warring parties. Wilson reasoned that he could best achieve these aims by protecting US neutrality and keeping the United States out of the war. Assuring America's nonaligned position, however, was almost impossible because neutrality required the forfeiture of US international business interests, something Washington and the US public were unwilling to do. Additionally the president's partisanship distorted his conception of neutrality and efforts to fulfill his lofty goals. Accordingly, in the first year of the war, Wilson failed to understand that many of the decisions he considered neutral undermined his position.

In the debates over the Declaration of London, the United States proposed using the decree as an established set of rules for neutral traders. The

Wilson administration acknowledged that Britain had rejected the treaty in 1911 and that in the Orders in Council of August and October of 1914 the Asquith government had applied a policy that the United States had used during the American Civil War. Thus when Britain refused to accept the document, Wilson and his advisors deduced that international law favored Britain and that their options for negotiating over neutral rights at sea were limited. As an industrial power, the United States could have threatened to sever trade relations with the Allies, but this would certainly have exacerbated the already reeling US financial outlook in 1914. Additionally such action might have eliminated even the minute chance for the administration to satisfy its ardent desire to mediate an end to the war. Regardless Wilson plausibly did not realize the economic leverage that he could have used against Britain because he gave no indication that he considered any other options after then State Department Counselor Robert Lansing told him that they had no real choice but to acquiesce. The president, therefore, accepted Britain's Orders in Council and surmised that he was still defending US neutrality by protesting against British seizures of American cargoes on a case-by-case basis.

To keep his country out of the war, Wilson not only tried to reach an agreement on a set of regulations for global trade, he sought ways to avoid complications with the belligerents. On the advice of then Secretary of State William Jennings Bryan, Wilson took actions that went beyond the legal construction of neutrality. By initially opposing American loans to the belligerents, Wilson and the secretary of state assumed they could bring about a quick end to the war. They also feared that loans would divide the United States and result in domestic strife. But in pursuing this objective, the administration inadvertently jeopardized the US economy. Britain was dependent on American goods, and the reliance intensified as the war continued. In deterring loans, the president placed his own country's economic health at risk because the Allies could not continue making enormous purchases without borrowing money in the United States.

As president, Wilson made several executive decisions that he reasoned would protect US neutrality. At the same time, he also tried to manipulate the outcomes of legislation being debated on Capitol Hill. He proposed a bill that would allow for the establishment of a government-owned merchant marine. Wilson asserted that increasing the size of the US commercial fleet would alleviate America's dependence on Britain and open up new markets for US exports. The shipping bill faced major opposition in Congress as well as from existing shipping interests, which favored laissez-faire capitalism. Wilson also opposed measures that would ban the sale of war materiel to the belligerents. He and Bryan argued that the United States had the legal right to sell arms and held the illogical assumption that cutting off Britain's access to them would threaten America's position as a nonaligned outsider. Despite the president's and Congress's intentions, the defeat of the shipping and munitions bills inadvertently drew the United States closer to the Allies.

Just as Wilson's decisions moved America nearer to Britain, the latter's incessant demand for arms and munitions intensified its interest in American friendship. As early as the fall of 1914, Britain confronted a major shortage of munitions. Decreases in the flow of weaponry and munitions across the ocean threatened the Asquith government and the outcome of the war. Therefore Britain paid close attention to US domestic politics. Willingness to cooperate with the Wilson administration was first evident in Britain's decision to replace its August Order in Council and keep cotton on the free list. Foreign Secretary Edward Grey and the cabinet appreciated both cotton's value to the American South and the connection between the region's economic health and its political support for the American president. Turning the South against Britain could have had a detrimental effect on the flow of munitions to the Allies because Congress might demand retaliation against Allied policies. To prevent US pressure from threatening the blockade of Germany and the flow of munitions, Britain continued making cordial gestures toward the United States, such as purchasing goods otherwise destined for Germany, feigning interest in Wilson's calls for mediation, and employing propaganda to cultivate pro-Allied feelings in the United States.

By late 1915, choices made since the beginning of the war had enmeshed Britain's success with the political and economic goals of the United States. The two countries became clearly dependent on each other, a reality that neither side was naïve enough to miss. When it became apparent in August 1915 that Britain needed loans to continue purchasing American goods, Wilson discretely and deliberately ended his opposition to lending to the Allies. This added another layer to their relationship. Not only were the Allies reliant on US industry, they became reliant on American funding as well.

At the same time, and in large part because of the expanding Anglo-American commercial and political bonds, Wilson's perception of Germany and his approach to mediation efforts changed. He opposed Berlin's February 1915 decision to use submarines against merchant vessels around the British Isles. Unlike the British blockade, which was intended to starve German civilians, U-boat attacks endangered Americans, and the death of US citizens during the summer of 1915 evidently convinced Wilson that Germany was brazenly callous toward the lives of his countrymen. In addition, German and German–American activities in the United States persuaded many Americans that the Imperial Government had brought the war across the Atlantic. Such events drove a wedge between the United

States and Germany and convinced Wilson to rethink his position on US preparedness and mediation.

Wilson did not realize that the German U-boat campaign and sabotage on American soil were in many ways reactions to his very own policies. Regardless of his apparent belief that he was acting impartially, Wilson's pro-Allied partisanship led him to condemn German operations that were often less appalling than British actions. By late 1915, the president's desire to assure US economic prosperity and his conclusion that Berlin was the sole barrier to peace convinced him to provide calculated support for the Allies. Consequently Wilson rationalized that neutrality was no longer in America's best interest and abandoned it.

Britain and the United States faced additional hurdles in 1916 and 1917, but they were not divisive enough to endanger the rapport established by the end of 1915. London eventually rejected Colonel Edward House's proposal to pressure Germany into peace talks. The British and French were not seriously interested in what became known as the House-Grey Memorandum. The Allies held out hope that they could defeat Germany in the field. Grey told House that they might be able to put the mediation strategy into effect sometime in late 1916. Yet after the failure of the Allied offensive at the Battle of the Somme, London delayed the proposal for mediation indefinitely. Once Chancellor of the Exchequer David Lloyd George became prime minister in December 1916, mediation was no longer possible; he believed that the Allies had to defeat Germany, not talk with it.[1] Thus even Wilson's appeal for "peace without victory" in early 1917 had no real chance for success.

Over the same period, the Foreign Office tightened the blockade by establishing a commercial blacklist of neutral firms that traded with the Central Powers. The policy angered many Americans, including the president, who on July 24, 1916, told House, "I am, I must admit, about to the end of my patience with Great Britain and the Allies. This black list business is the last straw." He threatened cutting off foreign loans because Britain was trying to prevent the United States from gaining "a foothold in markets which Great Britain has hitherto controlled and all but dominate" and to write a letter of protest to the Foreign Office that was "as sharp and as final as the one to Germany on the submarines."[2]

These issues certainly tested Anglo-American relations; however, they were not enough to break the bonds that had developed since August 1914. While the blacklist angered Wilson, he refused to allow it to disrupt the growing US economy. Wilson did send a stern message to London but eschewed any strong action for the rest of 1916. In a letter to Maurice B. Blumenthal, attorney for the Association to Resist British Domination of American Commerce, Wilson asserted that he saw no reason to address the blacklist until after he was reelected in the upcoming November election.[3] Regardless of his failed mediation efforts and irritation over the blacklist, he refused to jeopardize ties with the United States' most valuable economic partner. Speaking in Topeka, Kansas, on February 2, 1916, Wilson emphasized the importance he placed on American prosperity when he stated, "There is a moral obligation laid upon us to keep out of this war if possible. But, by the same token there is a moral obligation upon us to keep free the courses of our commerce and our finance." The total value of US exports jumped almost 300 percent between August 1914 and December 1915. The largest increase occurred in the latter half of 1915, concurrent with Wilson's changing approach to neutrality. By the end of the year, the Allies had purchased munitions in the United States valued at $508,269,245.00. Trade with Britain continued to rise throughout 1916 and into January 1917 when the dollar amount of America's overseas commerce reached an all-time high of $613.3 million.[4]

Britain's reliance on foreign credit increased significantly in 1916. During the first 18 months of the war, Britain was furnishing the credit for Russia's, and eventually Italy's, materiel purchases in the United States, and in 1916, France joined the list of dependents. These obligations, along with its own, led Chancellor of the Exchequer Reginald McKenna to fear that Britain's government could be bankrupt by June. French and British estimates suggested that they would need $1,500,000,000 to subsidize the war effort between September 1916 and April 1917, and the ability to finance the war further was questionable. The ongoing financial crisis forced Britain to seek additional loans in the United States.[5] Thus because of Britain's continued demand for war materiel and credit, the United States became the most powerful exporting country on the planet. Endangering the two states' economic interdependence was something that neither could afford.

Notes

Introduction

1. Hew Strachan, *The Outbreak of the First World War* (Oxford: Oxford University Press, 2004), 132–40; Richard Van Emden and Steve Humphries, *All Quiet on the Home Front: An Oral History of Life in Britain during the First World War* (London: Headline Book Publishing, 2003), 9–10; John Keegan, *The First World War* (New York: Vintage Books, 2000), 75.
2. Robert Lansing, *War Memoirs of Robert Lansing* (Westport, CT: Greenwood, 1970), 35.
3. Arthur Link, *Wilson the Diplomatist: A Look as His Major Foreign Policies* (Chicago, IL: Quadrangle Paperbacks, 1957), 3–5; Jan Willem Schulte Nordholt, *Woodrow Wilson: A Life for World Peace* (Berkley: University of California Press, 1991), 133; H. W. Brands, *Woodrow Wilson* (New York: Henry Holt, 2003), 41–42.
4. H. C. Engelbrecht and F. C. Hanighen, *Merchants of Death* (New York: Dodd, Mead, 1934).
5. For arguments that emphasize the influence of economics on Wilson's foreign policy, see Charles Beard, *The Devil Theory of War: An Inquiry into the Nature of History and the Possibility of Keeping out of War* (New York: Greenwood, 1977); Charles Callan Tansill, *America Goes to War* (New York: Little, Brown, 1963 reprint); Sidney Bell, *Righteous Conquest: Woodrow Wilson and the Evolution of New Diplomacy* (New York: Kennikat, 1972); William Diamond, *The Economic Thought of Woodrow Wilson* (Baltimore, MD: Johns Hopkins Press, 1943); Jeffrey J. Safford, *Wilsonian Maritime Diplomacy, 1913–1921* (New Brunswick, NJ: Rutgers University Press, 1978); William Appleman Williams, *The Tragedy of American Diplomacy* (New York: W. W. Norton, 1988); Carl P. Parrini, *Heir to Empire: United States Economic Diplomacy, 1916–1923* (Pittsburgh, PA: University of Pittsburgh Press, 1969); Ross Gregory, *The Origins of American Intervention in the First World War* (New York: W. W. Norton, 1971); John W. Coogan, *The End of Neutrality: The United States, Britain, and Maritime Rights, 1899–1915* (Ithaca, NY: Cornell University Press, 1981).
6. For arguments by historians who assert that Wilson's foreign policy was driven by the visionary goal of collective security and a desire to protect and spread democracy around the globe, see Arthur Link, *Wilson: The Struggle for Neutrality, 1914–1915* (Princeton, NJ: Princeton University Press, 1960); Kendrick A. Clements, *The Presidency of Woodrow Wilson* (Lawrence: University Press of Kansas, 1992); John Milton Cooper Jr., *Woodrow Wilson* (New York: Alfred A.

Knopf, 2009); Thomas J. Knock, *To End All Wars: Woodrow Wilson and the Quest for a New World Order* (Princeton, NJ: Princeton University Press, 1992); Lloyd E. Ambrosius, *Wilsonian Statecraft: Theory and Practice of Liberal Internationalism during World War I* (New York: Scholarly Resources, 1991); George F. Kennan, *American Diplomacy: 1900–1950* (Chicago, IL: University of Chicago Press, 1951); Robert W. Tucker, *Woodrow Wilson and the Great War: Reconsidering America's Neutrality 1914–1917* (University of Virginia Press, 2007).

7. For works that focus on national security, see Ross A. Kennedy, *The Will to Believe: Woodrow Wilson, World War I, and America's Strategy for Peace and Security* (Kent, OH: Kent State University Press, 2009); and Daniel M. Smith, *The Great Departure: The United States and World War I, 1914–1920* (New York: John Wiley and Sons, 1965).
8. Historians including Robert Ferrell, *Woodrow Wilson and World War I, 1917–1919* (Bloomington: Indiana University Press, 1985); Kennedy, *The Will to Believe*; Coogan, *The End of Neutrality*; Bell, *Righteous Conquest*; and Tansill, *America Goes to War*, assert that Wilson was never neutral or at best made no effort to remain neutral once the war began.
9. Woodrow Wilson to Associated Press, April 20, 1915, Arthur S. Link, ed., *The Papers of Woodrow Wilson* (Princeton, NJ: Princeton University Press, 1980), 33: 37–41.
10. Kennedy, *The Will to Believe*, 43.
11. Wilson's speech at the Annual Banquet of the New York Economic Club, May 23, 1912, Ray Stannard Baker, ed., *The Public Papers of Woodrow Wilson*, Volume 2 (New York: Harper and Brothers, 1925), 471; Diamond, *The Economic Thought of Woodrow Wilson*, 132–13; Safford, *Wilsonian Maritime Diplomacy, 1913–1921*, 18–20.

Chapter 1

1. Page to Wilson, August 2, 1914, Arthur S. Link, ed., *The Papers of Woodrow Wilson* (Princeton, NJ: Princeton University Press, 1979), 30: 329–30.
2. Thomas J. Knock, *To End All Wars: Woodrow Wilson and the Quest for a New World Order* (Princeton University Press, 1992), 23; Alexander L. George and Juliette L. George, *Woodrow Wilson and Colonel House: A Personality Study* (New York: Dover, 1964), 93–94.
3. House to Wilson, May 29, 1914, Link, ed., *The Papers of Woodrow Wilson*, 30: 108–9.
4. Page to Wilson, August 2, 1914, ibid., 30: 329–30.
5. Ross Gregory, *Walter Hines Page: Ambassador to the Court of St. James's* (Lexington: University Press of Kentucky, 1970), 56.
6. Page to Wilson, July 29, 1914, Link, *The Papers of Woodrow Wilson*, 30: 314–15. For more on the intricacies of the July Crisis and the interworking of the Triple Alliance, which included Germany, Austria-Hungary, and Italy (Italy remained neutral when the war broke out), and on the Triple Entente, see

Ian F. W. Beckett, *The Great War, 1914–1918* (London: Pearson, 2001), 19–21, 27–32; Joachim Remak, *1914–The Third Balkan War: Origins Reconsidered*, in H. W. Koch, ed., *The Origins of the First World War: Great Power Rivalries and German War Aims* (Macmillan, 1984), 86–100; Zara Steiner, *Britain and the Origins of the First World War* (New York: St. Martin's Press, 1977), 99–100; Hew Strachan, *The Outbreak of the First World War*, 81–127.

7. Trevor Wilson, *The Myriad Faces of War: Britain and the Great War, 1914–1918* (Cambridge: Polity Press, 1986), 30.
8. John H. Maurer, *The Outbreak of the First World War: Strategic Planning, Crisis Decision Making, and Deterrence Failure* (London: Prager, 1995), 105; David French, *British Strategy and War Aims 1914–1916* (London: George Allen and Unwin, 1986), 6–8, 21.
9. Wilson, *The Myriad Faces of War*, 30.
10. Wilson to House, August 3, 1914, Link, *The Papers of Woodrow Wilson*, 30: 336. Revisionist historian Charles Tansill asserts that Wilson missed a real opportunity to stop the war before it began. However, Tansill's assessment suggests that Wilson had more power and influence over world affairs than he actually did in August 1914. In the first days of the war, the United States had little if any substantial leverage with which to stop decades of tension from erupting in Europe. See Charles Callan Tansill, *America Goes to War* (New York: Little, Brown, 1963 reprint), 435.
11. Niels Aage Thorsen, *The Political Thought of Woodrow Wilson 1875–1910* (Princeton University Press, 1988), 5–6.
12. John Morton Blum, *Woodrow Wilson and the Politics of Morality* (Little, Brown, 1956), 6, 11.
13. Wilson's speech at the Annual Banquet of the New York Economic Club, May 23, 1912, Baker, ed., *The Public Papers of Woodrow Wilson: College and State*, Volume 2, 432; Thorsen, *The Political Thought of Woodrow Wilson 1875–1910*, 6–7.
14. Knock, *To End All Wars*, 8.
15. Arthur S. Link, *The Higher Realism of Woodrow Wilson* (Nashville, TN: Vanderbilt, University Press, 1971), 6–10; Ernest May, *The World War and American Isolation, 1914–1917* (Cambridge: Harvard University Press, 1966), 41; "The Schoolmaster in Politics as the Wits See Him," *New York Times*, February 4, 1912, SM14.
16. Blum, *Woodrow Wilson and the Politics of Morality*, 15; Wilson to Mary Allen Hulbert, August 23, 1914, Link, *The Papers of Woodrow Wilson*, 30: 437.
17. Blum, *Woodrow Wilson and the Politics of Morality*, 15; Patrick Devlin, *Too Proud to Fight: Woodrow Wilson's Neutrality* (New York: Oxford University Press, 1975, c1974), 225–27; Wilson to House, August 17, 1914, Link, 30: 390; Wilson to House, August 18, 1914, *The Woodrow Wilson Papers*, 30: 395; George C. Osborn, *Woodrow Wilson: The Early Years* (Baton Rouge: Louisiana State University Press, 1968), 103. For more on Wilson's emotional stress related to Ellen Wilson's failing health and death, see Edwin A. Weinstein, *Woodrow Wilson: A Medical and Psychological Biography* (Princeton, NJ:

Princeton University Press, 1981), 254–62; Cary T. Grayson, *Woodrow Wilson: In Intimate Memoir* (New York: Holt, Rinehart and Winston, 1960), 32–36.

18. Wilson in Press Release, August 4, 1914, Link, *The Papers of Woodrow Wilson*, 30: 342.
19. Yale Law School, Lillian Goldman Library, 2008, "Washington's Farewell Address," The Avalon Project: Documents in Law, History, and Diplomacy, accessed July 2012, http://avalon.law.yale.edu/18th_century/washing.asp.
20. John Milton Cooper Jr., *The Vanity of Power: American Isolationism and the First World War, 1914–1917* (Westport, CT: Greenwood, 1969), 2.
21. "Multitudes Cheer at Bulletin Boards," *New York Times*, August 5, 1914, 7.
22. US Census Bureau, "Country of Origin of the Foreign White Stock," 1910 Census, Chapter 8, accessed July 2012, http://www.census.gov/prod/www/abs/decennial/1910.htm.
23. Wilson, "An Appeal to the American People," August 18, 1914, Link, *The Papers of Woodrow Wilson*, 30: 393–94.
24. Robert W. Tucker, *Woodrow Wilson and the Great War: Reconsidering America's Neutrality 1914–1917* (University of Virginia Press, 2007), 30; Kendrick A. Clements, *William Jennings Bryan: Missionary Isolationist* (Knoxville: University of Tennessee Press, 1982), 66; LeRoy Ashby, *William Jennings Bryan: Champion of Democracy* (Boston: Twayne, 1987), 153–55.
25. Clements, *William Jennings Bryan*, xii.
26. Bryan to Wilson, August 10, 1914, Link, *The Papers of Woodrow Wilson*, 30: 372–73.
27. Ibid.
28. The Secretary of State to J. P. Morgan and Company, August 15, 1914, *Foreign Relations of the United States: 1914. Supplement, The World War* (Washington, DC: Government Printing Office, 1928), 580, (hereafter cited as *FRUS*).
29. H. C. Peterson, *Propaganda for War: The Campaign against American Neutrality, 1914–1917* (Port Washington, NY: Kennikat, 1939), 13.
30. Ibid., 16–18.
31. George Robb, *British Culture and the First World War* (New York: Palgrave, 2002), 97–98; Peterson, *Propaganda for War*, 32; See also: M. L. Sanders, "Wellington House and British Propaganda during the First World War," *The Historical Journal*, Vol. 18, No. 1 (March 1975), 119–46.
32. "President Advises Nation to be Calm," *New York Times*, August 3, 1914, 3.
33. US Census Bureau, "No. HS-44. Agriculture–Farms, Acreage, Income, and Foreign Trade: 1900 to 2002, Statistical Abstracts of the United States," accessed May 2008, http://www.census.gov/statab/hist/HS-44.pdf.
34. Carl P. Parrini, *Heir to Empire: United States Economic Diplomacy, 1916–1923* (Pittsburgh, PA: University of Pittsburgh Press, 1969), 19; Department of Commerce, Bureau of Foreign and Domestic Commerce, *Statistical Abstract of the United States: 1914* (Washington, DC: Government Printing Office, 1915), 37: 320, 326.

35. Kathleen Burk, *Britain, America, and the Sinews of War 1914–1918* (Boston: George Allen and Unwin, 1985), 55; David M. Kennedy, *Over Here: The First World War and American Society* (Oxford University Press, 1980), 301.
36. Burk, *Britain, America, and the Sinews of War 1914–1918*, 56.
37. Wilson to Congress, September 4, 1914, Baker, ed. *The Public Papers of Woodrow Wilson*, Volume 2, 160–61.
38. Cecil Spring-Rice to Grey, September 24, 1914, FO 368 / 1159, National Archives, Kew, UK.
39. Arthur Jacob Marder, *The Anatomy of British Sea Power: A History of British Naval Policy in the Pre-Dreadnought Era, 1880–1905* (New York: Alfred A. Knopf, 1940), 84, 204, 358.
40. Arthur J. Marder, *From Dreadnought to Scapa Flow* (New York: Oxford University Press, 1961), 367–69, 382–83.
41. The Ambassador in Great Britain (Page) to the Secretary of State, August 5, 1914, *FRUS: 1914. Supplement, The World War*, 215–16; Paul Haggie, "The Royal Navy and War Planning in the Fisher Era," in Paul Kennedy, ed. *The War Plans of the Great Powers 1880–1914* (London: George Allen and Unwin, 1979), 122.

    Establishing a distant blockade that stretched from Scotland to Norway was illegal based on the 1856 Declaration of Paris, which stated that for a blockade to be legitimate it must be "maintained by a force sufficient really to prevent access to the coast of the enemy" (The Avalon Project: Documents in Law, History and Diplomacy, "Laws of War: Declaration of Paris; April 16, 1856," accessed October 2009, http://avalon.law.yale.edu/19th_century/decparis.asp). Preventing "access to the coast of an enemy" demanded close and constant guard by a blockading navy. Remaining at a distance made a blockade porous and thus ineffective. British officials believed the conditions of war had changed and made close blockades too dangerous. During the Napoleonic era, the British used the close blockade of French ports to bottle up French sea traffic. It would use frigates to prevent ships from entering or leaving France's ports and stationed the slower ships-of-the-line further out. This was easier in the early 1800s than in the early 1900s because sailing ships did not need to refuel and the advent of submarines and mines made the distant blockade Britain's only real option. According to the "General Instructions" of November 25, 1912, a "distant blockade will inflict injury upon German interests, credit, and prestige sufficient to cause serious economic consequences to Germany." Marder, *From Dreadnought to Scapa Flow*, 367–69, 382–83; Marder, *The Anatomy of British Sea Power*, 84, 204, 358.
42. The Secretary of State to the Ambassador in Great Britain (Page), August 6, 1914, *FRUS: 1914. Supplement, The World War*, 216; The Ambassador in Great Britain (Page) to the Secretary of State, August 19, 1914 (received August 20), *FRUS*, 217; Marion C. Siney, *The Allied Blockade of Germany 1914–1916* (Ann Arbor, MI: The University of Michigan Press, 1957), 21; Avner Offer, *The First World War: An Agrarian Interpretation* (Oxford: Oxford University Press, 1989), 276–81. There are two forms of contraband: absolute and conditional. Absolute contraband includes materials that are solely used by military forces.

They include munitions, arms, and any other equipment deemed military in nature. Conditional contraband includes goods that could be used by both civilians and the military such as foodstuffs that could be confiscated only if they were destined for an enemy government to further its war effort. C. Paul Vincent, *Politics of Hunger: The Allied Blockade of Germany, 1915–1919* (Athens, OH: Ohio University Press, 1985), 30–33. What was labeled as absolute or conditional contraband was subject to the needs and whims of the labeler; Tansill, *America Goes to War*, 135–36.

43. Ernest R. May, *The World War and American Isolation, 1914–1917* (Cambridge, MA: Harvard University Press, 1966), 8–12.
44. John W. Coogan, *The End of Neutrality: The United States, Britain, and Maritime Rights, 1899–1915* (Ithaca, NY: Cornell University Press, 1981),156–60, 186. Devlin points out that McKenna's evidence is suspect. It was never produced for review during or after the war. Devlin, *Too Proud to Fight*, 193; Reginald McKenna to Grey, August 19, 1914, FO 372 / 584, National Archives, Kew, UK. The doctrine of continuous voyage defines a cargo based on its final destination, not the intermediate ports along its overseas route. In the War of 1812, the US merchants used the tactic known as the broken voyage. According to the British Rule of 1756, ports closed in peacetime to foreign vessels due to protectionist policies were also closed in time of war. To circumvent this issue, shippers would load French goods into their vessels and travel to a US port to change the cargo's status to neutral before sailing to their final destination. David S. Heidler and Jeanne T. Heidler, *The War of 1812* (Westport, CT: Greenwood Press, 2002), 19–20.
45. The Ambassador in Great Britain (Page) to the Secretary of State, August 22, 1914 (received August 24, 1914), *FRUS: 1915. Supplement, The World War* (Washington, DC: Government Printing Office, 1928), 218; Orders in Council are a form of English legislation proposed by the sovereign or public ministers. In emergencies, the Orders in Council often are decrees that can circumvent the need for parliamentary approval.
46. Lansing to the Director of the Bureau of War Risk Insurance William C. Delanoy, September 15, 1914, Robert Lansing Papers, Manuscript Division, Library of Congress, Washington, DC.
47. Ibid.
48. "New Shipping Bill Will Be Pushed through Today," printed in *New York World*, August 2, 1914, Link, *The Papers of Woodrow Wilson*, 30: 325–26; Elizabeth Greenhalgh, *Victory through Coalition: Britain and France during the First World War* (Cambridge, UK: Cambridge University Press, 2005), 104.
49. Charles Gilbert, *American Financing of World War I* (Westport, CT: Greenwood Publishing Corporation, 1970), 23.
50. "Put World Trade under Flag of US, President's Plan," *New York World*, July 31, 1914, Link, *The Papers of Woodrow Wilson*, 324–25; Jeffrey J. Safford, *Wilsonian Maritime Diplomacy, 1913–1921* (New Brunswick, NJ: Rutgers University Press, 1978), 35.
51. Safford, *Wilsonian Maritime Diplomacy, 1913–1921*, 41–45.

52. Ibid., 45–47, 50.
53. William H. Libby (for Standard Oil Company of New Jersey) to the Secretary of State, August 18, 1914, *FRUS: 1914 Supplement, The World War*, 486–87.
54. "Transfer of German Merchant Ships to Neutral Flag," August 29, 1914, FO 372 / 578, National Archives, Kew, UK.
55. Grey to Barclay, August 21, 1914, British Cabinet Papers, CAB 37–121, National Archives, Kew, UK.
56. Lansing to Wilson, with Enclosure, August 22, 1914, Link, *The Papers of Woodrow Wilson*, 30:435–36; Lansing to Wilson, August 24, 1914, ibid., 30: 447–48.
57. Wilson to Lansing, August 25, 1914, ibid., 30: 451.
58. Historian Ross Kennedy provides a different perspective on Wilson's decision to comply with Britain's position. He asserts that in accepting Britain's stipulation, Wilson proved his "willingness to defer to the British" and that the decision was an example of his "limited informal cooperation with the Allied effort." Ross A. Kennedy, *The Will to Believe: Woodrow Wilson, World War I, and America's Strategy for Peace and Security* (Kent, OH: Kent State University Press, 2009), 66.
59. A Press Release by Joseph Patrick Tumulty, August 19, 1914, Link, *The Woodrow Wilson Papers*, 402; "US Will Buy Ships to Move the Crops," *New York Times*, August 20, 1914, 1; "Wilson Will Push the Shipping Bill," *New York Times*, August 25, 1914, 8.
60. Safford, *Wilsonian Maritime Diplomacy, 1913–1921*, 43–46, 76–77; *New York Times*, August 20, 1914; Spring-Rice to Grey, FO 372 / 578, August 29, 1914, National Archives, Kew, UK.
61. Handwritten notes attached to letter from Spring-Rice to Grey, August 29, 1914, FO 372 / 582, National Archives, Kew, UK.
62. "President Advises Nation to Be Calm," *New York Times*, August 4, 1914, 3.
63. From the Diary of Colonel House, August 30, 1914, Link, *The Papers of Woodrow Wilson*, 30: 461–64.
64. Ibid.
65. Spencer C. Tucker, *The Great War 1914–1918* (Bloomington: Indiana University Press, 1998), 26; Hew Strachan, *The First World War* (London: Viking Penguin, 2004), 48–51.
66. Bryan to Wilson, August 28, 1914, Link, *The Papers of Woodrow Wilson*, 30: 457–58.
67. President Wilson to the Secretary of State, September 4, 1914, *FRUS: 1915. Supplement, The World War*, 33; See also Laurence W. Martin, *Peace without Victory: Woodrow Wilson and British Liberals* (Port Washington, NY: Kennikat, 1973 reprint), 89.
68. George and George, *Woodrow Wilson and Colonel House*, 85; House to Wilson, August 1, 1914, Link, *The Papers of Woodrow Wilson*, 30: 327.
69. House to Wilson, August 5, 1914, *The Papers of Woodrow Wilson*, 30: 349–50.
70. House to Arthur Zimmermann, September 5, 1914, ibid., 30: 489.

71. For an argument discussing Wilson's national security concerns, see Ross A. Kennedy, *The Will to Believe: Woodrow Wilson, World War I, and America's Strategy for Peace and Security* (Kent, OH: Kent State University Press, 2009).
72. Grey to Spring-Rice, September 3, 1914, Link, *The Papers of Woodrow Wilson*, 30: 473.
73. French, *British Strategy and War Aims 1914–1916*, 36, 57–58; Jean Jules Jusserand to the French Foreign Ministry, September 8, 1914, Link, *The Papers of Woodrow Wilson*, 31: 15–16.
74. Gerard to German Foreign Office, September 8, 1914, *The Papers of Woodrow Wilson*, 31: 15–16.
75. Grey to Spring-Rice, September 9, 1914, David Stevenson, ed., *British Documents on Foreign Affairs: Reports and Papers from the Foreign Office Confidential Print.* Part 2, *From the First to the Second World War.* Series H. *The First World War, 1914–1918*, Volume 1, *The Allied and Neutral Powers: Diplomacy and War Aims, I: August 1914–July 1915* (Frederick, MD: University Publications of America, 1989), 1: 74–5; Page to Bryan, September 10, 1914, Link, *The Papers of Woodrow Wilson*, 31: 21–22.
76. Beckett, *The Great War, 1914–1918*, 56; Keegan, *The First World War*,122–23.
77. Bryan to Wilson, September 16, 1914, Link, *The Papers of Woodrow Wilson*, 31: 37.
78. Page to House, September 15, 1915, Charles Seymour, ed., *The Intimate Papers of Colonel House: Behind the Political Curtain, 1912–1915* (Boston: Houghton Mifflin, 1926), 1: 333.
79. House to Wilson, September 18, 1914, Link, *The Papers of Woodrow Wilson*, 31: 45.
80. Spring-Rice to Wilson, with Enclosure, September 19, 1914, ibid., 31: 58–59.
81. Bryan to Wilson, September 19, 1914, ibid., 31: 56–57.
82. House to Wilson, September 19, 1914, ibid., 31: 55.
83. House to Wilson, ibid., 60–61; Rice to Grey, September 20, 1914, ibid., 62; Spring-Rice to Grey, September 20, 1914, FO 800 / 84, National Archives, Kew, UK.
84. House to Wilson, September 22, 1914, Link, *The Papers of Woodrow Wilson*, 31: 75–76.

Chapter 2

1. Wilson to Hugo Münsterberg, November 10, 1914, Arthur S. Link, ed., *The Papers of Woodrow Wilson* (Princeton, NJ: Princeton University Press, 1980), 31: 293.
2. The Acting Secretary of State to the Ambassador in Great Britain (Page), September 26, 1914, *FRUS: 1914. Supplement, The World War*, 225–32.
3. Ibid.
4. Ibid.
5. Ibid.

6. Lansing to Wilson, September 27, 1914, Link, *The Papers of Woodrow Wilson*, 31: 85–86.
7. Diary of Colonel House, September 27, 1914, ibid., 31: 86–87.
8. Ibid., September 28, 1914, ibid., 31: 91–96.
9. Ibid.
10. Ibid.; Arthur Link, *Wilson: The Struggle for Neutrality, 1914–1915* (Princeton, NJ: Princeton University Press, 1960), 110–11.
11. Lansing to Wilson, September 28, 1914, Link, *The Papers of Woodrow Wilson*, 31: 90–91; Diary of Colonel House, September 28, 1914, ibid., 31: 91–96. Link italicized a portion of the letter to show the additions made by Wilson.
12. See also John Milton Cooper Jr., *Woodrow Wilson* (New York: Alfred A. Knopf, 2009), 265–66.
13. Spring-Rice to Grey, September 28, 1914, ibid., 31: 96.
14. Grey to Spring-Rice, September 29, 1914, FO 800 / 84.
15. Page to the Secretary of State, September 29, 1914, *FRUS: 1915. Supplement, The World War*, 233.
16. Diary of Colonel House, September 30, 1914, Link, *The Papers of Woodrow Wilson*, 31: 108–9.
17. Ibid.
18. Spring-Rice to Wilson, September 30, 1914, ibid., 31: 109–10.
19. Page to Bryan, September 30, 1914, *FRUS: 1914. Supplement, The World War*, 235.
20. Spring-Rice to Wilson (with enclosure), October 1, 1914, Link, *The Papers of Woodrow Wilson*, 31: 115–16.
21. Lansing to Wilson, October 8, 1914, ibid., 31: 133.
22. Ibid., 31: 133–37.
23. Revisionist author Charles Tansill asserts that by providing this interpretation of the Declaration of London to Grey, Lansing was "painfully anxious to conciliate the British Government." Charles Callan Tansill, *America Goes to War* (New York: Little, Brown, 1963 reprint), 158–62.
24. Spring-Rice in Embassy Diary, October 4, 1914, FO 800 / 84. During the American Civil War, the United States seized a British ship headed to Nassau that was carrying sabers destined for the Confederacy. In doing so, the United States not only upheld the idea of continuous voyage, it accepted the British understanding of the principle. Washington asserted that intent to break the blockade was pretext enough to seize a neutral vessel. John W. Coogan, *The End of Neutrality: The United States, Britain, and Maritime Rights, 1899–1915* (Ithaca, NY: Cornell University Press, 1981), 23.
25. Spring-Rice to Wilson (with enclosure), October 5, 1914, Link, *The Papers of Woodrow Wilson*, 31: 125–26.
26. Viscount Grey of Fallodon, KG, *Twenty-Five Years 1892–1916*, Volume 2 (New York: Frederick A. Stokes, 1925), 107–8.
27. Grey to Spring-Rice, October 10, 1914, Link, *The Papers of Woodrow Wilson*, 31: 145–47.
28. Ibid.; Siney, *The Allied Blockade of Germany*, 26–29.

29. Spring-Rice to Wilson, October 15, 1914, Link, *The Papers of Woodrow Wilson*, 31: 154–56.
30. Ibid.
31. Daniel M. Smith, *Robert Lansing and American Neutrality, 1914–1917* (Berkeley: University of California Press, 1958), 27.
32. Lansing to Wilson, October 15, 1914, Link, *The Papers of Woodrow Wilson*, 31: 158–59.
33. Page to Bryan, October 15, 1914, ibid., 31: 159–60.
34. Ross Gregory, *Walter Hines Page: Ambassador to the Court of St. James's* (Lexington: University Press of Kentucky, 1970), 66–68.
35. Wilson to Page, October 16, 1914, Link, *The Papers of Woodrow Wilson*, 31: 166.
36. Ibid.
37. Wilson and Lansing wrote the letter to Page, but Lansing signed it. Lansing to Page, October 16, 1914, Link, *The Papers of Woodrow Wilson*, 31: 163–66; Herbert Whittaker Briggs, *The Doctrine of Continuous Voyage* (Buffalo, NY: William S. Hein, 2003), 110–11; William A. Shepherd, *The Protection of Neutral Rights at Sea: Documents on Naval Warfare* (New York: Sturgis and Walton, 1915), 10.
38. Grey to Spring-Rice, October 17, 1914, FO 800 / 84.
39. Ibid.
40. Bryan to Lansing, November 2, 1914, Robert Lansing Papers, Library of Congress; Spring-Rice to Lansing, October 20, 1914, FO 800 / 241, National Archives, Kew, UK.
41. Lance E. Davis and Stanley L. Engerman, *Naval Blockades in War and Peace: An Economic History since 1750* (Cambridge, UK: Cambridge University Press, 2006), 118; Spring-Rice to Lansing, October 20, 1914, FO 800 / 241, National Archives, Kew, UK.
42. Spring-Rice to Lansing, October 20, 1914, FO 800 / 241, National Archives, Kew, UK.
43. Lansing to Wilson, October 20, 1914, Link, *The Papers of Woodrow Wilson,* 31: 188–90.
44. Coogan, *The End of Neutrality*, 20; Daniel M. Smith, "Robert Lansing and the Formulation of American Neutrality Policies, 1914–1915," *The Mississippi Valley Historical Review,* Vol. 43, No. 1 (June 1956), 63; Precedent and state interests not only directed international law, but also, as the Wilson administration would learn, laws pertaining to the confiscation of contraband and decisions made by prize courts. While prize courts were supposed to provide unbiased verdicts about contraband and neutral vessels, they usually would not make rulings that were counter to military strategy. See Devlin, *Too Proud to Fight*, 159–60.
45. Lansing to Wilson, October 20, 1914, Link, *The Papers of Woodrow Wilson,* 31: 188–90.
46. The Acting Secretary of State to Page, October 22, 1914, *FRUS: 1914. Supplement, The World War*, 257–58. For a different view on the conclusion to the

Declaration of London debate, see Coogan, *The End of Neutrality*, 210–11 and Ross A. Kennedy, *The Will to Believe: Woodrow Wilson, World War I, and America's Strategy for Peace and Security* (Kent, OH: Kent State University Press, 2009), 68. They assert that US acquiescence was an unneutral act that intentionally favored the Allies.

47. Lansing to Senator William J. Stone, Chair of the Foreign Relations Committee, January 8, 1915, *FRUS: 1914. Supplement, The World War*, 6–10.
48. Ibid.
49. Ibid.
50. Ibid.
51. Woodrow Wilson, *A History of the American People: The Founding of the Government*, Volume 3 (London: Harper and Brothers, 1908), 194; See also William Diamond, *The Economic Thought of Woodrow Wilson* (Baltimore, MD: Johns Hopkins Press, 1943), 156.
52. Lansing to Page, October 22, 1914, *Papers Relating to the Foreign Relations of the United States: 1914. Supplement, The World War* (Washington, DC: Government Printing Office, 1928), 257–58.
53. Page to Wilson, October 28, 1914, ibid., 31: 244.
54. McAdoo to Lansing, October 14, 1914, Lansing Papers, Library of Congress.
55. The Assistant Secretary of the Treasury (Peters) to the Acting Secretary of State (Lansing), October 14, 1914, *FRUS: The Lansing Papers, 1914–1920*, Volume 1, *The World War* (Washington, DC: Government Printing Office, 1928), 103–4. Peters to the Acting Secretary of State, October 14, 1914, ibid., 103–4.
56. Acting Secretary of State to Wilson, October 19, 1914, ibid., 104–5.
57. *New York Times*, October 19, 1914, 1.
58. Lansing to Wilson, October 20, 1914, Lansing Papers, Library of Congress.
59. Spring-Rice to Wilson (with enclosures), October 24, 1914, Link, *The Papers of Woodrow Wilson*, 31: 229–31.
60. Lansing to Peters, October 26, 1914, Lansing Papers, Library of Congress.
61. Wilson to Lansing, November 23, 1914, Link, *The Papers of Woodrow Wilson*, 31: 345–46.
62. Lansing to Wilson, November 23, 1914, ibid., 31: 347–49.
63. Ibid.
64. Joseph A. Fry, *Dixie Looks Abroad: The South and U.S. Foreign Relations, 1789–1973* (Baton Rouge: Louisiana State University Press, 2002), 150–51; "The Cotton Crisis, The South, and Anglo-American Diplomacy, 1914–1915," in Arthur S. Link, *The Higher Realism of Woodrow Wilson* (Nashville, TN: Vanderbilt University Press, 1971), 309; Martin T. Olliff, ed., *The Great War in the Heart of Dixie: Alabama during World War I* (Tuscaloosa: University of Alabama Press, 2008), 6.
65. The President of the Galveston Cotton Exchange and Board of Trade (I. H. Kemper) to the Solicitor for the State Department, October 20, 1914, *FRUS: 1914. Supplement, The World War*, 285–86.
66. The President of the New York Chamber of Commerce (Seth Low) to the Secretary of State, October 24, 1914, ibid., 287.

67. Lansing to Page, October 24, 1914, ibid., 288–89.
68. Grey of Fallodon, KG, *Twenty-Five Years 1892–1916*, Volume 2 (New York: Frederick A. Stokes, 1925), 109.
69. Ibid., 115–16.
70. Spring-Rice to Grey, October 20, 1914, FO 800 / 84.
71. US Senate Website, Party Divisions in the Senate 1789–Present, accessed June 2012, http://www.senate.gov/pagelayout/history/one_item_and_teasers/partydiv.htm.
72. *New York Times*, February 21, 1915, 3; United States House of Representatives, "Congressional Profiles," accessed July 2, 2013, http://history.house.gov/Congressional-Overview/Profiles/63rd/.
73. Dudley M. Hughes (Georgia), October 21, 1914, 63rd Congress, *Congressional Record, Appendix*, 1262–63.
74. Link, "The Cotton Crisis, The South, and Anglo-American Diplomacy, 1914–1915," in *The Higher Realism of Woodrow Wilson* (Nashville, TN: Vanderbilt University Press, 1971), 310; Justus D. Doenecke, *Nothing Less than War: A New History of America's Entry into World War I* (Lexington: The University Press of Kentucky, 2011), 42.
75. Jackson M. Young to John H. Bankhead, August 27, 1914, Senator John Bankhead Files, Alabama Department of Archives and History, Montgomery, Alabama.
76. Ibid. At the beginning of the war, Congress approved funds to send ships to Europe to help Americans evacuate the continent.
77. Diary of Colonel House, Link, *The Papers of Woodrow Wilson*, 31: 95; John Milton Cooper Jr., *The Warrior and the Priest* (Cambridge, MA: Belknap Press of Harvard University Press, 1985), 275.
78. Page to Bryan, October 26, 1914, *FRUS: 1914. Supplement, The World War*, 289.
79. Grey, *Twenty-Five Years*, 2: 109; George and George, *Woodrow Wilson and Colonel House*, 161; Spring-Rice to the Acting Secretary of State, October 26, 1914, *FRUS: 1914. Supplement, The World War*, 290.
80. Remarks at a Press Conference, October 26, 1914, Link, *The Papers of Woodrow Wilson*, 31: 233–35.
81. *New York Times*, February 21, 1915, 3; Biographical Directory of the United States Congress, 1774–2005, accessed July 2008, http://www.gpoaccess.gov/serialset/cdocuments/hd108-222/64th.pdf; Extension of Remarks of Hon. Simeon D. Fess of Ohio, January 23, 1915, *Congressional Record, Appendix*, 63rd Congress, 204–7; Cooper, *The Warrior and the Priest*, 250–51.
82. From the Diary of Colonel House, November 4, 1914, Link, *The Papers of Woodrow Wilson*, 31: 263–66.
83. Spring-Rice to Grey, November 3, 1914, FO 115 / 1770, National Archives, Kew, UK; Spring-Rice to Grey, November 9, 1914, Link, *The Papers of Woodrow Wilson*, 31: 292.
84. Spring-Rice to Grey, September 21 (received September 30), David Stevenson, ed., *British Documents on Foreign Affairs*, 101–2.
85. Ibid.
86. Spring-Rice to Grey, September 22, 1914, FO 800 / 84.

87. Hugo Münsterberg to Wilson, November 6, 1914, Link, *The Papers of Woodrow Wilson*, 31: 276–79.
88. Wilson to Münsterberg, November 10, 1914, ibid., 31: 293.
89. Ernest R. May *The World War and American Isolation 1914–1919* (Cambridge: Harvard University Press, 1966), 42–45.

Chapter 3

1. An Annual Address to Congress, December 8, 1914, Arthur S. Link, ed., *The Papers of Woodrow Wilson* (Princeton, NJ: Princeton University Press, 1979), 31: 414–24.
2. FO 368 / 1159 October 10, 1914, National Archives, Kew, UK.
3. Samuel J. Hurwitz, *State Intervention in Great Britain: A Study of Economic Control and Social Response, 1914–1919* (New York: Columbia University Press, 1949), 148–49; Kathleen Burk, *Britain, America, and the Sinews of War 1914–1918* (Boston: George Allen and Unwin, 1985), 14–15; Kitchener to French as cited in R. J. Q. Adams, *Arms and the Wizard: Lloyd George and the Ministry of Munitions, 1915–1916* (College Station: Texas A&M University Press, 1978), 15.
4. Lansing to Wilson (with enclosure), October 23, 1914, Link, *The Papers of Woodrow Wilson*, 31: 217–19.
5. A Memorandum by Robert Lansing, October 23, 1914, ibid., 31: 219.
6. Ibid.; Patrick Devlin, *Too Proud to Fight: Woodrow Wilson's Neutrality* (New York: Oxford University Press, 1975, c1974), 176; Henry Blumenthal, *Illusion and Reality in Franco-American Diplomacy: 1914–1945* (Baton Rouge, Louisiana State University Press, 1986), 12; William Diamond, *The Economic Thought of Woodrow Wilson* (Baltimore, MD: Johns Hopkins Press, 1943), 157.
7. Arthur Link, *Wilson: The Struggle for Neutrality, 1914–1915* (Princeton, NJ: Princeton University Press, 1960), 136; Ernest R. May *The World War and American Isolation 1914–1919* (Cambridge: Harvard University Press, 1966), 45–47.
8. Spring-Rice to Grey, November 3, 1914, FO 800 / 84.
9. Ibid.
10. Ibid.
11. Ibid.
12. Grey to Spring-Rice, November 6 1914, *FRUS: 1914. Supplement, The World War*, 338–39.
13. Pfeiffer to Bryan, November 6, 1914, ibid., 278–79.
14. Lansing to Spring-Rice, November 7, 1914, ibid., 339–41.
15. *Punch*, January 6, 1915, as cited in Armin Rappaport, *The British Press and Wilsonian Neutrality* (Gloucester, Massachusetts: Stanford University Press, 1965), 13.
16. Grey, *Twenty-Five Years*, 109–10.
17. Grey to the British Ambassador at Rome J. Rennell Rodd, November 8, 1914, *FRUS:1914. Supplement, The World War*, 342; Grey to Spring-Rice, November 8, 1914, FO 115 / 1770, National Archives, Kew, UK.

18. Acting Secretary of Commerce (William J. Harris) to Bryan, October 30, 1914, *FRUS: 1914. Supplement, The World War*, 420.
19. Lansing to Page, November 3, 1914, ibid., 422; Page to Lansing, November 6, 1914 (received November 7), ibid., 423.
20. Spring-Rice to Grey, November 13, 1914, Link, *The Papers of Woodrow Wilson*, 315–16.
21. Burk, *Britain, America, and the Sinews of War 1914–1918*, 14–15.
22. Wilson to Page, November 10, 1914, *The Papers of Woodrow Wilson*, 294.
23. Hew Strachan, *The First World War* (London: Viking Penguin, 2004), 139.
24. Grey to Spring-Rice, December 1, 1914, FO 115 / 1771, National Archives, Kew, UK.
25. Ibid.
26. Grey to Spring-Rice, December 22, 1914, FO 115 / 1771, National Archives, Kew, UK.
27. "Restriction of Enemy Supplies through US," December 1, 1914, FO 368 / 1162.
28. Page to Bryan, December 6, 1914 (received December 7, 1914), *FRUS: 1914. Supplement, The World War*, 356–57; Grey to Spring-Rice, December 6, 1914, FO 368 / 1162.
29. Page to Wilson, November 30, 1914, Link, *The Papers of Woodrow Wilson*, 31: 370–72.
30. British Cabinet Minutes, British Cabinet Papers, December 1914, Kew, National Archives, Kew, UK.
31. Lansing to Spring-Rice, December 7, 1914, FO 368 / 1162.
32. Sir A. Johnstone to Grey, November 18, 1914 (received November 20), David Stevenson, ed., *British Documents on Foreign Affairs: Reports and Papers from the Foreign Office Confidential Print*. Part 2, *From the First to the Second World War*. Series H. *The First World War, 1914–1918*, Volume 5, *Blockade and Economic Warfare, 1: August 1914–July 1915* (Frederick, MD: University Publications of America, 1989), 6–8.
33. Marjorie Milbank Farrar, *Conflict and Compromise: The Strategy, Politics and Diplomacy of the French Blockade, 1914–1918* (The Hague: Martinus Nijhoff, 1974), 60–62; Consul General at Rotterdam Soren Listoe to Bryan, December 21, 1914 (received January 4, 1915), *FRUS: 1915. Supplement, The World War*, 268–69; Marion C. Siney, *The Allied Blockade of Germany 1914–1916* (Ann Arbor, MI: The University of Michigan Press, 1957), 40–41; *New York Times* February 22, 1916, 4. The trusts were set up as nonprofit organizations. If the governments allowed the trusts to profit from their exploits, neutral exporters would have cause for complaint that could damage international relations. Therefore, any income accumulated by the trusts was to go to humanitarian relief efforts. The Minister in the Netherlands Henry van Dyke to Bryan, January 9, 1915, *FRUS: 1915. Supplement, The World War*, 269–70.
34. Grey to Spring-Rice, November 11, 1914, Link, *The Papers of Woodrow Wilson*, 31: 297–98.
35. Ibid.

36. Diary of Colonel House, November 14, 1914, Link, *The Papers of Woodrow Wilson*, 31: 317–20. On the advice of Dr. Grayson, the President tried to play golf regularly as a means of reducing his stress. Grayson, *Woodrow Wilson*, 46–47.
37. Diary of Colonel House, November 14, 1914, Link, *The Papers of Woodrow Wilson*, 31: 317–20.
38. Hugo Münsterberg to Wilson, November 19, 1914, ibid., 31: 336–40.
39. Ibid.
40. Wilson to Lansing, December 1, 1914, *The Papers of Woodrow Wilson*, 31: 376.
41. Lansing to Wilson, December 9, 1914, ibid., 31: 432–33.
42. Ibid.; Smith, "Robert Lansing and the Formulation of American Neutrality Policies, 1914–1915," *The Mississippi Valley Historical Review*, Vol. 43, No. 1 (June 1956), 67.
43. Wilson to Lansing, Link, *The Papers of Woodrow Wilson*, 31: 447.
44. Nancy Gentile Ford, *The Great War and America: Civil-Military Relations during World War I* (Westport, CT: Prager Security International, 2008), 2, 9–11; Charles Seymour, ed., *The Intimate Papers of Colonel House: Behind the Political Curtain, 1912–1915* (Boston: Houghton Mifflin, 1926), 1: 296–98. At the beginning of the war the US Army was less than 100,000 men strong. John Patrick Finnegan, *Against the Specter of a Dragon: The Campaign for American Military Preparedness, 1914–1917* (Westport, CT: Greenwood Press, 1974), 5–6.
45. Diary of Colonel House, November 4, 1914, Link, *The Papers of Woodrow Wilson*, 31: 263–66.
46. Diary of Colonel House, November 8, 1914, ibid., 31: 281.
47. Ibid.
48. Seymour, ed., *The Intimate Papers of Colonel House*, 1: 296–98; November 25, 1914, ibid., 31: 354–57; John Patrick Finnegan, *Against the Specter of a Dragon: The Campaign for American Military Preparedness, 1914–1917* (Westport, CT: Greenwood Press, 1974), 28.
49. Gaddis Smith, *Britain's Clandestine Submarines: 1914–1915* (New Haven: Yale University Press, 1964), 30–39.
50. Lansing to Bryan, November 12, 1914, Lansing Papers, Library of Congress.
51. Bryan to Wilson, November 12, 1914, *FRUS: The Lansing Papers, 1914–1920*, Volume 1, *The World War* (Washington, DC: Government Printing Office, 1928), 114.
52. Lansing to Wilson, November 28, 1914, Link, *The Papers of Woodrow Wilson*, 31: 359.
53. Wilson to Lansing, November 30, 1914, ibid., 31: 369.
54. Howard Jones, *Union in Peril: The Crisis Over British Intervention in the Civil War* (Chapel Hill: University of North Carolina Press, 1992), 146–47.
55. Frank J. Merli, *The Alabama, British Neutrality, and the Civil War*, ed. David M. Fahey (Bloomington: Indiana University Press, 2004), 141–42; "CSS *Alabama*," Naval Historical Center (Washington, DC: Department of the Navy), accessed July 2012, www.history.navy.mil/branches/org12-1.htm.

56. Jones, *Union in Peril*, 229; Adrian Cook, *The Alabama Claims: American Politics and Anglo-American Relations, 1865–1872* (Ithaca, NY: Cornell University Press, 1975), 239.
57. Lansing to James H. Hayden, December 1, 1914, *FRUS: 1914. Supplement, The World War*, 577–78; Smith, *Britain's Clandestine Submarines*, 46.
58. Spring-Rice to Bryan, December 16, 1914, FO 372 / 584, National Archives Kew, UK.
59. Spring-Rice to Grey, December 3, 1914, FO 371 / 2226.
60. An Annual Address to Congress, December 8, 1914, Link, *The Papers of Woodrow Wilson*, 31: 414–24.
61. Ibid.
62. Ibid.
63. Ibid.
64. Ibid.; Finnegan, *Against the Specter of a Dragon*, 28.

Chapter 4

1. Bryan to Wilson, December 1, 1914, Arthur S. Link, ed., *The Papers of Woodrow Wilson* (Princeton, NJ: Princeton University Press, 1979), 31: 378–79.
2. Ibid.
3. Ibid.
4. House to Wilson (with enclosures), December 27, 1914, ibid., 31: 540–41. Link suggests it was received around December 15; Patrick Devlin, *Too Proud to Fight: Woodrow Wilson's Neutrality* (New York: Oxford University Press, 1975, c1974), 245–46.
5. As quoted in Arthur Link, *Wilson: The Struggle for Neutrality, 1914–1915* (Princeton, NJ: Princeton University Press, 1960), 209.
6. Diary of Colonel House, December 16, 1914, Link, *The Papers of Woodrow Wilson*, 31: 468–71.
7. Ibid.; Charles Seymour, ed., *The Intimate Papers of Colonel House: Behind the Political Curtain, 1912–1915* (Boston: Houghton Mifflin, 1926), December 17, 1914, 1: 340–41.
8. Diary of Colonel House, December 18, 1914, Link, *The Papers of Woodrow Wilson*, 31: 489–90.
9. David M. Esposito, *The Legacy of Woodrow Wilson: American War Aims in World War I* (Westport, CT: Praeger, 1996), 20; Lady A. G. Lennox, ed., *The Diary of Lord Bertie of Thame 1914–1918* (London: Hodder and Stoughton, 1924), 81–82.
10. Diary of Colonel House, December 20, 1914, Link, *The Papers of Woodrow Wilson*, 31: 499–501.
11. Ibid.
12. Spring-Rice to Grey, December 10, 1914, FO 368 / 1161, National Archives, Kew, UK.
13. Spring-Rice to Grey, December 11, 1914, ibid.

14. Page to Bryan, December 13, 1914 (received December 14), *FRUS: 1914. Supplement, The World War*, 362–63.
15. Bryan to Wilson (with enclosure), December 17, 1914, Link, *The Papers of Woodrow Wilson,* 31: 458–60.
16. Diary of Colonel House, December 18, 1914, ibid., 31: 489–90.
17. Ibid.
18. Spring-Rice to Wilson (with enclosures), December 21, 1914, ibid., 31: 505–6.
19. Wilson to Spring-Rice, December 23, 1914, ibid., 31: 514.
20. Grey to Spring-Rice, December 19, 1914, FO 800 / 84; Grey to Spring-Rice, December 20, 1914, ibid.; Hew Strachan, *Financing the First World War* (Oxford: Oxford University Press, 2004), 188; Roberta A Dayer, "Strange Bedfellows: J. P. Morgan and Co. Whitehall, and the Wilson Administration during World War I," *Business History*, Vol. 18, No. 2 (1976), 128; Kathleen Burk, "The Treasury: From Impotence to Power," in Kathleen Burk, ed. *War and the State: The Transformation of the British Government, 1914–1919* (London: George Allen and Unwin, 1982), 89–90.
21. Grey to Spring-Rice, December 20, 1914, FO 800 / 84; Secretary of Commerce William C. Redfield's report on US munitions exports, December 18, 1914, *Congressional Record*, 63d Congress, 3d Session, Senate.
22. Clifton J. Child, "German-American Attempts to Prevent the Exportation of Munitions of War, 1914–1915," *The Mississippi Valley Historical Review*, Vol. 25, No. 3 (December 1938), 352.
23. *Wall Street Journal,* October 15, 1914, 7.
24. Frederick C. Luebke, *Bonds of Loyalty: German-Americans and World War I* (DeKalb: Northern Illinois University Press, 1974), 98; Child, "German-American Attempts to Prevent the Exportation of Munitions of War, 1914–1915," 355.
25. Justus D. Doenecke, *Nothing Less than War: A New History of America's Entry into World War I* (Lexington: The University Press of Kentucky, 2011), 53–54; *Atlanta Journal-Constitution*, December 16, 1914, 11.
26. Grey to Spring-Rice, December 13, 1914, FO 372 / 584, National Archives, Kew, UK.
27. Spring-Rice to Grey, December 11, 1914, FO 372 / 582, ibid.
28. Cabinet notes, December 28, 1914, British Cabinet Papers, CAB 37 / 122, National Archives, Kew, UK.
29. Lloyd George to Asquith, December 31, 1914, David Lloyd George Papers, C/6/11/24, Parliamentary Archives, London, UK.
30. "Convention (V) Respecting the Rights and Duties of Neutral Powers and Persons in Case of War on Land. The Hague, 18 October 1907," International Committee of the Red Cross, accessed July 2012, http://www.icrc.org/ihl.nsf/full/200?opendocument.
31. Ernest R. May, *The World War and American Isolation, 1914–1917* (Cambridge, MA: Harvard University Press, 1966), 47–50; Spring-Rice to Grey, December 11, 1914, FO 372 / 584, National Archives, Kew, UK.
32. Spring-Rice to Grey, January 5, 1915, FO 372 / 735, National Archives, Kew, UK.

33. Diary of Colonel House, December 23, 1914, Link, *The Papers of Woodrow Wilson*, 31: 517–20.
34. Ibid.
35. Ibid.
36. Bryan to Wilson, December 24, 1914, ibid., 31: 521–22; Wilson to Bryan (with enclosure), December 26, 1914, ibid., 31: 524–30.
37. Ibid.
38. Remarks at a Press Conference, December 29, 1914, ibid., 31: 543–45.
39. Diary of Colonel House, December 29, 1914, ibid., 31: 548–51.
40. House to Wilson (with enclosure), December 31, 1914, ibid., 31: 553.
41. Grey, *Twenty-Five Years*, 110. In 1923, to express their appreciation for Page's pro-British sentiments, London officials approved the installation of a memorial plaque at Westminster Abby for the former US ambassador. During the ceremony, Grey asserted that Page had been "the friend of Britain in her sorest need." *Daily Telegraph* (London), June 23, 1923; *Times* (London), July 4, 1923.
42. Page to Bryan, January 5, 1915, *FRUS: 1915. Supplement, The World War*, 182.
43. Page to Bryan, January 7, 1915, ibid., 299–302.
44. Ibid.
45. Lansing to Wilson, January 11, 1915, Link, *The Papers of Woodrow Wilson* (Princeton, NJ: Princeton University Press, 1979), 32: 54.
46. Remarks at a Press Conference, January 12, 1915, ibid., 32: 55.
47. Bryan to Wilson (with enclosure), January 12, 1915, ibid. One month later, Grey sent a second response that buttressed his first message. This is discussed further in Chapter 5. CASR 4–2, February 10, 1915.
48. Spring-Rice to Grey, January 15, 1915, FO 800 / 85, National Archives, Kew, UK.
49. Ibid.
50. "Purchase of the Steamship 'Dacia': Statement of the Motives and Facts Concerning the Purchase of the Steamship 'Dacia,'" by E. N. Breitung, February 19, 1915, *Congressional Record*, 63rd Congress, 3d Session, Senate.
51. *New York Times*, January 5, 1915, 1.
52. Devlin, *Too Proud to Fight*, 187; Grey, *Twenty-Five Years*, 111–12.
53. Spring-Rice to Bryan, January 12, 1915, *FRUS: 1915. Supplement, The World War*, 677.
54. Bryan to Spring-Rice, January 13, 1915, ibid., 678–79.
55. Page to Bryan, January 15, 1915, ibid., 679–80.
56. Ibid.
57. Spring-Rice to Bryan, January 15, 1915, ibid., 680–81.
58. Bryan to Wilson (with enclosure), January 19, 1915, Link, *The Papers of Woodrow Wilson*, 32: 91–93; On November 8, 1861, Captain Charles Wilkes of the USS *San Jacinto* stopped the neutral British merchant vessel the *Trent* after it left Havana, Cuba in order to remove two Confederate emissaries. Declaring the ministers, John Slidell and James Mason, "the embodiment of dispatches," Wilkes essentially considered the men contraband and placed them in custody. The captain's actions were unprecedented in maritime law. The

affair provoked many people in Britain to demand a declaration of war on the Union. Ultimately, the crisis was resolved because the Palmerston government wanted to remain neutral and Washington released the two Confederate diplomats. For an in-depth discussion of the *Trent* affair see Howard Jones, *Blue and Gray Diplomacy: A History of Union and Confederate Foreign Relations* (Chapel Hill: University of North Carolina Press, 2010), 83–111.

59. Page to Bryan, January 19, 1915 (received January 20, 8:15 a.m.), *FRUS: 1915. Supplement, The World War*, 6–7.
60. Bernstorff to Bryan, December 15, 1914, *FRUS:1914. Supplement, The World War*, 646–47.
61. Spring-Rice to Grey, December 11, 1914, FO 372 / 584, National Archives, Kew, UK.
62. Spring-Rice to Grey, January 19, 1915, FO 800 / 85; Bryan to the Chairman of the Senate Committee on Foreign Relations, January 20, 1915, *FRUS: 1914. Supplement, The World War*, 7–14; Avalon Project: Documents in Law, History and Diplomacy, "Convention Respecting the Rights and Duties of Neutral Powers and Persons in Case of War on Land (Hague 5); October 18, 1907," accessed June 2011, http://avalon.law.yale.edu/20th_century/hague05.asp.
63. Spring-Rice to Grey, January 15, 1915, FO 382 / 735.
64. Spring-Rice to Grey, February 2, 1915, FO 800 / 241, Spring-Rice Papers, Churchill Archives Center, Cambridge University, Cambridge, UK.
65. House to Wilson (with enclosure), January 22, 1915, Link, *The Papers of Woodrow Wilson* 32: 107–11; Grey to Spring-Rice, January 18, 1915, FO 800 / 85. Spring-Rice received the original dispatch from Grey on January 18, 1915 and strengthened some of the criticisms and softened others before giving it to House.
66. Wilson to Bryan (with enclosure), January 22, 1915, Link, *The Papers of Woodrow Wilson*, 32: 100–105.
67. Link, *Wilson: The Struggle for Neutrality*, 186–87. Once the French captured the *Dacia* on February 27, the prize court took control of the ship and commissioned it as a French vessel. To prevent confrontation over the cargo, Paris elected to purchase the entire cotton shipment.
68. Grey, *Twenty-Five Years*, 111–12.
69. Link, *Wilson: The Struggle for Neutrality*, 148.
70. Henry Lee Higginson to Wilson, January 27, 1915, Link, *The Papers of Woodrow Wilson*, 32: 140–41.
71. Charles Williams Eliot to Wilson, February 15, 1915, ibid., 32: 238–39.
72. Wilson to Eliot, February 18, 1915, ibid., 32: 244–45.
73. Theodore Roosevelt to Spring-Rice, February 5, 1915, FO 800 / 85.
74. Spring-Rice to Grey, February 12, 1915, ibid.
75. Ibid.
76. Senator Asle J. Gronna of North Dakota, February 18, 1915, *Congressional Record*, Senate, 63rd Congress, 3rd Session, 4006.
77. Safford, *Wilsonian Maritime Diplomacy 1913–1921*, 64; Link, *Wilson: The Struggle for Neutrality*, 170.

78. Spring-Rice to Grey, March 16, 1915, FO 800 / 241.
79. Wilson to House, January 5, 1915, Link, *The Papers of Woodrow Wilson,* 32: 17–18.
80. House to Wilson, January 8, 1915, ibid., 32: 41–42.
81. Diary of Chandler Parsons Anderson, January 9, 1915, ibid., 32: 44–50; C.M.Mason"Anglo-American Relations: Mediation and 'Permanent Peace,'" in F. H. Hinsley, ed., *British Foreign Policy under Sir Edward Grey* (Cambridge, UK: Cambridge University Press, 1977), 467.
82. Diary of Colonel House, January 12, 1915, ibid., 32: 61.
83. Diary of Colonel House, January 13, 1915, ibid., 32: 63–67.
84. Ibid.
85. Ibid.
86. Seymour, ed., *The Intimate Papers of Colonel House,* 1: 356.
87. Diary of Colonel House, January 24, 1915, Link, *The Papers of Woodrow Wilson,* 32: 117–18.
88. Wilson to House, January 28, 1915, ibid., 32: 144–45. According to Link, Wilson added the italics and marked the entire paragraph for emphasis.
89. Seymour, ed., *The Intimate Papers of Colonel House,* 1: 359.

Chapter 5

1. Excerpt from Page's diary as cited in Jan Willem Schulte Nordholt, *Woodrow Wilson: A Life for World Peace* (Berkley: University of California Press, 1991), 169.
2. Charles Seymour, ed., *The Intimate Papers of Colonel House: Behind the Political Curtain, 1912–1915* (Boston: Houghton Mifflin, 1926), February 6, 1915, 1: 361–62.
3. Lansing to Wilson, February 5, 1915, Arthur S. Link, ed., *The Papers of Woodrow Wilson* (Princeton, NJ: Princeton University Press, 1979), 32: 193.
4. Gerard to Bryan, February 2, 1915, *FRUS: 1915. Supplement, The World War,* 93.
5. Lansing to Wilson, February 7, 1915, Link, *The Papers of Woodrow Wilson*, 32: 195–96; Paul G. Halpern, *A Naval History of the First World War* (Annapolis, MD: Naval Institute Press, 1995), 295.
6. Bernstorff to Bryan, February 6, 1915, *FRUS: 1915. Supplement, The World War*, 94–95.
7. Paul G. Halpern, *A Naval History of the First World War* (Annapolis, MD: Naval Institute Press, 1995), 23, 293–94; Naval War College, *International Law Documents: Neutrality: Breaking of Diplomatic Relations: War* (Washington, DC: Government Printing Office, 1918), 126–27; Lance E. Davis and Stanley L. Engerman, *Naval Blockades in War and Peace: An Economic History since 1750* (Cambridge, UK: Cambridge University Press, 2006), 165; Philip K. Lundeberg, The German Naval Critique of the U-Boat Campaign, 1915–1918, *Military Affairs*, Vol. 27, No. 3 (Autumn 1963), 105–18; Holger H. Herwig, *Politics*

of Frustration: The United States in German Naval Planning, 1889–1941 (Boston: Little, Brown, 1976), 116–18.

8. Lansing to Wilson, February 5, 1915, *The Papers of Woodrow Wilson* 32: 193; Tucker, *Woodrow Wilson and the Great War*, 96.
9. Bryan to Gerard, February 10, 1915, *The Papers of Woodrow Wilson* 32: 207–10.
10. Ibid.; See also Kendrick A. Clements and Eric A. Cheezum, *Woodrow Wilson* (Washington, DC: CQ Press), 2003, 172; John Milton Cooper Jr., *Woodrow Wilson* (New York: Alfred A. Knopf, 2009), 275.
11. Spring-Rice to Grey, February 20, 1915, FO 800 / 85.
12. Page to Bryan, February 8, 1915, *FRUS: 1915. Supplement, The World War*, 97–98.
13. Remarks at a press conference, February 9, 1915, Link, *The Papers of Woodrow Wilson*, 32: 199–202.
14. Spring-Rice to Grey, February 12, 1915, FO 800 / 241.
15. Memorandum communicated by United States Ambassador, February 11, 1915, British Cabinet Papers, CAB 37 / 124, National Archives, Kew, UK.
16. Cabinet meeting notes, February 17, 1915, ibid.
17. Grey to Page, February 19, 1915, CASR 4–2, Spring-Rice Papers, Churchill Archives Centre, Churchill College, Cambridge, UK.
18. Wilson to House, February 13, 1915, Link, *The Papers of Woodrow Wilson,* 32: 230–31; Tucker, *Woodrow Wilson and the Great War*, 98.
19. For more discussion about Wilson's perception that Germany had ample supplies of food and the effect it had on US policy see Chapter 6.
20. Zimmermann to House, February 4, 1915, Link, *The Papers of Woodrow Wilson*, 32: 254.
21. House to Wilson, February 9, 1915, ibid., 32: 204–5.
22. Page to Wilson, February 10, 1915, ibid., 32: 211–12. Page added the italics to emphasize the British view on peace negotiations.
23. Ibid.; Excerpt from Page's diary as cited in Nordholt, *Woodrow Wilson: A Life for World Peace*, 169.
24. House to Wilson, February 11, 1915, Link, *The Papers of Woodrow Wilson*, 32: 220–21.
25. House to Wilson, February 15, 1915, Ibid., 32: 237–38.
26. Account of conversation between House and Grey, February 18, 1915, Edward M. House Diary, Alderman Library, University of Virginia; Nordholt, *Woodrow Wilson: A Life for World Peace*, 169.
27. Account of conversation between House and Grey, February 20, 1915, ibid. David French, *British Strategy and War Aims 1914–1916* (London: Allen and Unwin, 1986), 79; Jeffry D. Wallin, *By Ships Alone: Churchill and the Dardanelles*, (Durham: Carolina Academic Press, 1981), 52–53, 137.
28. Seymour, ed., *Intimate Papers of Colonel House*, February 18, 1915, 1: 378–79.
29. House to Zimmermann, February 17, 1915, Link, *The Papers of Woodrow Wilson*, 32: 256–57.
30. Wilson to House, February 20, 1915, ibid., 32: 265.

31. House to Wilson, February 20, 1915, ibid., 32: 266.
32. House to Wilson, February 21, 1915, ibid., 32: 267–68.
33. Seymour, ed., *Intimate Papers of Colonel House*, February 23, 1915, 1: 380–83.
34. Ibid.
35. House to Wilson, Link, *The Papers of Woodrow Wilson*, February 9, 1915, 32: 204–5.
36. Diary of Colonel House, Link, *The Papers of Woodrow Wilson*, 31: 517–20; Lloyd E. Ambrosius, *Wilsonian Statecraft: Theory and Practice of Liberal Internationalism during World War I* (New York: Scholarly Resources, 1991), 36–37.
37. Seymour, ed., *Intimate Papers of Colonel House*, February 23, 1915, 1: 380–83.
38. House to Wilson, February 11, 1915, Link, *The Papers of Woodrow Wilson*, 32: 220–21.
39. In mid-1916, Wilson began promoting the idea that the United States should join an "association of nations" that could ensure the maintenance of peace. Thomas J. Knock, *To End All Wars: Woodrow Wilson and the Quest for a New World Order* (Princeton University Press, 1992), 75–77.
40. Gerard to Bryan, February 12, 1915 (received February 13), *FRUS: 1915. Supplement, The World War*, 102.
41. Page to Bryan, January 27, 1915, ibid., 317.
42. Two letters from Bryan to Wilson, February 15, 1915, Link, 32: 235–37.
43. Bryan to Wilson, February 15, 1915, William Jennings Bryan Papers, Manuscript Division, Library of Congress, Washington, DC.
44. Bryan to Page, February 15, 1915, *FRUS: 1915. Supplement, The War*, 105–7.
45. Bryan to Page, February 16, 1915, ibid., 107.
46. Gerard to Bryan, February 16, 1915, ibid., 110.
47. Page to Bryan, February 17, 1915, ibid., 111.
48. Bryan to Wilson (with enclosure), February 18, 1915, *The Papers of Woodrow Wilson*, 32: 248–52. Italics added by Bryan.
49. Wilson to Bryan, February 19, 1915, ibid., 32: 258.
50. Page to Bryan, February 20, 1915, *FRUS: 1915. Supplement, The World War*, 118–19.
51. Page to Bryan, February 19, 1915, ibid., 335–37.
52. Ibid.
53. Ibid. Page had Grey's message published in newspapers so that the public could see Britain's defense of its actions.
54. C. J. B. Hurst to Grey, February 22, 1915, British Cabinet Papers CAB 37 / 124, National Archives, Kew, UK; Crowe to Grey, February 23, 1915, ibid.
55. "Observations Upon the United States Note of the 22nd February, 1915," February 28, 1915, British Cabinet Papers, CAB 37 / 124, National Archives, Kew, UK; Avner Offer, *The First World War: An Agrarian Interpretation* (Oxford: Oxford University Press, 1989), 271. In the first quarter of 1915, the calorie intake of the German civilian population had not dropped significantly since the beginning of the war. Britain had only just completed its agreements with continental neutrals to prevent the re-export of goods. Therefore, the full

effect of the blockade had not yet been realized in Germany and the admiralty certainly did not want to see its efforts go to naught. Offer, *The First World War*, 45, 230; David and Engerman, *Naval Blockades in Peace and War*, 162; C. Paul Vincent, *Politics of Hunger: The Allied Blockade of Germany, 1915–1919* (Athens: Ohio University Press, 1985), 36–43.

56. "Draft of possible reply to the suggestions of the United States Government for an arrangement between Germany and Great Britain of the conduct of the war," March 1, 1915, British Cabinet Papers, CAB 37 / 125, National Archives, Kew, UK.
57. Vincent, *The Politics of Hunger*, 42.
58. "Declaration made by His Majesty's Government and communicated to Neutral Governments," March 1, 1915, Stevenson, ed., *British Documents on Foreign Affairs: Reports and Papers from the Foreign Office Confidential Print.* Part 2, *From the First to the Second World War.* Series H. *The First World War, 1914–1918*, Volume 5, *Blockade and Economic Warfare, 1: August 1914–July 1915*, 34; Marion C. Siney, *The Allied Blockade of Germany 1914–1916* (Ann Arbor, MI: The University of Michigan Press, 1957), 66–67.
59. "Declaration made by His Majesty's Government and communicated to Neutral Governments," March 1, 1915, Stevenson, ed., *British Documents on Foreign Affairs: Reports and Papers from the Foreign Office Confidential Print.* Part 2, *From the First to the Second World War.* Series H. *The First World War, 1914–1918*, Volume 5, *Blockade and Economic Warfare, 1: August 1914–July 1915*, 34.
60. Gerard to Bryan, March 1, 1915 (received March 2, midnight), *FRUS: 1915. Supplement, The World War*, 129–30.
61. Gerard to Bryan, March 4, 1915, ibid., 132; For more on the struggle to gain control of German policy see Martin Kitchen, "Civil-Military Relations in Germany," in R. J. Q. Adams, ed., *The Great War, 1914–1918: Essays on the Military, Political and Social History of the First World War* (College Station: Texas A&M University Press, 1990), 39–41.
62. Page to Wilson, March 10, 1915, Link, *The Papers of Woodrow Wilson*, 32: 357–63.
63. Robert F. Rose to Bryan, May 21, 1915, *FRUS: 1915. Supplement, The World War*, 216–21. First names for Mr. L. Wolf and Mr. Beer were unavailable.
64. Spring-Rice to Bryan, March 19, 1915 (received March 23), ibid., 691.
65. Ibid.
66. Lansing to Bryan, March 2, 1915, *FRUS: The Lansing Papers, 1914–1920*, Volume 1, *The World War*, 270–71.
67. Bryan to Wilson March 3, 1915, ibid., 271–72.
68. Wilson to Bryan, March 4, 1915, ibid., 273.
69. Page to Bryan, March 15, 1915 (received 11 p.m.), *The Papers of Woodrow Wilson*, 32: 378–82.
70. Page to Bryan, March 15, 1915 (received March 16, 8 a.m.), *FRUS: 1915. Supplement, The World War*, 143–45; Devlin, *Too Proud to Fight*, 202–4; Siney, *The Allied Blockade of Germany*, 66–67.
71. Grey to Spring-Rice, March 15, 1915, Spring-Rice Papers, CASR 4–2.

72. Wilson to Bryan (with enclosure), March 19, 1915, Link, *The Papers of Woodrow Wilson*, 32: 399–401.
73. Page to Bryan, March 21, 1915, *FRUS: 1915. Supplement, The World War*, 146–47.
74. Bryan to Wilson, March 22, 1915, *The Papers of Woodrow Wilson*, 32: 412–13; Bryan to Wilson (with enclosure), March 22, 1915, *FRUS: The Lansing Papers, 1914–1920*, Volume 1, *The World War*, 279–81.
75. Coogan, *The End of Neutrality*, 22.
76. Ibid.
77. Bryan to Wilson, March 22, 1915, *FRUS: The Lansing Papers, 1914–1920*, Volume 1, *The World War*, 285–86.
78. Five letters from Wilson to Bryan, March 24, 1915, Link, *The Papers of Woodrow Wilson*, 32: 424–27.
79. Bryan to Wilson, March 24, 1915, ibid., 32: 428–29.
80. Wilson to Lansing, March 28, 1915, ibid., 32: 443–49.
81. Ibid.; Adrian Cook, *The Alabama Claims: American Politics and Anglo-American Relations, 1865–1872* (Ithaca, NY: Cornell University Press, 1975), 26; Howard Jones, *Blue and Gray Diplomacy: A History of Union and Confederate Foreign Relations* (Chapel Hill: University of North Carolina Press, 2010), 290; Naval Historical Center, "USS *Vanderbilt* (1862–1873)," Department of the Navy, accessed June 2008, http://www.history.navy.mil/photos/sh-usn/usnsh-v/vanderbt.htm.
82. Wilson to Lansing, March 28, 1915, Link, 32: 443–49; Wilson to Bryan, March 30, 1015, ibid., 32: 457–58.
83. House to Wilson, March 1, 1915, Link, ibid., 32: 303–4.
84. Zimmermann to House, March 2, 1915, ibid., 32: 351.
85. House to Wilson, March 20, 1915, ibid., 32: 402–3.
86. House to Wilson, March 29, 1915, ibid., 32: 455–56.
87. Seymour, ed., *Intimate Papers of Colonel House*, 1: 410–11; Wilson to House, April 1, 1915, Link, *The Papers of Woodrow Wilson*, 32: 462.
88. See Sidney Bell, *Righteous Conquest: Woodrow Wilson and the Evolution of New Diplomacy* (New York: Kennikat, 1972), 154–55; Daniel M. Smith, *The Great Departure: The United States and World War I, 1914–1920* (New York: John Wiley and Sons, 1965), 52.
89. Bryan to Gerard, February 10, 1915, *The Papers of Woodrow Wilson* 32: 207–10.

Chapter 6

1. Personal Memoranda, May 3, 1915, Lansing Papers, Library of Congress, Washington, DC.
2. Wilson to Edith Bolling Galt, May 8, 1915, Arthur S. Link, ed., *The Papers of Woodrow Wilson* (Princeton, NJ: Princeton University Press, 1979), 33: 128–29. Italics added by Wilson.

3. Spring-Rice to Cabinet, April 2, 1915, FO 372 / 762, National Archives, Kew, UK.
4. Bryan to Wilson (with enclosure), April 2, 1915, *The Papers of Woodrow Wilson*, 32: 464–66.
5. Ibid.; Avalon Project: Documents in Law, History and Diplomacy, "Convention Relating to the Status of Enemy Merchant Ships at the Outbreak of Hostilities (Hague 6); October 18, 1907," accessed August 2012, www.avalon.law.yale.edu/20th_century/hague06.asp; See also: Natalino Ronzitti, ed. *The Law of Naval Warfare: A Commentary on the Relevant Agreements and Documents* (Dordrecht, The Netherlands: Martinus Nijhoff, 1988), 353–54.
6. Four letters to Bryan, April 3, 1915, ibid., 32: 469.
7. Lansing to Bryan (with enclosure), April 5, 1915, ibid., 32: 483–86.
8. Bryan to Wilson, April 6, 1915, ibid., 32: 487.
9. Bryan to Wilson (with enclosures), April 6, 1915, ibid., 32: 490–93.
10. Bryan to Wilson, April 7, 1915, ibid., 32: 488–90.
11. Robert Skinner to Bryan, April 7, 1915, *FRUS: 1915. Supplement, The World War*, 32: 359–60.
12. Two letters from Lansing, April 10, 1915, Link, *The Papers of Woodrow Wilson*, 32: 503–4.
13. Two Letters from Bryan, April 16, 1915, ibid., 32: 526–27.
14. Wilson to Bryan, April 16, 1915, ibid., 32: 527.
15. Three letters from Bryan, April 19, 1915, Arthur S. Link, ed., *The Papers of Woodrow Wilson* (Princeton, NJ: Princeton University Press, 1980), 33: 28–29.
16. Wilson to Bryan, April 22, 1915, ibid., 33: 61–62.
17. Two letters from Bryan, April 23, 1915, ibid., 33: 65–67.
18. Bryan to Wilson (with enclosures), April 27, 1915, ibid., 33: 71–77.
19. Two letters from Wilson to Bryan, April 28, 1915, ibid., 33: 85–86.
20. Bryan to Wilson (with enclosure), May 1, 1915, ibid., 33: 91–92; *New York Times*, May 1, 1915, 1.
21. *New York Times*, May 1, 1915, 1.
22. Bryan to Wilson (with enclosure), May 1, 1915, Link, *The Papers of Woodrow Wilson*, 33: 91–93.
23. Bryan to Wilson (with enclosure), May 3, 1915, ibid., 33: 93–95.
24. Bryan to Wilson (with enclosure), May 5, 1915, ibid., 33: 106–8.
25. Page to Bryan, May 7, 1915, *FRUS: 1915. Supplement, The World War*, 384.
26. *New York Times*, May 8, 1915, 1.
27. Howard Jones, *Crucible of Power: A History of American Foreign Relations from 1897*, 2nd ed. (Lanham, MD: Rowman and Littlefield, 2008), 72; *New York Times*, May 8, 1915, 6.
28. Spring-Rice to Grey, May 12, 1915, FO 115 / 1998, National Archives, Kew, UK. (Microfilm located at University of North Carolina at Chapel Hill).
29. Spring-Rice to Grey, May 20, 1915, FO 800 / 241, National Archives, Kew, UK.
30. House to Wilson, May 9, 1914, Seymour, *Intimate Papers of Colonel House*, 1: 433–34; House to Wilson, May 11, 1915, Link, *The Papers of Woodrow Wilson*, 33: 158–59; Armin Rappaport, *The British Press and Wilsonian Neutrality*

(Gloucester, Massachusetts: Stanford University Press, 1965), 34; Glasgow *Herald*, May 10, 1915 as cited in Rappaport, *The British Press and Wilsonian Neutrality*, 35.

31. Joseph P. Tumulty, *Woodrow Wilson as I Know Him* (Garden City, New York: Doubleday, Page, 1921), 232.
32. Tucker, *Woodrow Wilson and the Great War*, 109; Wilson to Edith Bolling Galt, May 8, 1915, *The Papers of Woodrow Wilson*, 33: 128–29. Edith Galt and Wilson were courting and had just started writing letters to each other days before the *Lusitania* crisis.
33. "An Address in Philadelphia to Newly Naturalized Citizens," May 10, 1915, ibid., 33: 147–50.
34. Ibid.
35. Spring-Rice to Grey, May 20, 1915, FO 800 / 241.
36. Lansing, *War Memoirs of Robert Lansing*, 28.
37. Bryan to Wilson, May 9, 1915, Link, *The Papers of Woodrow Wilson*, 33: 134–35.
38. Bryan to Wilson (with enclosures), May 10, 1915, ibid., 33: 142–45.
39. Gerard to Bryan, May 10, 1915 (received May 11, 1915, 1: 10 p.m.), *FRUS: 1915. Supplement, The World War*, 389; Paul G. Halpern, *A Naval History of the First World War* (Annapolis, MD: Naval Institute Press, 1995), 298.
40. Wilson to Bryan, May 11, 1915, Link, *The Papers of Woodrow Wilson*, 33: 155–58.
41. Wilson to Bryan, May 11, 1915, Link, *The Papers of Woodrow Wilson*, 33: 155–58.
42. H. C. Peterson, *Propaganda for War: The Campaign against American Neutrality, 1914–1917* (Port Washington, NY: Kennikat, 1939), 38; James Morgan Read, *Atrocity Propaganda, 1914–1919* (New Haven, CT: Yale University Press, 1941), 204–5, 211–15; Trevor Wilson, *The Myriad Faces of War: Britain and the Great War, 1914–1918* (Cambridge: Polity Press, 1986), 184–85. While the Bryce Report was probably the apex of British propaganda sent to the United States, there seems to have been limited discussion about the Bryce Report in the White House. The Bryce Report did not seem to influence Wilson's conversations with the Department of State or Col. House during the much more pressing submarine crisis. Additionally, as discussed in previous chapters, the administration had already agreed that the time for protesting against the German treatment of Belgian civilians had passed and that new protests could endanger the peace process. Therefore, while it may have bolstered the British population and pro-Allied Americans, it did not seem play a significant role in Wilson's policies. In July 1918, Assistant Secretary of Navy Franklin Delano Roosevelt confirmed the lack of popular support when he sat down with King George V and expressed that Americans doubted the report's claims. Thomas Fleming, *The Illusions of Victory: America in World War I* (New York: Basic Books, 2003), 255.
43. *New York Times*, May 12, 1915, 2.

44. Bryan to Wilson, May 12, 1915, Link, *The Papers of Woodrow Wilson*, 33: 165–67.
45. Bryan to Wilson (with enclosure), May 12, 1915, ibid., 33: 167–73.
46. Bryan to Wilson, May 12, 1915, ibid., 33: 173–74; Wilson to Bryan, May 13, 1915, ibid., 33: 181.
47. Bryan to Wilson (with enclosure), May 13, 1915, ibid., 33: 182–83.
48. Arthur Link, *Wilson: The Struggle for Neutrality, 1914–1915* (Princeton, NJ: Princeton University Press, 1960), 385–89.
49. Wilson to Bryan, May 13, 1915, Link, *The Papers of Woodrow Wilson*, 33: 183–84.
50. Bryan to Wilson, May 13, 1915, ibid., 33: 185.
51. Wilson to Bryan, May 13, 1915, ibid., 185–86.
52. Two letters from Bryan to Wilson, May 13, 1915, ibid., 33: 186.
53. Wilson to Bryan, May 13, 1915, ibid., 33: 187.
54. Spring-Rice to Grey, April 8, 1915, FO 115 / 1857, National Archives, Kew, UK.
55. Skinner to Bryan, April 14, 1915 (received April 27), *FRUS: 1915. Supplement, The World War*, 373–74.
56. Page to Bryan, May 20, 1915, ibid., 423–27.
57. Wilson to House, May 5, 1915, Link, *The Papers of Woodrow Wilson*, 33: 105–6.
58. Spring-Rice to Grey, April 16, 1915, FO 800 / 85.
59. Spring-Rice to Grey, April 20, 1915 (received on May 5), Stevenson, ed., *British Documents on Foreign Affairs: Reports and Papers from the Foreign Office Confidential Print.* Part 2, *From the First to the Second World War.* Series H. *The First World War, 1914–1918*, Volume 5, *Blockade and Economic Warfare, 1: August 1914–July 1915*, 145–46; Stephen Broadberry and Mark Harrison, eds., *The Economics of World War I* (New York: Cambridge University Press, 2005), 12.
60. Henry Asquith, the Earl of Oxford, and Asquith, KG, *Memories and Reflections, 1852–1927* (Boston: Little, Brown, 1928), 2: 90.
61. War Office Armaments Output Committee to George, April 20, 1915, David Lloyd George Papers, C/14/3/13, Parliamentary Archives, London, UK.
62. Arthur Marwick, *The Deluge: British Society and the First World War* (London: Bodley Head, 1965), 56–58. At the beginning of the war, Secretary of State for War Lord Kitchener convinced Asquith's cabinet to drastically increase the size of the British ground forces and by the spring of 1915 the number of men available to work in munitions factories had dropped by one-third. See David French's chapter "The Rise and Fall of 'Business as Usual,'" in Kathleen Burk, ed., *War and the State: The Transformation of the British Government, 1914–1919* (London: Allen and Unwin, 1982), 21.
63. "List of Orders Placed or Being Executed in U.S.A. From 4th August to 15th May 1915," June 14, 1915, FO 115 / 1847, National Archives, Kew, UK.
64. Chris Wrigley, "The Ministry of Munitions: an Innovatory Department," in Kathleen Burk, ed., *War and the State*, 38; David Lloyd George, *War Memoirs of David Lloyd George, 1914–1915* (Boston: Little, Brown, 1933), 115.

65. "Munitions Crisis," May 19, 1915, David Lloyd George Papers, C/1/2/17, Parliamentary Archives, London, UK.
66. Ibid.; Lloyd George, *War Memoirs of David Lloyd George, 1914–1915*, 124.
67. House to Wilson (with enclosure), April 18, 1915, Link, *The Papers of Woodrow Wilson*, 33: 12–14.
68. Lloyd George, *War Memoirs of David Lloyd George, 1914–1915*, 175–79; Peter Roland, *David Lloyd George: A Biography* (New York: Macmillan, 1976), 307.
69. For more on the failure of the Royal Navy attack on the Turkish defenses see Jeffrey D. Wallin, *By Ships Alone: Churchill and the Dardanelles* (Durham: Carolina Academic Press, 1981), 161–95; Halpern, *A Naval History of World War I*, 111–16; Hew Strachan, *The First World War* (London: Viking Penguin, 2004), 115–23; Paolo E. Colette, *Sea Power in the Atlantic and Mediterranean in World War I* (London: University Press of America, 1989), 19–23.
70. *Morning Post*, May 12, 1915, as cited in Peter Fraser, "British War Policy and the Crisis of Liberalism in May 1915," *The Journal of Modern History*, Vol. 54, No. 1 (March 1982), 9.
71. John Turner, ed., "British Politics and the Great War," in John Turner, ed., *Britain and the First World War* (London, UK: Unwin Hyman, 1988), 120–22; John Turner, *British Politics and the Great War: Coalition and Conflict, 1915–1918* (New Haven, CT: Yale University Press, 1992), 61.
72. Grey, *Twenty-Five Years*, 2: 243.
73. Turner, *British Politics and the Great War*,120–22; Wilson, *The Myriad Faces of War*, 192–94; R. J. Q. Adams, *Arms and the Wizard: Lloyd George and the Ministry of Munitions, 1915–1916* (College Station: Texas A&M University Press, 1978), 28; Samuel J. Hurwitz, *State Intervention in Great Britain: A Study of Economic Control and Social Response, 1914–1919* (New York: Columbia University Press, 1949), 154–55.
74. Charles Seymour, ed., *The Intimate Papers of Colonel House: Behind the Political Curtain, 1912–1915* (Boston: Houghton Mifflin, 1926), 1: 424–26.
75. Ibid.; Devlin, *Too Proud To Fight*, 278–79.
76. Two letters from House, May 14, 1915, Link, *The Papers of Woodrow Wilson*, 33: 197–99.
77. Wilson to House, May 16, 1915, ibid., 33: 205.
78. Bryan to Wilson (with enclosure), May 14, 1915, ibid., 33: 192–94.
79. Four letters to Bryan from Wilson, May 14, 1915, ibid., 33: 194.
80. Personal Memoranda, May 3, 1915, Lansing Papers, Library of Congress, Washington, DC.
81. Ibid.
82. Ibid.
83. Bryan to Wilson (with enclosures), May 16, 1915, Link, *The Papers of Woodrow Wilson*, 33: 205–9.
84. Wilson to House, May 18, 1915, ibid., 33: 217.
85. House to Wilson, May 19, 1915, ibid., 33: 222.
86. Three letters to Bryan from Wilson, May 20, 1915, ibid., 33: 223–24.
87. Ibid.

88. Page to Bryan, May 20, 1915, *FRUS: 1915. Supplement, The World War*, 427–30; Spring-Rice to Foreign Office, May 22, 1915, FO 382 / 9, National Archives, Kew, UK.
89. Grey to Spring-Rice, May 24, 1915, ibid.
90. Page to Bryan, undated (received May 26, 1915 10: 10 a.m.), *FRUS: 1915. Supplement, The World War*, 414.
91. Eyre Crowe's handwritten notes in Foreign Office interoffice document, May 26, 1915, FO 382 / 9.
92. Foreign Office to Spring-Rice, May 29, 1915, ibid.
93. Spring-Rice to Grey, June 2, 1915, ibid.
94. Gerard to Bryan, May 15, 1915 (received May 17, 8am), *FRUS: 1915. Supplement, The World War*, 396.
95. House to Wilson, May 25, 1915, Link, *The Papers of Woodrow Wilson*, 33: 253–54.
96. Wilson to Bryan (with enclosure), May 27, 1915, ibid., 33: 264–66.
97. Von Jagow to Gerard, May 28, 1915, James Brown Scott, ed., *Diplomatic Correspondence between the United States and Germany, 1914–1917* (Oxford University Press, 1918), 47–50.
98. Spring-Rice to Grey, June 2, 1915, FO 800 / 85.
99. Spring-Rice to Grey, June 2, 1915 (received June 14), Stevenson, David, ed., *British Documents on Foreign Affairs: Reports and Papers from the Foreign Office Confidential Print.* Part 2, *From the First to the Second World War.* Series H. *The First World War, 1914–1918*, Volume 1, *The Allied and Neutral Powers: Diplomacy and War Aims, 1: August 1914–July 1915* (Frederick, MD: University Publications of America, 1989), 361–62.
100. Ibid.
101. Three letters to Bryan from Wilson, June 2, 1915, Link, *The Papers of Woodrow Wilson*, 33: 308–9.
102. Lansing's Personal Memorandums, June 1915, Lansing Papers.
103. Bryan to Wilson (with enclosure), June 2, 1915, Link, *The Papers of Woodrow Wilson*, 33: 310–13.
104. Ibid.
105. Wilson to Bryan, June 2, 1915, ibid., 33: 314.
106. Bryan to Wilson, June 3, 1915, ibid., 33: 321–26; In April 1914, several USN sailors were arrested in Tampico, Mexico when they went ashore to locate fuel for the USS *Dolphin*, stationed near the city, during the Mexican Revolution. The Wilson administration used the affair to justify an eight-month long occupation of Vera Cruz, Mexico's main port on the Gulf of Mexico, to force Mexican President Victoriano Huerta from power. In preparing for the occupation, the State Department advised Americans living in Tampico to leave because of the threat of reprisal by the Mexican people. Robert S. Quirk, *An Affair of Honor: Woodrow Wilson and the Occupation of Vera Cruz, Mexico* (New York: W. W. Norton, 1962), 20–22.
107. Mary Baird Bryan and William Jennings Bryan, *The Memoirs of William Jennings Bryan* (Chicago, IL: John C. Winston, 1925), 419–24. Mary Bryan added the italics to emphasize her husband's distress.

108. Bryan to Wilson, June 5, 1915, Link, *The Papers of Woodrow Wilson*, 33: 342–43.
109. House to Wilson, May 25, 1915, ibid., 33: 253–54.
110. Wilson to Bryan, June 5, 1915, ibid., 33: 343.
111. Kendrick A. Clements, *The Presidency of Woodrow Wilson* (Lawrence: University Press of Kansas, 1992), 126; Mary Baird Bryan and William Jennings Bryan, *The Memoirs of William Jennings Bryan*, 422–24; August Heckscher, *Woodrow Wilson* (New York; Charles Scribner's Sons, 1991), 366–68.
112. Link, *Wilson: The Struggle for Neutrality*, 421; Galt to Wilson, June 5, 1915, Link, *The Papers of Woodrow Wilson*, 33: 346–47.
113. Paolo E. Coletta, *William Jennings Bryan: 2. Progressive Politician and Moral Statesman, 1909–1915* (Lincoln: University of Nebraska Press, 1969), 311; House diary entry, June 24, 1915, Edward M. House Diary, Alderman Library, University of Virginia.
114. Lansing to Gerard, June 9, 1915, *FRUS: 1915. Supplement, The World War*, 436–38.
115. Ibid.
116. Tansill, *America Goes to War*, 450.

Chapter 7

1. Wilson to Galt, September 6, 1915, Arthur S. Link, ed., *The Papers of Woodrow Wilson* (Princeton, NJ: Princeton University Press, 1979), 34: 423–24.
2. Spring-Rice to Grey, June 10, 1915, FO 800 / 85.
3. Spring-Rice to Grey, June 22, 1915, FO 800 / 85.
4. Wilson to Galt, June 12, 1915, Link, *The Papers of Woodrow Wilson*, 33: 388–89.
5. Charles Seymour, ed., *The Intimate Papers of Colonel House: From Neutrality to War 1915–1917* (Boston: Houghton Mifflin, 1926), 2: 12.
6. House to Wilson, June 16, 1915, Link, *The Papers of Woodrow Wilson*, 33: 409; Patrick Devlin, *Too Proud to Fight: Woodrow Wilson's Neutrality* (New York: Oxford University Press, 1975, c1974), 303; Arthur Link, *Wilson: The Struggle for Neutrality, 1914–1915* (Princeton, NJ: Princeton University Press, 1960), 427.
7. Diary of House, June 24, 1915, Link, *The Papers of Woodrow Wilson*, 33: 448–53.
8. Grey to Spring-Rice, June 10, 1915, FO 800 / 85.
9. Spring-Rice to Grey, June 11, 1915, ibid.
10. Lansing to Wilson (with enclosures), June 12, 1915, Link, *The Papers of Woodrow Wilson*, 33: 385–87.
11. Spring-Rice to Grey, June 15, 1915, FO 800 / 85.
12. Grey to Spring-Rice, June 16, 1915, ibid. The British liked Lansing as Wilson's choice to head the State Department because of his decidedly pro-Allied leanings. Writing Grey on June 25, the day after Lansing's appointment, Spring-Rice promoted the new secretary: "He is cool-headed and has been the

President's chief advisor in dealing with policy of all problems arising from the war. He is friendly toward us." Spring-Rice to Grey, June 25, 1915, ibid.

13. House to Wilson (with enclosures), June 16, 1915, Link, *The Papers of Woodrow Wilson*, 33: 405–9.
14. Von Jagow to Gerard, July 8, 1915, Scott, ed., *Diplomatic Correspondence between the United States and Germany, August 1, 1914–April 6, 1917*, 56–60.
15. As cited in Link, *Wilson: The Struggle for Neutrality*, 440–41.
16. House to Wilson (with enclosure), July 1, 1915, Link, *The Papers of Woodrow Wilson*, 33: 461–63.
17. Wilson to House, July 3, 1915, ibid., 33: 469–70.
18. Seymour, ed., *The Intimate Papers of Colonel House*, 2: 15–16.
19. Wilson to Lansing, July 13, 1915, Link, *The Papers of Woodrow Wilson*, 33: 499–500.
20. Gerard to Lansing, July 13, 1915, *FRUS: 1915. Supplement, The World War*, 43–44. The *Mauretania* was the sister ship of the *Lusitania*. Both had four funnels and were listed as British auxiliary cruisers. Paul G. Halpern, *A Naval History of the First World War* (Annapolis, MD: Naval Institute Press, 1995), 298.
21. Lansing to Wilson, July 14, 1915, Link, *The Papers of Woodrow Wilson*, 33: 507–8.
22. Lansing to Wilson, July 15, 1915, ibid., 33: 509–10.
23. Lansing to Wilson (with enclosure), July16, 1915, ibid., 33: 527–29.
24. Lansing to Wilson (with enclosure), July 19, 1915, ibid., 33: 529–32.
25. Wilson to Lansing (with enclosure), July 21, 1915, ibid., 33: 545–48.
26. Seymour, *The Intimate Papers of Colonel House*, 2: 12.
27. Ibid., 2: 19–20.
28. Wilson to Josephus Daniels, July 21, 1915, Arthur S. Link, ed., *The Papers of Woodrow Wilson* (Princeton, NJ: Princeton University Press, 1980), 34: 4–5. The general staff responded to Garrison's call for an estimate on the necessary size of the military through the *Statement of a Proper Military Policy for the United States*. The general staff asserted that the United States needed at minimum a 218,000 man regular army and a 500,000 man reserve force under federal control. Garrison revised the report before sending it on to the president but still called for a significant increase in the size of the army and reserves. Nancy Gentile Ford, *Civil-Military Relations during World War I* (Westport, CT: Prager Security International, 2008), 20.
29. Ford, *Civil-Military Relations during World War I*, 20; Link, *Wilson: The Struggle for Neutrality*, 591–92.
30. David French, *British Strategy and War Aims 1914–1916* (London: Allen and Unwin, 1986), 1; Eric Drummond to Crewe, June 11, 1915, FO 800 / 95. Lord Crewe temporarily replaced Grey because he was having trouble with his eyesight.
31. George Macaulay Trevelyan, *The Life and Letters of Sir Edward Grey* (Boston: Houghton Mifflin, 1937), 362–64.
32. Winston Churchill, *The World in Crisis, 1915* (New York, Charles Scribner's Sons, 1929), 292.

33. Grey to Cabinet, July 17, 1915, Grey Papers, FO 800 / 95, National Archives, Kew, UK.
34. Memorandum communicated to Page, June 17, 1915 (sent out several days later), Stevenson, ed., *British Documents on Foreign Affairs: Reports and Papers from the Foreign Office Confidential Print.* Part 2, *From the First to the Second World War.* Series H. *The First World War, 1914–1918,* Volume 5, *Blockade and Economic Warfare, 1: August 1914–July 1915,* 270; Page to Lansing, June 22, 1915, *FRUS: 1915. Supplement, The World War,* 443–46.
35. Memorandum communicated to Page, June 17, 1915 (sent out several days later), Stevenson, ed., *British Documents on Foreign Affairs: Reports and Papers from the Foreign Office Confidential Print.* Part 2, *From the First to the Second World War.* Series H. *The First World War, 1914–1918,* Volume 5, *Blockade and Economic Warfare, 1: August 1914–July 1915,* 270.
36. Skinner to Lansing, June 11, 1915 (received June 22), ibid., 448–49.
37. Skinner to Lansing, June 29, 1915, ibid., 455–56.
38. The Galveston Commercial Association to Lansing, July 2, 1915, ibid., 192.
39. Lansing to Page, July 16, 1915, Link, *The Papers of Woodrow Wilson,* 33: 515–16.
40. Grey to Spring-Rice, July 19, 1915, Stevenson, ed., *British Documents on Foreign Affairs: Reports and Papers from the Foreign Office Confidential Print.* Part 2, *From the First to the Second World War.* Series H. *The First World War, 1914–1918,* Volume 5, *Blockade and Economic Warfare, 1: August 1914–July 1915,* 366–67.
41. Page to Lansing, July 19, 1915, Link, *The Papers of Woodrow Wilson,* 534.
42. Handwritten comments by Crowe written in interoffice papers concerning a London *Times* article, "Blockade and Cotton," July 20, 1915, FO 382 / 12, National Archives, Kew, UK.
43. Grey to Cabinet, July 22, 1915, CAB 37 / 131, National Archives, Kew, UK. The *Neches* was a merchant vessel detained by the Royal Navy on suspicion that at least some of its cargo had originated in occupied Belgium. Simon D. Fess, *The Problems of Neutrality When the World Is at War: A History of Our Relations with Germany and Great Britain as Detailed in Documents That Passed between the United States and the Two Great Powers, Part One the Submarine Controversy* (Washington, DC: Government Printing Office, 1917), 314.
44. Page to Lansing, July 24, 1915, *FRUS: 1915. Supplement, The World War,* 168–71.
45. Spring-Rice to Grey, August 6, 1915, FO 382 / 464, National Archives, Kew, UK.
46. Letter to Lord Moulton from numerous signers, March 11, 1915, Bonar Law Papers, Parliamentary Archives, London, UK.
47. Memorandum respecting cotton as contraband, July 3, 1915, Stevenson, David, ed., *British Documents on Foreign Affairs: Reports and Papers from the Foreign Office Confidential Print.* Part 2, *From the First to the Second World War.* Series H. *The First World War, 1914–1918,* Volume 5, *Blockade and Economic Warfare, 1: August 1914–July 1915,* 333–35.
48. Ibid.
49. Grey to Cabinet (No Date), David Lloyd George Papers, D/25/8/3.

50. Ibid.; Spring-Rice to Grey, July 6, 1915, Stevenson, ed., *British Documents on Foreign Affairs: Reports and Papers from the Foreign Office Confidential Print.* Part 2, *From the First to the Second World War.* Series H. *The First World War, 1914–1918*, Volume 5, *Blockade and Economic Warfare, 1: August 1914–July 1915*, 333–35.
51. Spring-Rice to Grey, July 6, 1915, FO 800 / 85.
52. Spring-Rice to Grey July 6, 1915, Stevenson, ed., *British Documents on Foreign Affairs: Reports and Papers from the Foreign Office Confidential Print.* Part 2, *From the First to the Second World War.* Series H. *The First World War, 1914–1918*, Volume 5, *Blockade and Economic Warfare, 1: August 1914–July 1915*, 333–34.
53. Spring-Rice to Grey, July 7, 1915, ibid., 334.
54. Spring-Rice to Grey, July 15, 1915, FO 800 / 85; Arthur S. Link, *The Higher Realism of Woodrow Wilson* (Nashville, TN: Vanderbilt, University Press, 1971), 327.
55. Spring-Rice to Grey, July 21, 1915, FO 800 / 85.
56. Page to Lansing, July 22, 1915, *FRUS: 1915. Supplement, The World War*, 193; Devlin, *Too Proud to Fight*, 353.
57. Grey to the cabinet, July 1915, David Lloyd George Papers, D/25/9/4, Parliamentary Archives, London, UK.
58. Wilson to House, July 19, 1915, Link, *The Papers of Woodrow Wilson*, 33: 526.
59. Lansing to Wilson, July 28, 1915, Link, *The Papers of Woodrow Wilson*, 34: 34–35.
60. Spring-Rice to Grey, July 29, 1915, FO 382 / 464.
61. Letter to G. S. Barkdale from Bankhead, July 30, 1915, John H. Bankhead Files, LPR 49 Box 29 File 1, Alabama Department of Archives. Dr. Barkdale's first name is unstated.
62. Spring-Rice to Grey, July 31, 1915, FO 382 / 464.
63. Spring-Rice to Grey, August 3, 1915, ibid.
64. Spring-Rice to Grey, August 9, 1915, ibid.; Grey to Spring-Rice, August 11, 1915, ibid.
65. Skinner to Lansing, July 28, 1915 (received August 9, 1915), *FRUS: 1915. Supplement, The World War*, 502–3.
66. Ibid.
67. House to Wilson, August 14, 1915, Link, *The Papers of Woodrow Wilson*, 34: 200; Link, *The Higher Realism of Woodrow Wilson*, 328.
68. Spring-Rice to Grey, August 14, 1915, FO 382 / 464.
69. Link, *The Higher Realism of Woodrow Wilson*, 328.
70. Link, *Wilson: The Struggle for Neutrality*, 611–14; *Times-Picayune* (New Orleans), August 23, 1915, 8, as cited in Pearson, *The South and the European War, 1914–1917*, 44–45.
71. Cabinet Report, June 1915, CAB 37 / 129, National Archives, Kew, UK.
72. March 10, 1915, FO 368; between 1914 and 1917, 70 percent of all Entente loans went to aid Russia. Hew Strachan, *Financing the First World War* (Oxford: Oxford University Press, 2004), 181.
73. Burk, *Britain, America, and the Sinews of War, 1914–1918*, 61–64; John Milton Cooper Jr., "The Command of Gold Reserved: American Loans to Britain, 1915–1917," *The Pacific Historical Review*, Vol. 45, No. 2, May 1976, 211.

74. Cabinet Report, June 1915, CAB 37 / 129.
75. Burk, *Britain, America, and the Sinews of War 1914–1918*, 63, 66; Burk, "The Diplomacy of Finance: British Financial Missions to the United States, 1914–1918," *The Historical Journal*, Vol. 22, No. 2 (June 1979), 353; Link, *Wilson: The Struggle for Neutrality*, 616. Britain attempted to meet its financial obligations through domestic borrowing but discovered that it could not raise enough money at home. French, *British Strategy and War Aims 1914–1916*, 121.
76. Spring-Rice to Grey, June 13, 1915, FO 800 / 85.
77. Lloyd George to the Cabinet, August 14, 1915, David Lloyd George Papers, D/3/3/19, Parliamentary Archives, London, UK. The number of rounds produced in June 1915 is an average for the first three weeks of the month.
78. Lloyd George to Crewe, August 13, 1915, Lloyd George Papers, D/3/5/18, ibid.
79. Lloyd George at the War Policy Cabinet Committee meeting, August 16, 1915, CAB 37 / 132, National Archives, Kew, UK.
80. R. J. Q. Adams, *Arms and the Wizard: Lloyd George and the Ministry of Munitions, 1915–1916* (College Station: Texas A&M University Press, 1978), 167–68.
81. Spring-Rice to Grey, May 22, 1915, FO 115 / 1997.
82. Ibid.
83. Crowe to Spring-Rice, June 18, 1915, Spring-Rice Papers, CASR 1 / 26.
84. McKenna to Cabinet, October 22, 1915, CAB 37 / 136, National Archives, Kew, UK.
85. McKenna to Churchill, August 23, 1915, CAB 37 / 132.
86. McAdoo to Wilson, August 21, 1915, Link, *The Papers of Woodrow Wilson*, 34: 275; Link, *Wilson: The Struggle for Neutrality*, 618–19.
87. McAdoo to Wilson, August 21, 1915, Link, *The Papers of Woodrow Wilson*, 34: 275.
88. Spring-Rice to Grey, August 19, 1915, CAB 37/132.
89. Lansing's private memorandum, July 1915, Lansing Papers.
90. Vice Consul at Cork Lewis Thompson to Lansing, August 19, 1915, *FRUS: 1915. Supplement, The World War*, 516; Devlin, *Too Proud to Fight*, 319.
91. Wilson to Galt, August 19, 1915, Link, *The Papers of Woodrow Wilson*, 34: 253–63.
92. Ibid.
93. Lansing to Wilson, August 20, 1915, ibid., 34: 264–66.
94. Wilson to Lansing, August 21, 1915, ibid., 34: 271.
95. Wilson to House, August 21, 1915, ibid., 34: 271–72.
96. Seymour, *The Intimate Papers of Colonel House*, 2: 30–32.
97. Wilson to Galt (with enclosures), August 23, 1915, Link, *The Papers of Woodrow Wilson*, 34: 296–98.
98. Wilson to Galt (with enclosures), August 22, 1915, Link, *The Papers of Woodrow Wilson*, 34: 287–92.
99. Bernstorff to Lansing, August 24, 1915, *FRUS: 1915. Supplement, The World War*, 524.

100. Wilson to Galt (with enclosure), August 24, 1915, Link, *The Papers of Woodrow Wilson*, 34: 308–9; Gerard to Lansing, August 24, 1915 (received August 25 1: 30 p.m.), *FRUS: 1915. Supplement, The World War*, 525.
101. Wilson to House, August 25, 1915, Link, *The Papers of Woodrow Wilson*, 34: 315–16.
102. Page to Lansing, August 29, 1915, *FRUS:1915. Supplement, The World War*, 528–29. To deal with the German submarine attacks Britain started using Q-ships. Q-ships were British naval vessels disguised as merchant ships that carried hidden guns. Their strategy was to lure German submarines in close and fire on them once they surfaced. Halpern, *A Naval History of the World War I*, 300.
103. Wilson to Galt (with enclosure), August 30, 1915, Link, *The Papers of Woodrow Wilson*, 34: 367–68.
104. Bernstorff to Lansing, September 1, 1915, ibid., 34: 400–401. He received letters of congratulation from Herbert Hoover, Josephus Daniels, Franklin Knight Lane, and others. Herbert Clark Hoover to Wilson, ibid., 34: 409–10; Josephus Daniels to Wilson, ibid., 34: 410–11; Franklin Knight Lane to Wilson, ibid., 34: 411.
105. *New York Times*, Current History: A Monthly Magazine of the New York Times, Volume 3, October 1915–March 1916 (New York: New York Times, 1916), 9; Wilson to Galt, September 6, 1915, Link, *The Papers of Woodrow Wilson*, 34: 423–24; Link, *Wilson: The Struggle for Neutrality*, 652.
106. Wilson to Lansing, August 26, 1915, Link, *The Papers of Woodrow Wilson*, 34: 329; Link, *Wilson: The Struggle for Neutrality*, 621–22.
107. Lansing to McAdoo, August 26, 1915, Link, *The Papers of Woodrow Wilson*, 34: 330.
108. Lansing to Wilson, September 6, 1915, ibid., 34: 421–23.
109. Ibid.
110. Wilson to Lansing, September 8, 1915, ibid., 34: 432.
111. For a different view on the impact of the loan, see Kendrick A. Clements, *The Presidency of Woodrow Wilson* (Lawrence: University Press of Kansas, 1992), 129.

Chapter 8

1. Grey to Spring-Rice, November 6, 1915, CAB 37 / 136, National Archives, Kew, UK.
2. Robert Lansing, *War Memoirs of Robert Lansing* (Westport, CT: Greenwood, 1970), 63.
3. Page to Lansing, August 31, 1915, *FRUS: 1915. Supplement, The World War*, 932; Page to Lansing, September 1, 1915 (received September 2), ibid., 932–33.
4. Grey to Spring-Rice, September 4, 1915, FO 800 / 85; *New York Times*, September 6, 1915, 1.
5. Spring-Rice to Grey, September 6, 1915, FO 800 / 241.
6. Lansing, *War Memoirs of Robert Lansing*, 65.

7. Bernstorff to Lansing, September 8, 1915 (received September 9), *FRUS: 1915. Supplement, The World War*, 540. As early as June 5, Berlin ordered its U-boat captains not to attack passenger vessels of any nationality. Paul G. Halpern, *A Naval History of the First World War* (Annapolis, MD: Naval Institute Press, 1995), 299.
8. Gerard to Lansing, September 7, 1915 (received September 9 at 8 a.m.), *FRUS: 1915. Supplement, The World War*, 539–40; Arthur Link, *Wilson: The Struggle for Neutrality, 1914–1915* (Princeton, NJ: Princeton University Press, 1960), 655–56.
9. Gerard to Lansing, September 9, 1915 (received September 10 at 2 p.m.), ibid., 543; Gerard to Lansing, September 10, 1915 (received September 11 at 10:15 a.m.), ibid., 545; Link, *Wilson: The Struggle for Neutrality*, 655–56.
10. Lansing to Gerard, September 11, 1915, ibid., 545.
11. Gerard to Lansing, September 14, 1915 (received September 15 at 8 p.m.), ibid., 548.
12. Lansing to Wilson, September 11, 1915, Link, Arthur S. Link, ed., *The Papers of Woodrow Wilson* (Princeton, NJ: Princeton University Press, 1979), 34: 448–52; Link, *Wilson: The Struggle for Neutrality*, 659–60.
13. Lansing to Wilson, September 13, 1915, ibid., 34: 461–62.
14. Lansing to Gerard, September 14, 1915, *FRUS: 1915. Supplement, The World War*, 547–48; Frank L. Polk to Gerard, September 20, 1915, ibid., 549–50.
15. Diary of Colonel House, September 22, 1915, Link, *The Papers of Woodrow Wilson*, 34: 505–8.
16. Polk to Penefield, September 22, 1915 (received 9 p.m.), *FRUS: 1915. Supplement, The World War*, 941.
17. Bernstorff to Lansing, October 2, 1915, Link, *The Papers of Woodrow Wilson*, 35: 13; Patrick Devlin, *Too Proud to Fight: Woodrow Wilson's Neutrality* (New York: Oxford University Press, 1975, c1974), 329–30.
18. Memorandum by Lansing, October 5, 1915, ibid., 35: 25–26.
19. Bernstorff to Lansing, October 5, 1915, *FRUS: 1915. Supplement, The World War*, 560; Link, *Wilson: The Struggle for Neutrality*, 675–76.
20. Memorandum by Lansing, October 5, 1915, Link, *The Papers of Woodrow Wilson* 35: 25–26; Bernstorff to Lansing, October 5, 1915, ibid., 35: 26–27.
21. Wilson to Galt, ibid., 35: 27.
22. Skinner to Lansing, September 16, 1915 (received October 2), *FRUS: 1915. Supplement, The World War*, 559–60.
23. Messrs. Henry Veeder, Charles J. Faulkner Jr., and Luther M. Walter, counsel for American packers to Lansing, October 6, 1915, ibid., 561. The ships involved were the *Kim*, *Alfred Nobel*, *Bjornstjerne Bjornson*, and *Fridland.*
24. Spring-Rice to Lansing, October 6, 1915 (received October 9), ibid., 564–66.
25. Spring-Rice to Lansing (received October 12), ibid., 566–69.
26. Wilson to Lansing, October 21, 1915, Link, *The Papers of Woodrow Wilson*, 35: 91–92.
27. Lansing to Page, October 21, 1915, *FRUS: 1915. Supplement, The World War*, 578–601.

28. Link, *Wilson: The Struggle for Neutrality*, 691.
29. House to Wilson (with enclosure), October 31, 1915, Link, *The Papers of Woodrow Wilson*, 35: 144–45.
30. Grey to Spring-Rice, November 6, 1915, CAB 37 / 136, National Archives, Kew, UK.
31. Mason, "Anglo-American Relations: Mediation and 'Permanent Peace,'" in F. H. Hinsley, ed., *British Foreign Policy Under Sir Edward Grey*, 474; Diary of Colonel House, October 8, 1915, Link, *The Papers of Woodrow Wilson*, 35: 43–44.
32. Diary of Colonel House, October 8, 1915, Link, *The Papers of Woodrow Wilson*, 35: 43–44.
33. Ibid.
34. Charles Seymour, ed., *The Intimate Papers of Colonel House: Behind the Political Curtain, 1912–1915* (Boston: Houghton Mifflin, 1926), 2: 86.
35. Diary of Colonel House, October 13, 1915, Link, *The Papers of Woodrow Wilson*, 35: 59–60.
36. Diary of Colonel House, October 15, 1915, ibid., 35: 69–72; Mason, "Anglo-American Relations: Mediation and 'Permanent Peace,'" in F. H. Hinsley, ed., *British Foreign Policy Under Sir Edward Grey*, 474.
37. Wilson to House (with enclosure), October 18, 1915, Link, *The Papers of Woodrow Wilson*, 35: 80–82.
38. Ibid. Italics added by author for emphasis.
39. Tucker, *Woodrow Wilson and the Great War*, 149–50.
40. Lansing to Wilson, November 2, 1915, ibid., 35: 158–59.
41. Bernstorff to Lansing (with enclosure), October 2, 1915, ibid., 35: 14–15.
42. Lansing to Wilson, November 19, 1915, ibid., 35: 218–19.
43. Wilson to Lansing, November 21, 1915, ibid., 35: 233–34.
44. *New York Times*, November 12, 1915, 2.
45. Devlin, *Too Proud to Fight*, 368. After the war, evidence proved that the Germans had conducted the attack; however, in 1915 Austria had taken responsibility for the assault.
46. Wilson to House, November, 12 1915, Link, *The Papers of Woodrow Wilson*, 35: 192.
47. Lansing, *The War Memoirs of Robert Lansing*, 89.
48. House to Wilson, November 21, 1915, Link, *The Papers of Woodrow Wilson*, 35: 234–35.
49. Diary of Colonel House, November 28, 1915, ibid., 35: 258–60.
50. Ibid.
51. Ibid.; Spring-Rice to Grey, August 21, 1915, FO 115 / 1958, National Archives, Kew, UK.
52. Lansing, *The War Memoirs of Robert Lansing*, 73.
53. *New York Times*, November 19, 1915, 4.
54. *New York Herald* as cited in Link, *The Papers of Woodrow Wilson*, 35: 222.
55. Tumulty to Wilson, November 19, 1915, *The Papers of Woodrow Wilson*, 35: 221–22.

56. The Wilson administration discovered as early as the winter of 1914–15 that the German embassy was aiding reservists by providing false passports, which was a violation of US neutrality. As a result, the government arrested several of the main instigators. In early 1915, however, Wilson did not make this a serious problem and tried to prevent information about the passport issue from reaching the public. Link, *Wilson: The Struggle for Neutrality*, 558–59; William G. McAdoo, *Crowded Years: The Reminiscences of William G. McAdoo* (New York: Houghton Mifflin, 1931), 324–28.
57. McAdoo, *Crowded Years: The Reminiscences of William G. McAdoo*, 324–28.
58. Lansing, *The War Memoirs of Robert Lansing*, 76–77; Devlin, *Too Proud to Fight*, 318–19.
59. Frederick C. Luebke, *Bonds of Loyalty: German-Americans and World War I* (DeKalb: Northern Illinois University Press, 1974), 145; *New York Times*, October 12, 1915, 1.
60. Katie Pickles, *Transnational Outrage: The Death and Commemoration of Edith Cavell* (New York: Palgrave Macmillan, 2007), 81.
61. *New York Evening Herald* as cited in Pickles, *Transnational Outrage*, 81.
62. Lansing to Wilson, November 29, 1915, Link, *The Papers of Woodrow Wilson*, 35: 264.
63. Lansing to Wilson (with enclosure), December 1, 1915, ibid., 35: 276–78.
64. Wilson to Lansing, December 2, 1915, ibid., 35: 281.
65. Wilson, "An Annual Message on the State of the Union," December 7, 1915, ibid., 35: 293–310.
66. Ibid.
67. Ibid.
68. Spring-Rice to Grey, December 9, 1915, FO 800 / 85.
69. Ibid.
70. Diary of Colonel House, December 15, 1915, *The Papers of Woodrow Wilson*, 35: 355–61.

Conclusion

1. Hew Strachan, Strachan, *The First World War* (London: Viking Penguin, 2004), 192; Robert H. Ferrell, *American Diplomacy: A History* (New York: W. W. Norton, 1975), 467; See also John Milton Cooper Jr., "The British Response to the House-Grey Memorandum: New Evidence and New Questions," *The Journal of American History* Vol. 59, No. 4 (March 1973), 958–66.
2. Wilson to House, July 24, 1916, Arthur S. Link, ed., *The Papers of Woodrow Wilson* (Princeton, NJ: Princeton University Press, 1979), 37: 466–67.
3. Wilson to Blumenthal, October 30, 1916, Link, ed., *The Papers of Woodrow Wilson* (Princeton, NJ: Princeton University Press, 1982), 38: 562.
4. As cited in Ernest R. May *The World War and American Isolation 1914–1919* (Cambridge: Harvard University Press, 1966), 41; Tansill, *America Goes to War*, 52–53; Charles Gilbert, *American Financing of World War I*, 33.
5. Strachan, *Financing the First World War*, 195–202.

Bibliography

Primary Sources

Unpublished Sources

United Kingdom

Bodleian Library, University of Oxford, Oxford
  H. Henry Asquith Papers
Churchill Archives Center, Cambridge University, Cambridge
  Cecil Spring-Rice Papers
National Archives of the United Kingdom, Kew
  Cabinet Office Papers
  Cecil Spring-Rice Papers
  Edward Grey Papers
  Foreign Office Papers
Parliamentary Archives, London
  Bonar Law Papers
  David Lloyd George Papers

United States

Alabama Department of Archives and History, Montgomery
  John H. Bankhead Papers
Library of Congress, Washington, DC
  Chandler Anderson Papers
  Robert Lansing Papers
  William Jennings Bryan Papers
  William McAdoo Papers
  Woodrow Wilson Papers
University of North Carolina at Chapel Hill
  Great Britain, Foreign Office, Confidential Print: *War (General), 1914–1940.*
  Great Britain, Foreign Office, Embassy and Consular Archives. Correspondence, 1903–1940, United States of America
  Great Britain, Foreign Office, Political Files
University of Virginia, Charlottesville, Virginia
  Edward Mandell House Papers, 1885–1938
  Papers of Sir Cecil Spring-Rice, 1859–1918
  Papers of Sir Edward Grey as Foreign Secretary, 1905–1916

Published Documentary Collections, Congressional Documents, and Periodicals

Baker, Ray Stannard, ed. *The Public Papers of Woodrow Wilson: College and State: Educational, Literary, and Political Papers (1875–1913)*. Volume 1. New York: Harper and Brothers, 1925.

———. *The Public Papers of Woodrow Wilson: College and State: Presidential Messages, Addresses, and Other Papers (1913–1917)*. Volume 2. New York: Harper and Brothers, 1925.

Bleck, Edward C., and Edward Parkes. *British and Foreign State Papers, 1915*. London: His Majesty's Stationary Office, 1919.

Cambridge University Press. "Historical Statistics of the United States Millennial Edition Online." June 2008. http://hsus.cambridge.org.libdata.lib.ua.edu/HSUSWeb/table/seriesnext.do?id=Ee533–50.

Cronon, E. David, ed. *The Cabinet Diaries of Josephus Daniels*. Lincoln: University of Nebraska Press, 1963.

Department of Commerce, Bureau of Foreign and Domestic Commerce. *Statistical Abstract of the United States: 1914*. Volume 37. Washington, DC: Government Printing Office, 1915.

Fess, Simon D., ed. *The Problems of Neutrality When the World Is at War: A History of Our Relations with Germany and Great Britain as Detailed in Documents that Passed between the United States and the Two Great Powers*. Part 1, *The Submarine Controversy*. Washington, DC: Government Printing Office, 1917.

Gwynn, Stephen, ed. *The Letters and Friendships of Sir Cecil Spring-Rice*. Volume 2. New York: Houghton Mifflin, 1929.

Hendrick, Burton J. *The Life and Letters of Walter H. Page*. Volume 1. Garden City, NY: Doubleday, Page, 1922.

———. *The Life and Letters of Walter H. Page*. Volume 2. Garden City, NY: Doubleday, Page, 1922.

International Committee of the Red Cross. "Convention (V) Respecting the Rights and Duties of Neutral Powers and Persons in Case of War on Land. The Hague, 18 October 1907." http://www.icrc.org/ihl.nsf/full/200?opendocument.

Link, Arthur S., ed. *The Papers of Woodrow Wilson*. Volume 30. Princeton, NJ: Princeton University Press, 1979.

———. *The Papers of Woodrow Wilson*. Volume 31. Princeton, NJ: Princeton University Press, 1979.

———. *The Papers of Woodrow Wilson*. Volume 32. Princeton, NJ: Princeton University Press, 1980.

———. *The Papers of Woodrow Wilson*. Volume 33. Princeton, NJ: Princeton University Press, 1980.

———. *The Papers of Woodrow Wilson*. Volume 34. Princeton, NJ: Princeton University Press, 1980.

———. *The Papers of Woodrow Wilson*. Volume 35. Princeton, NJ: Princeton University Press, 1981.

———. *The Papers of Woodrow Wilson*. Volume 36. Princeton, NJ: Princeton University Press, 1981.

———. *The Papers of Woodrow Wilson*. Volume 37. Princeton, NJ: Princeton University Press, 1982.

———. *The Papers of Woodrow Wilson*. Volume 38. Princeton, NJ: Princeton University Press, 1982.

Naval War College. *International Law Documents: Neutrality, Breaking of Diplomatic Relations, War*. Washington, DC: Government Printing Office, 1918.

New York Times. *Current History: A Monthly Magazine of the New York Times. Volume 3*. New York: New York Times, 1916.

Scott, James Brown. *Declaration of London February 26, 1909: A Collection of Official Papers and Documents Relating to the International Conference Held in London, December, 1908–February, 1909*. New York: Oxford University Press, 1919.

———, ed. *Diplomatic Correspondence between the United States and Germany, August 1, 1914–April 6, 1917*. New York: Oxford University Press, 1918.

Seymore, Charles, ed. *The Intimate Papers of Colonel House*. Volume 1. New York: Houghton Mifflin, 1926.

———. *The Intimate Papers of Colonel House*. Volume 2. New York: Houghton Mifflin, 1926.

Stevenson, David, ed. *British Documents on Foreign Affairs: Reports and Papers from the Foreign Office Confidential Print*. Part 2, *From the First to the Second World War*. Series H, *The First World War, 1914–1918*. Volume 1, *The Allied and Neutral Powers: Diplomacy and War Aims, I: August 1914–July 1915*. Frederick, MD: University Publications of America, 1989.

———. *British Documents on Foreign Affairs: Reports and Papers from the Foreign Office Confidential Print*. Part 2, *From the First to the Second World War*. Series H, *The First World War, 1914–1918*. Volume 5, *Blockade and Economic Warfare, I: August 1914–July 1915*. Frederick, MD: University Publications of America, 1989.

US Census Bureau. "Census of Population and Housing: 1910 Census." Accessed August 15, 2008. http://www.census.gov/prod/www/abs/decennial/1910.htm.

———. "No. HS-44. Agriculture–Farms, Acreage, Income, and Foreign Trade: 1900 to 2002." Accessed August 15, 2008. Statistical Abstracts of the United States. www.census.gov/statab/hist/HS-44.pdf.

US Congressional Record, 63D Congress 3d Session, Senate.

US Department of State. *Papers Relating to the Foreign Relations of the United States. The Lansing Papers, 1914–1920*. Volume 1. Washington, DC: Government Printing Office, 1939.

———. *Papers Relating to the Foreign Relations of the United States. The Lansing Papers, 1914–1920*. Volume 2. Washington, DC: Government Printing Office, 1940.

———. *Papers Relating to the Foreign Relations of the United States, 1915. Supplement, The World War*. Washington, DC: Government Printing Office, 1928.

———. *Papers Relating to the Foreign Relations of the United States, 1914. Supplement, The World War (1914)*. Washington, DC: Government Printing Office, 1928.

US Government Printing Office. "Biographical Directory of the United States Congress, 1774–2005." Accessed July 8, 2008. http://www.gpoaccess.gov/serialset/cdocuments/hd108-222/64th.pdf.

US House of Representatives. "Congressional Profiles." Accessed July 2, 2013. http://history.house.gov/Congressional-Overview/Profiles/63rd.

Yale Law School, Lillian Goldman Library. "Laws of War: Declaration of Paris; April 16, 1856." The Avalon Project: Documents in Law, History, and Diplomacy. Accessed October 21, 2009. http://avalon.law.yale.edu/19th_century/decparis.asp.

Periodicals

Atlanta Journal-Constitution
Daily Telegraph (London)
Times (London)
Times-Picayune (New Orleans)
New York Times
Wall Street Journal
Washington Post

Memoirs and Personal Accounts

Asquith, Henry, the Earl of Oxford, and Asquith, KG. *Memories and Reflections, 1852–1927*. Boston: Little, Brown, 1928.

Bernstorff, Johann Heinrich. *My Three Years in America*. London: Skeffington and Son, 1920.

Bryan, William Jennings, and Mary Baird Bryan. *The Memoirs of William Jennings Bryan*. Philadelphia: John C. Winston, 1925.

Churchill, Winston S. *The World Crisis, 1911–1914*. New York: Charles Scribner's Sons, 1928.

———. *The World Crisis, 1915*. New York: Charles Scribner's Sons, 1929.

George, David Lloyd. *War Memoirs of David Lloyd George, 1914–1915*. Boston: Little, Brown, 1933.

———. *War Memoirs of David Lloyd George, 1915–1916*. Boston: Little, Brown, 1933.

Grayson, Rear Admiral Cary T. *Woodrow Wilson: An Intimate Memoir*. New York: Holt, Rinehart, and Winston, 1960.

Grey, Edward, Viscount of Fallodon, *Twenty-Five Years, 1892–1916*. Volume 1. New York: Frederick A. Stokes, 1925.

———. *Twenty-Five Years, 1892–1916*. Volume 2. New York: Frederick A. Stokes, 1925.

Haldane, Richard Burdon. *An Autobiography*. Garden City, NY: Doubleday, Doran, 1929.

Lansing, Robert. *War Memoirs of Robert Lansing*. Westport, CT: Greenwood, 1970.
Lennox, Lady A. G., ed. *The Diary of Lord Bertie of Thame 1914–1918*. London: Hodder and Stoughton, 1924.
McAdoo, William G. *Crowded Years: The Reminiscences of William G. McAdoo*. Boston: Houghton Mifflin, 1931.
Trevelyan, George. *The Life and Letters of Sir Edward Grey*. Boston: Houghton Mifflin, 1937.
Tumulty, Joseph P. *Woodrow Wilson as I Know Him*. New York: Doubleday, Page, 1921.
Wilson, Edith Bolling. *My Memoir*. New York: Bobbs-Merrill, 1938.
Wilson, Woodrow. *A History of the American People: The Founding of the Government*. Volume 3. London: Harper and Brothers, 1908.

Secondary Cited and Consulted Sources

Adams, R. J. Q. *Arms and the Wizard: Lloyd George and the Ministry of Munitions, 1915–1916*. College Station: Texas A&M University Press, 1978.
———. *The Great War, 1914–1918: Essays on the Military, Political, and Social History of the First World War*. College Station: Texas A&M University Press, 1990.
Ambrosius, Lloyd E. *Wilsonian Statecraft: Theory and Practice of Liberal Internationalism during World War I*. New York: Scholarly Resources, 1991.
Ashby, LeRoy. *William Jennings Bryan: Champion of Democracy*. Boston: Twayne, 1987.
Beard, Charles. *The Devil Theory of War: An Inquiry into the Nature of History and the Possibility of Keeping Out of War*. New York: Greenwood, 1977 ed.
Beckett, Ian F. W. *The Great War, 1914–1918*. London: Pearson Education, 2001.
Bell, Sidney. *Righteous Conquest: Woodrow Wilson and the Evolution of New Diplomacy*. New York: Kennikat, 1972.
Blum, John Morton. *Woodrow Wilson and the Politics of Morality*. Boston: Little, Brown, 1956.
Bond, Brian, ed. *The First World War and British Military History*. Oxford: Clarendon, 1991.
Brands, H. W. *Woodrow Wilson*. New York: Henry Holt, 2003.
Briggs, Herbert Whittaker. *The Doctrine of Continuous Voyage*. Buffalo, NY: William S. Hein, 2003.
Broadberry, Stephen, and Mark Harrison, eds. *The Economics of World War I*. New York: Cambridge University Press, 2005.
Buehrig, Edward H., ed. *Wilson's Foreign Policy in Perspective*. Bloomington: Indiana University Press, 1970.
Burk, Kathleen. *Britain, America, and the Sinews of War, 1914–1918*. London: George Allen and Unwin, 1985.
———. "The Diplomacy of Finance: British Financial Missions to the United States, 1914–1918." *The Historical Journal*. Vol. 22, No. 2 (June 1979): 351–72.
———, ed. *War and the State: The Transformation of British Government, 1914–1919*. London: Allen and Unwin, 1982.

Burton, David H. *Cecil Spring-Rice: A Diplomat's Life*. London: Associated University Presses, 1990.

Child, Clifton J. "German-American Attempts to Prevent the Exportation of Munitions of War, 1914–1915." *The Mississippi Valley Historical Review*. Vol. 25, No. 3 (December 1938): 351–68.

Clements, Kendrick A. *The Presidency of Woodrow Wilson*. Lawrence: University Press of Kansas, 1992.

———. *William Jennings Bryan: Missionary Isolationist*. Knoxville: University of Tennessee Press, 1982.

Clements, Kendrick A., and Eric Cheezum, *Woodrow Wilson*. Washington, DC: CQ Press, 2003.

Coles, Harry L. *The War of 1812*. Chicago, IL: University of Chicago Press, 1965.

Coletta, Paolo. *Sea Power in the Atlantic and Mediterranean in World War I*. New York: University Press of America, 1989.

———. *William Jennings Bryan: Volume 2. Progressive Politician and Moral Statesman, 1909–1915*. Lincoln: University of Nebraska Press, 1969.

Conyne, G. R. *Woodrow Wilson: British Perspectives 1912–1921*. New York: Palgrave Macmillan, 2003.

Coogan, John W. *The End of Neutrality: The United States, Britain, and Maritime Rights, 1899–1915*. Ithaca, NY: Cornell University Press, 1981.

Cook, Adrian. *The Alabama Claims: American Politics and Anglo-American Relations, 1865–1872*. Ithaca, NY: Cornell University Press, 1975.

Cooper, John Milton, Jr. "The British Response to the House-Grey Memorandum: New Evidence and New Questions." *The Journal of American History*. Vol. 59, No. 4 (March 1973): 958–66.

———. "The Command of Gold Reserved: American Loans to Britain, 1915–1917." *The Pacific Historical Review*. Vol. 45, No. 2 (May 1976): 209–30.

———. *The Vanity of Power: American Isolationism and the First World War, 1914–1917*. Westport, CT: Greenwood, 1969.

———. *Walter Hines Page: The Southerner as American, 1855–1918*. Chapel Hill: University of North Carolina Press, 1977.

———. *The Warrior and the Priest: Woodrow Wilson and Theodore Roosevelt*. Cambridge, MA: Belknap Press of Harvard University Press, 1983.

———. *Woodrow Wilson*. New York: Alfred A. Knopf, 2009.

Davis, Lance E., and Stanley L. Engerman. *Naval Blockades in War and Peace: An Economic History since 1750*. Cambridge: Cambridge University Press, 2006.

Dayer, Roberta A. "Strange Bedfellows: J. P. Morgan & Co., Whitehall, and the Wilson Administration during World War I." *Business History*. Vol. 18, No. 2 (1976): 127–51.

Devlin, Patrick. *Too Proud to Fight: Woodrow Wilson's Neutrality*. New York: Oxford University Press, 1975, c1974.

Diamond, William. *The Economic Thought of Woodrow Wilson*. Baltimore, MD: Johns Hopkins University Press, 1943.

Doenecke, Justus D. *Nothing Less Than War: A New History of America's Entry into World War I*. Lexington: University Press of Kentucky, 2011.

Emden, Richard van, and Steve Humphries. *All Quiet on the Home Front: An Oral History of Life in Britain during the First World War*. London: Headline Book Publishing, 2003.
Engelbrecht, H. C., and F. C. Hanighen. *Merchants of Death*. New York: Dodd, Mead: 1934.
Esposito, David M. *The Legacy of Woodrow Wilson: American War Aims in World War I*. Westport, CT: Praeger, 1996.
Evera, Stephen van. "The Cult of the Offensive and the Origins of the First World War." In *Military Strategy and the Origins of the First World War*, edited by Steven E. Miller. Princeton, NJ: Princeton University Press, 1985.
Farrar, Marjorie Milbank. *Conflict and Compromise: The Strategy, Politics, and Diplomacy of the French Blockade, 1914–1918*. The Hague, Netherlands: Martinus Nijhoff, 1974.
Ferrell, Robert H. *American Diplomacy: A History*. New York: W. W. Norton, 1975.
———. *Woodrow Wilson and World War I, 1917–1919*. Bloomington: Indiana University Press, 1985.
Finnegan, John Patrick. *Against the Specter of a Dragon: The Campaign for American Military Preparedness, 1914–1917*. Westport, CT: Greenwood, 1974.
Fischer, Fritz. *Germany's War Aims in the First World War*. New York: W. W. Norton, 1967.
Fleming, Thomas. *The Illusions of Victory: America in World War I*. New York: Basic Books, 2003.
Ford, Nancy Gentile. *The Great War and America: Civil-Military Relations during World War I*. Westport, CT: Praeger Security International, 2008.
Fordham, Benjamin O. "Revisionism Reconsidered: Exports and American Intervention in World War I." *International Organization*. Vol. 61, No. 2 (Spring 2007): 277–310.
Fraser, Peter. "British War Policy and the Crisis of Liberalism in May 1915." *The Journal of Modern History*. Vol. 54, No. 1 (March 1982): 1–26.
French, David. *British Strategy and War Aims 1914–1916*. London: George Allen and Unwin, 1986.
Fry, Joseph A. *Dixie Looks Abroad: The South and U.S. Foreign Relations, 1789–1973*. Baton Rouge: Louisiana State University Press, 2002.
Geiss, Imanuel. "Origins of the First World War." In *The Origins of the First World War: Great Power Rivalry and German War Aims*, edited by H. W. Koch. London: McMillian, 1984.
George, Alexander L., and Juliette L. George. *Woodrow Wilson and Colonel House: A Personality Study*. New York: Dover, 1964.
Gilbert, Charles. *American Financing of World War I*. Westport, CT: Greenwood, 1970.
Grady, Henry F. *British War Finance: 1914–1919*. New York: AMS, 1968.
Gray, Colin S. *The Leverage of Sea Power: The Strategic Advantage of Navies in War*. New York: Free Press, 1992.
Greenhalgh, Elizabeth. *Victory through Coalition: Britain and France during the First World War*. Cambridge: Cambridge University Press, 2005.

Gregory, Ross. *The Origins of American Intervention in the First World War*. New York: W. W. Norton, 1971.

———. *Walter Hines Page: Ambassador to the Court of St. James's*. Lexington: University Press of Kentucky, 1970.

Hagan, Kenneth J., ed. *In Peace and War: Interpretations of American Naval History, 1775–1978*. Westport, CT: Greenwood, 1978.

Haggie, Paul. "The Royal Navy and War Planning in the Fisher Era." In *The War plans of the Great Powers 1880–1914*, edited by Paul Kennedy. London: George Allen and Unwin, 1979.

Halpern, Paul G. *A Naval History of World War I*. Annapolis, MD: Naval Institute Press, 1995.

Harvey, A. D. *Collision of Empires: Great Britain in Three World Wars, 1793–1945*. London: Hambledon and London, 2003.

Hawkins, Nigel. *The Starvation Blockade*. South Yorkshire, UK: Leo Cooper, 2002.

Heckscher, August. *Woodrow Wilson*. New York: Charles Scribner's Sons, 1991.

Heidler, David S., and Jeanne T. Heidler *The War of 1812*. Westport, CT: Greenwood, 2002.

Hendrick, Burton J. *The Life and Letters of Walter Hines Page*. Garden City, NY: Doubleday, Page, 1924.

Hill, J. R., ed. *The Oxford Illustrated History of the Royal Navy. New York:* Oxford University Press, 1995.

Hinsley, F. H., ed. *British Foreign Policy under Sir Edward Grey*. New York: Cambridge University Press, 1977.

Hofstadter, Richard. *The Age of Reform: From Bryan to F. D. R.* New York: Vintage Books, 1955.

Hurwitz, Samuel J. *State Intervention in Great Britain: A Study of Economic Control and Social Response, 1914–1919*. New York: AMS, 1968.

Johnson, J. H. *Stalemate! The Great Trench Warfare Battles of 1915–1917*. London: Arms and Armor, 1995.

Jones, Howard. *Blue and Gray Diplomacy: A History of Union and Confederate Foreign Relations*. Chapel Hill: University of North Carolina Press, 2010.

———. *Crucible of Power: A History of American Foreign Relations from 1897*. 2nd ed. Lanham, MD: Rowman and Littlefield, 2008.

———. *Union in Peril: The Crisis over the British Intervention in the Civil War*. Lincoln: University of Nebraska Press, 1997.

Keegan, John. *The First World War*. New York: Vintage Books, 2000.

Kennan, George F. *American Diplomacy, 1900–1950*. Chicago, IL: University of Chicago Press, 1951.

Kennedy, David M. *Over Here: The First World War and American Society*. London: Oxford University Press, 1980.

Kennedy, Paul M., ed. *The War Plans of the Great Powers, 1880–1914*. London: George Allen and Unwin, 1979.

Kennedy, Ross A., *The Will to Believe: Woodrow Wilson, World War I, and America's Strategy for Peace and Security*. Kent, OH: Kent State University Press, 2009.

Knock, Thomas J. *To End All Wars: Woodrow Wilson and the Quest for a New World Order*. Princeton, NJ: Princeton University Press, 1992.

Koch, H. W., ed. *The Origins of the First World War: Great Power Rivalry and German War Aims*. London: Macmillan, 1984.

Levin, Norman Gordon. *Woodrow Wilson and World Politics: America's Response to War and Revolution*. New York: Oxford University Press, 1968.

Link, Arthur S. *The Higher Realism of Woodrow Wilson*. Nashville, TN: Vanderbilt University Press, 1971.

———. *Wilson the Diplomatist: A Look at His Major Foreign Policies*. Chicago, IL: Quadrangle Paperbacks, 1957.

———. *Wilson: The Struggle for Neutrality, 1914–1915*. Princeton, NJ: Princeton University Press, 1960.

Luebke, Frederick C. *Bonds of Loyalty: German-Americans and World War I*. DeKalb: Northern Illinois University Press, 1974.

Lundeberg, Philip K. "The German Naval Critique of the U-Boat Campaign, 1915–1918." *Military Affairs*. Vol. 27, No. 3 (Autumn 1963): 105–18.

Marder, Arthur Jacob. *The Anatomy of British Sea Power: A History of British Naval Policy in the Pre-Dreadnought Era, 1880–1905*. New York: Alfred A. Knopf, 1940.

———. *From Dreadnought to Scapa Flow*. New York: Oxford University Press, 1961.

Martin, Laurence W. *Peace without Victory: Woodrow Wilson and British Liberals*. Port Washington, NY: Kennikat, 1973 reprint.

Marwick, Arthur. *The Deluge: British Society and the First World War*. London: Bodley Head, 1965.

Mason, C. M. "Anglo-American Relations: Mediation and 'Permanent Peace.'" In *British Foreign Policy under Sir Edward Grey*, edited by F. H. Hinsley. Cambridge: Cambridge University Press, 1977.

Maurer, John H. *The Outbreak of the First World War: Strategic Planning, Crisis Decision Making, and Deterrence Failure*. London: Praeger, 1995.

May, Ernest R. *The World War and American Isolation, 1914–1917*. Cambridge, MA: Harvard University Press, 1966.

McWilliams, Tennant S. *The New South Faces the World: Foreign Affairs and the Southern Sense of Self, 1877–1950*. Baton Rouge: Louisiana State University Press, 1988.

Merli, Frank J., *The Alabama, British Neutrality, and the Civil War*. Edited by David M. Fahey. Bloomington: Indiana University Press, 2004.

Miller, Steven E. *Military Strategy and the Origins of the First World War*. Princeton, NJ: Princeton University Press, 1985.

Millman, Brock. *Managing Domestic Dissent in First World War Britain*. London: Frank Cass, 2000.

Mott, Col. T. Bently. *Myron T. Herrick: Friend of France, an Autobiographical Biography*. Garden City, NY: Doubleday, Doran, 1929.

Naval Historical Center. "USS *Vanderbilt* (1862–1873)." Accessed June 2008. http://www.history.navy.mil/photos/sh-usn/usnsh-v/vanderbt.htm.

Nordholt, Jan Willem Schulte. *Woodrow Wilson: A Life for World Peace*. Berkley: University of California Press, 1991.

Offer, Avner. *The First World War: An Agrarian Interpretation.* Oxford: Oxford University Press, 1989.

Olliff, Martin T. *The Great War in the Heart of Dixie: Alabama during World War I.* Tuscaloosa: University of Alabama Press, 2008.

Osborn, George Coleman. *Woodrow Wilson: The Early Years.* Baton Rouge: Louisiana State University, 1968.

Osgood, Robert Endicott. *Ideals and Self-Interest in American Foreign Relations: The Great Transformation of the Twentieth Century.* Chicago, IL: University of Chicago Press, 1953.

Parrini, Carl P. *Heir to Empire: United States Economic Diplomacy, 1916–1923.* Pittsburgh, PA: University of Pittsburgh Press, 1969.

Parsons, Edward B. *Wilsonian Diplomacy: Allied-American Rivalries in War and Peace.* St. Louis, MO: Forum Press, 1978.

Pearson, Sue Jones. "The South and the European War." Master's thesis, Samford University, 1967.

Peterson, Horace Cornelius. *Propaganda for War: The Campaign against American Neutrality, 1914–1917.* Port Washington, NY: Kennikat, 1968.

Pickles, Katie. *Transnational Outrage: The Death and Commemoration of Edith Cavell.* New York: Palgrave Macmillan, 2007.

Pugh, Martin D. "Asquith, Bonar Law, and the First Coalition." *The Historical Journal.* Vol. 17, No. 4 (December 1974): 813–36.

Quirk, Robert S. *An Affair of Honor: Woodrow Wilson and the Occupation of Vera Cruz, Mexico.* New York: W. W. Norton, 1962.

Rappaport, Armin. *The British Press and Wilsonian Neutrality.* Gloucester, MA: Stanford University Press, 1965.

Read, James Morgan. *Atrocity Propaganda, 1914–1919.* New Haven, CT: Yale University Press, 1941.

Robb, George. *British Culture and the First World War.* New York: Palgrave, 2002.

Roland, Peter. *David Lloyd George: A Biography.* New York: Macmillan, 1976.

Ronzitti, Natalino, ed. *The Law of Naval Warfare: A Commentary on the Relevant Agreements and Documents.* Dordrecht, Netherlands: Martinus Nijhoff, 1988.

Rosenberg, Emily S. *Spreading the American Dream: American Economic and Cultural Expansion, 1890–1945.* New York: Hill and Wang, 1982.

Safford, Jeffrey J. *Wilsonian Maritime Diplomacy, 1913–1921.* New Brunswick, NJ: Rutgers University Press, 1978.

Sanders, M. L. "Wellington House and British Propaganda during the First World War." *The Historical Journal.* Vol. 18, No. 1 (March 1975): 119–46.

Seymour, Charles. *American Diplomacy during the World War.* Hamden, CT: Archon Books, 1964.

Shepherd, William A. *The Protection of Neutral Rights at Sea: Documents on Naval Warfare.* New York: Sturgis and Walton, 1915.

Siney, Marion C. *The Allied Blockade of Germany, 1914–1916.* Ann Arbor: University of Michigan Press, 1957.

Smith, Daniel Malloy. *The Great Departure: The United States and World War I, 1914–1920.* New York: John Wiley and Sons, 1965.

———. *Robert Lansing and American Neutrality, 1914–1917*. Berkley: University of California Press, 1958.

———. "Robert Lansing and the Formulation of American Neutrality Policies, 1914–1915." *The Mississippi Valley Historical Review*. Vol. 43, No. 1 (June 1956): 59–81.

Smith, Gaddis. *Britain's Clandestine Submarines, 1914–1915*. New Haven, CT: Yale University Press, 1964.

Steiner, Zara. *Britain and the Origins of the First World War*. New York: St. Martin's, 1977.

Strachan, Hew. *Financing the First World War*. Oxford: Oxford University Press, 2004.

———. *The First World War*. London: Viking Penguin, 2004.

———. *The Outbreak of the First World War*. Oxford: Oxford University Press, 2004.

Stevenson, David. *French War Aims against Germany, 1914–1919*. Oxford, UK: Clarendon, 1982.

Tansill, Charles Callan. *America Goes to War*. New York: Little, Brown, 1963 reprint.

Thorsen, Niels Aage. *The Political Thought of Woodrow Wilson, 1875–1910*. Princeton, NJ: Princeton University Press, 1988.

Traxel, David. *Crusader Nation: The United States in Peace and the Great War, 1898–1920*. New York: Alfred A Knopf, 2006.

Trevelyan, George Macaulay. *Grey of Fallodon: The Life and Letters of Sir Edward Grey*. Boston: Houghton Mifflin, 1937.

Tucker, Robert W. *Woodrow Wilson and the Great War: Reconsidering America's Neutrality 1914–1917*. Charlottesville: University of Virginia Press, 2007.

Tucker, Spencer C. *The Great War 1914–1918*. Bloomington: Indiana University Press, 1998.

Tuchman, Barbara W. *The Zimmermann Telegram*. New York: Ballantine, 1958.

Tumulty, Joseph P. *Woodrow Wilson as I Know Him*. New York: Doubleday, Page, 1924.

Turner, John, ed. *Britain and the First World War*. London: Unwin Hyman, 1988.

———. *British Politics and the Great War: Coalition and Conflict, 1915–1918*. New Haven, CT: Yale University Press. 1992.

der Vat, Dan van. *Standard of Power: The Royal Navy in the Twentieth Century*. Volume 1. London: Hutchinson, 2000.

Vincent, C. Paul. *Politics of Hunger: The Allied Blockade of Germany, 1915–1919*. Athens: Ohio University Press, 1985.

Wagner, Dana M. "The Union Navy, 1861–1865." In *In Peace and War: Interpretations of American Naval History, 1775–1978*, edited by Kenneth J. Hagan. Westport, CT: Greenwood, 1978.

Wallin, Jeffrey D. *By Ships Alone: Churchill and the Dardanelles*. Durham, NC: Carolina Academic Press, 1981.

Weinstein, Edwin A. *Woodrow Wilson: A Medical and Psychological Biography*. Princeton, NJ: Princeton University Press, 1981.

Williams, Joyce Grigsby. *Colonel House and Sir Edward Grey: A Study in Anglo-American Diplomacy*. New York: University Press of America, 1984.

Williams, William Appleman. *The Tragedy of American Diplomacy*. New York: W. W. Norton, 1988.

Wilson, Trevor. *The Myriad Faces of War: Britain and the Great War, 1914–1918*. Cambridge, UK: Polity Press, 1986.

Winter, Denis. *25 April 1915: The Inevitable Tragedy*. St. Lucia, Australia: University of Queensland Press, 1994.

Winter, J. M. *The Great War and the British People*. Cambridge, MA: Harvard University Press, 1986.

Index

Printed in the United States of America